COSA
Recovery

Copyright © 2023 by ISO of COSA

All rights reserved.

No portion of this book may be reproduced in any form without written permission from the publisher or author, except as permitted by U.S. copyright law.

This publication is designed to provide accurate and authoritative information in regard to the subject matter covered. It is sold with the understanding that neither the author nor the publisher is engaged in rendering legal, investment, accounting, or other professional services. While the publisher and author have used their best efforts in preparing this book, they make no representations or warranties with respect to the accuracy or completeness of the contents of this book and specifically disclaim any implied warranties of merchantability or fitness for a particular purpose. No warranty may be created or extended by sales representatives or written sales materials. The advice and strategies contained herein may not be suitable for your situation. You should consult with a professional when appropriate. Neither the publisher nor the author shall be liable for any loss of profit or any other commercial damages, including but not limited to special, incidental, consequential, personal, or other damages.

Paperback ISBN: 979-8-218-34779-6
eBook ISBN: 979-8-218-34780-2

www.cosa-recovery.org

COSA Recovery

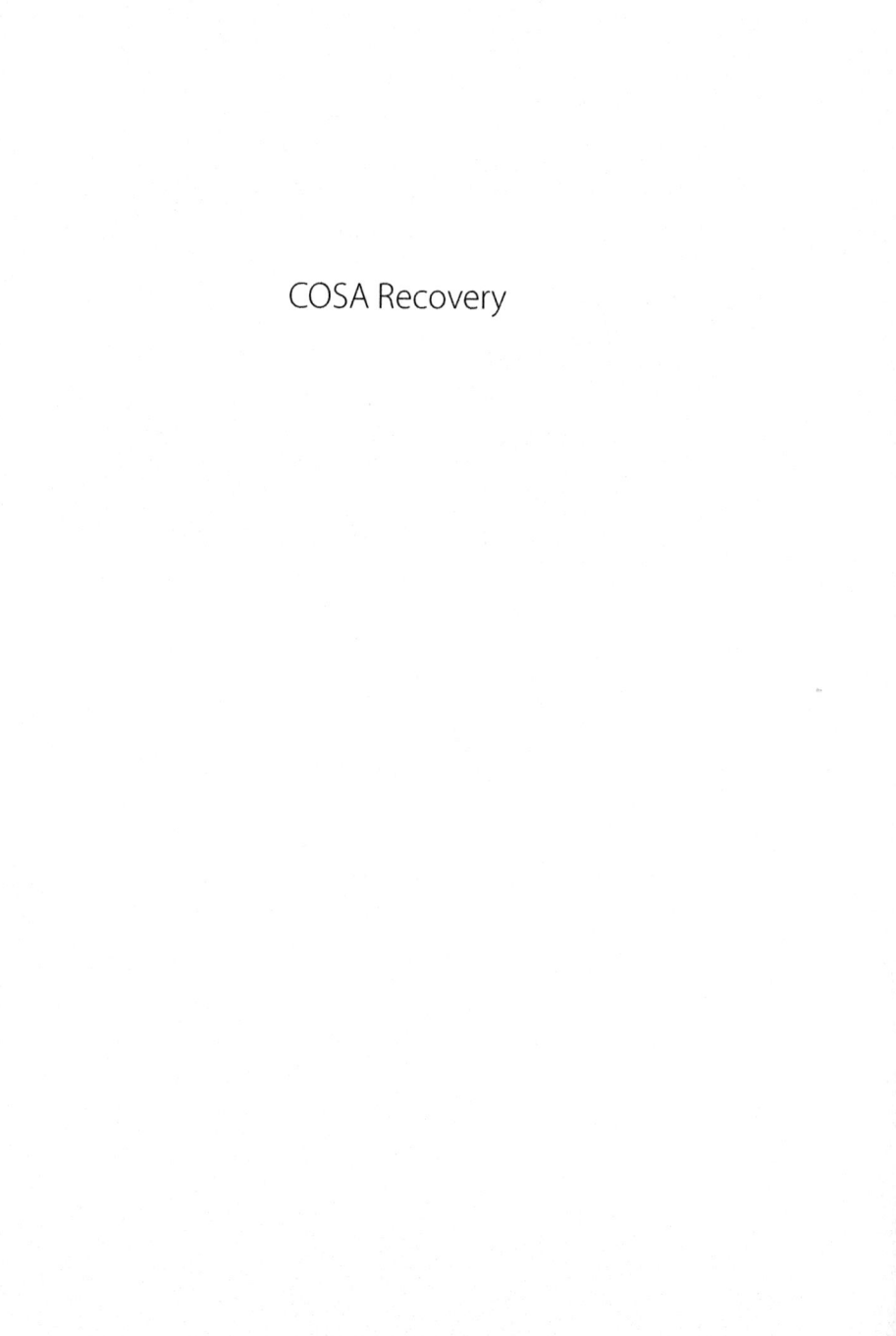

COSA DIVERSITY STATEMENT

- COSA Diversity is consistent with the Third Tradition of COSA, which states that the only requirement for COSA membership is that our lives have been affected by compulsive sexual behavior.

- The COSA Fellowship welcomes all genders, all varieties of relationship to the addict, all religious and spiritual preferences, all employment statuses, all marital statuses, all ethnicities, cultures, and languages. COSA does not discriminate on the basis of class, financial status, sexual orientation or gender identification, physical or mental challenges, race, or national origins.

- In COSA, we find hope whether or not there is a sexually addicted person currently in our lives.

- COSA Diversity is consistent with the First Tradition of COSA, which states that our common welfare should come first; personal recovery depends upon COSA unity.

Contents

What is COSA?	11
Welcome to COSA	14
Introduction	19
Acknowledgements	31
Introduction to the Twelve Steps of COSA	33
Step One	36
Step Two	43
Step Three	50
Step Four	55
Step Five	62
Step Six	69
Step Seven	75
Step Eight	81
Step Nine	87
Step Ten	96
Step Eleven	104
Step Twelve	111

Introduction to the Twelve Traditions of COSA	119
Tradition One	121
Tradition Two	127
Tradition Three	132
Tradition Four	137
Tradition Five	141
Tradition Six	144
Tradition Seven	148
Tradition Eight	152
Tradition Nine	156
Tradition Ten	160
Tradition Eleven	163
Tradition Twelve	168
Introduction to the Twelve Concepts of COSA	173
Concept One	175
Concept Two	178
Concept Three	181
Concept Four	185
Concept Five	189
Concept Six	192
Concept Seven	196
Concept Eight	199
Concept Nine	202
Concept Ten	205
Concept Eleven	208
Concept Twelve	211

Introduction to the Tools of COSA — 215

Abstinence and Celibacy	217
Acknowledging Grief	220
Anonymity and Confidentiality	224
Attending COSA Meetings	229
Boundaries	232
Defining and Maintaining Sobriety	237
Detachment	241
Honesty	245
Outreach Calls	251
Practicing Gratitude	255
Prayer and Meditation	259
Service	264
Slogans and Wise Sayings	267
Slogans and Wise Sayings with Explanatory Text	269
Slogans and Wise Sayings Categorical Index	284
Sponsorship	296
The Serenity Prayer	300
Using the Twelve Steps to Work Through a Specific Situation	304
Writing and Journaling	312

Appendix — 317

The Twelve Steps of COSA	318
The Twelve Traditions of COSA	321
The Twelve Concepts of COSA	324
The Three Circles	328
COSA Confidentiality Statement	329
The Inverted Triangle Structure of COSA	330

What is COSA?

COSA is an anonymous Twelve Step recovery program for anyone whose life has been impacted by the effects of compulsive sexual behavior. The COSA recovery program is adapted from the Twelve Steps, Twelve Traditions, and Twelve Concepts of Alcoholics Anonymous. The name COSA has evolved over time but is not an acronym.

COSA is a community of people with shared experiences and feelings that center around the unique effects of compulsive sexual behavior. We are an inclusive fellowship made up of partners, parents, children, friends, and anyone else affected by compulsive sexual behavior. We are also diverse in the ways in which our lives have been affected. Our community is open to all who seek relief, healing, and hope from these effects.. In this WE program we are no longer alone, and we can find real support to work on our own behaviors. We focus on ourselves and not on the behavior of others.

COSA meetings are a fundamental part of personal recovery. When we enter a COSA meeting we are no longer in painful isolation. We connect with the collective wisdom, experience, strength, and hope of our fellow COSA members. Meetings are safe and anonymous gatherings where we can be understood and accepted without judgment.

Meetings offer us the opportunity to share our stories and to hear specific examples of how others have applied the Steps and recovery principles to their lives. We listen for those who describe how their lives have changed for the better. They show clarity, serenity, and peace. Their healthy confidence is evident. We realize that we want what they have. When we find someone in the group who has the kind of recovery we admire, we can ask them to be our sponsor. Sponsors guide and support us as we work the Twelve Steps. They also lend their experience and wisdom through difficult situations along our recovery path.

The Twelve Steps are the spiritual foundation of our program. Working the Steps offers a way to explore our inner selves and develop a deeper self-awareness. As we work the Steps and use the principles within them, we begin to heal from the effects caused by compulsive sexual behavior. We begin to release and replace the self-defeating behaviors, attitudes, and beliefs we have unwittingly developed. As we continue to grow in our recovery, we gain new insights which help us make healthier choices. We find the courage to make positive changes that lead to greater empowerment and self-esteem, resulting in happier, more fulfilled lives.

The Steps also encourage a path to spiritual development, no matter what our religious or philosophical beliefs. Working the Twelve Steps helps us come to understand God, Higher Power, or a Power greater than ourselves, through our own evolving understanding, not in any prescribed way. Having a spiritual connection provides great comfort and meaningful support in our lives, in and outside of recovery.

COSA benefits from the structure and guidance of the Twelve Traditions and Twelve Concepts of COSA, which support cooperation within our groups and the fellowship as a whole. Additionally, COSA offers a myriad of tools for this healing journey.

Through recovery we move toward the best version of ourselves. We honor our inner voice, and we learn to make healthier choices. We begin to feel a sense of real peace and serenity. The gifts of our recovery begin to ripple out to all areas of our lives. Others may see our peace and serenity and discover they want that for themselves. And that is the primary purpose of COSA: to carry the COSA message of recovery, hope, and healing to all who suffer.

Welcome to COSA

If you are reading these words, then most likely your life has been affected by compulsive sexual behavior. COSA offers you a warm welcome and a safe place to heal. No matter how bleak or broken or infuriating your life may feel at this moment, we can assure you that you are not alone and that there is hope.

When we arrived at COSA, many of us felt as if the world as we knew it had been shattered. Some of us were simply surviving our days, struggling with fear, shame, anger, and confusion. Our losses were many; our grief was deep. We were grappling with quiet seething, intense rage, emotional numbness, or depression. Some of us developed addictions of our own, had physical accidents, or succumbed to illnesses as a result of trying to cope with the stress. Others of us experienced traumatic events that we feared would cripple us emotionally for the rest of our lives.

Initially, many of us wondered: "Why do I need a program when it is the sex addict who has the problem?" Some of us felt indignant at having to take time out of our lives to deal with what we thought of as "their issues." Yet even if we thought this way, when we heard others share in COSA meetings and we reflected on our own lives, we realized the depth of the traumas we had experienced. We gradually began to look at our reactions, and how our thoughts and behaviors were hurting us and others. We recognized our need for help and guidance.

Those of us who were open to the COSA program from the start were relieved to find a safe haven where we could talk openly about what we were experiencing. We met others who had faced similar circumstances, and we got support.

Some of us were hesitant to participate or were resistant at first. We feared judgment or questions we didn't feel ready to answer. We were concerned we might expose ourselves or others to greater risk. For those who had experienced abuse or manipulation in our relationships, trusting anyone seemed frightening or unhealthy. Others of us had seen or done things we believed we simply could not speak about; this made it difficult to open up. Regardless of our individual challenges, we reached out to the program.

When we were willing to stay with the COSA program, even for a short time, we came out of isolation. We began to feel comfort and strength. We connected with other COSAs because they understood, perhaps better than anyone else, what we were going through. COSA provided sanctuary and good, orderly direction. Gradually, we began to feel safe and at home.

A PATH TOWARD SELF-DISCOVERY

As newcomers, we sought ways to change the addict in our lives, or to stop or control that person's behavior. We were often obsessed with researching, diagnosing, and making discoveries. Those activities seemed to be the clearest way out of our pain. Accepting our powerlessness at that point was more than hard; it was nearly impossible.

As we continued in the program and contemplated the Serenity Prayer, we gradually discovered that we had no power to change another person, the past, or the effects of compulsive sexual behavior. This was hard to accept sometimes, as a newcomer and even well into our recovery, but it also brought relief. For those of us who embraced the COSA program and attempted, however imperfectly, to practice the principles of recovery, there was a new realization of just how helpful the program could be for us personally.

In COSA, we found healing, regardless of whether the sex addict or addicts were still in our lives, and whether or not they found recovery. Many of us also discovered that the situation that originally brought us to COSA was not the first such situation in our lives. We started to see our own life story in a new light.

Often, as we reflected and gained understanding, we were surprised to discover just how damaging our own COSA "disease" could be. In many cases, it was just as damaging for us as the addiction was for the sex addict. Perhaps we were struggling with compulsive behaviors of our own. We may have found ourselves riding a roller coaster of extreme or obsessive thoughts and feelings.

Some of us participated in behaviors that seemed harmless enough on the surface, such as being conscientious and responsible, or holding others or ourselves to high standards. These may have brought some reward or a sense of control. Yet such behaviors, when we took them to extremes, left us feeling weary and overwhelmed. Or we may have acted in ways that caused us to feel either superior or humiliated, sometimes one and then the other in quick succession.

Some of us lost our ability to express our feelings in a healthy way. We got lost in rage or in blaming others. Some shopped compulsively or worked too much without adequate rest. Some developed eating disorders in an effort to cope, or hurt ourselves by abusing alcohol or drugs. Some of us put ourselves in dangerous situations where our health or our lives were at risk. We may have participated in compulsive sexual behaviors ourselves. We may have contemplated or even acted on suicidal or violent thoughts.

It was tempting to attribute our turmoil to the hurt we felt over someone else's actions instead of our own ineffective coping skills. In recovery, we learn and continue to grow in the understanding that our behavior and our thinking are our own responsibility. Recovery helps us see our lives and ourselves more clearly and take specific steps to heal.

SAFE HAVEN AND RENEWAL

No matter who you are, what you have been through, or how you have attempted to cope, if your life has been affected by compulsive sexual behavior, you are welcome in COSA. This anonymous Twelve Step recovery program helps us to keep things simple as we work through the complexity of our challenges.

COSA offers us a safe place to sort through our thoughts and feelings and to share what we are going through. Within the COSA program we can set aside the fear of judgment, shame, or criticism. We learn that we don't need to be perfect. We attend meetings. We connect with sponsors and other recovering people. We learn how to have healthier relationships. We work the Twelve Steps and Twelve Traditions and learn how to use the many other tools of the COSA program. We engage in service work that brings new meaning into our lives. And we take full advantage of COSA literature and the other

COSA resources to learn about the nature of our dilemma and the possibilities for healing.

We are nurtured by the warmth and reassurance of being connected with a community of recovering people. We begin to feel the awe-inspiring strength of a power greater than our individual selves.

At the heart of our COSA recovery is an abiding trust in the guidance and grace of a Higher Power of our own understanding. For some, this is the revival of a longstanding faith, or a new concept of a Higher Power that is more gentle and nurturing than the one in which we once believed. For others, it is a sense of inner spiritual connection that we are feeling for the first time, or the recognition of the Higher Power that is the experience, strength, and hope (ESH) of our group.

In COSA recovery, we find joy and richness in lives that were once clouded by hopelessness and despair. We grow into feeling peaceful, grateful, empowered, and free. We wish the same for you. You no longer need to be alone.

This book is written solely by COSAs and for COSAs. We invite you to give yourself time to consider the words we share here with you, and to give yourself the gift of working the COSA program.

Introduction

Whoever you are, whatever you have experienced, and no matter how you have tried to cope, if your life has been affected by compulsive sexual behavior, then the COSA fellowship is here for you.

WHO ARE COSAS?

We are a richly diverse group of people. We come from all walks of life. We are of many races, religions, and ethnicities, and we live in all parts of the world. We have various levels of education and income. We are people of all genders and sexual orientations. We are engaged in a wide array of professions, and many of us are highly respected members of our communities. While our stories and our life experiences are unique to each of us, every single one of us has been affected in some way, at some point in our lives, by compulsive sexual behavior and the accompanying shame, trauma, and grief. This is our common challenge.

We vary widely in the types of relationships we have to sexually compulsive people and to their behaviors. Many of us are partners, former partners, adult children, parents, family members, or friends of sex addicts. Many of us are sexual abuse survivors. Some of us have been impacted by the compulsive sexual behavior of an authority figure, a colleague, an acquaintance, or a stranger. And some of us identify both as COSAs and as sex addicts. Regardless of the specifics of our stories, recovery from the effects of compulsive sexual behavior is our common goal.

Our stories may be different, but we find it helpful to listen for similarities rather than get distracted by differences. We can all relate to the distress of trying to manage an unmanageable situation. We can all identify with the very human desire to express anger or grief and to relieve pain.

Some of us refer to ourselves simply as COSA members or recovering COSAs. Although it was originally an abbreviation, today the term COSA refers only to the fact that our lives have been affected by compulsive sexual behavior. While some of us identify as codependent, codependent to a sex addict (or sex addicts), a co-sex addict, or a sexual codependent, these terms are not a requirement or meant to limit us but rather to acknowledge the ways we individually understand the effects of compulsive sexual behavior on our lives. Regardless of how we individually choose to identify ourselves, as members of COSA, we claim our connection to the shared purpose of the COSA Twelve Step fellowship: to recover, and to help others recover, from the effects of compulsive sexual behavior.

In the COSA recovery program, we begin to recognize the full extent of the damage caused by compulsive sexual behavior, by the deception and denial that surround it, and by our reactions to it. We find hope, whether or not there is a sexually compulsive person currently in our lives. By attending meetings, reading COSA literature, and working the Twelve Steps with a sponsor, we begin to recover from the effects of compulsive sexual behavior. The preoccupation with the addict decreases, and for some will disappear entirely. Through recovery, we move away from a life of emotional turmoil to a more serene and healthier living experience. As we gradually reclaim our lives and our sense of ourselves, we begin to find hope.

SEXUAL ADDICTION AND ITS IMPACT

Sexuality can be a rich and complex part of the human experience. Our perspectives on sexuality are as varied as we are, shaped by a tangle of divergent messages that come from our parents, our peers, our experiences, our cultures, our religions, and the media. In the best of circumstances, connecting sexually with another consenting adult can be a sensuous, pleasurable experience. It can be an opportunity to be open, intimate, and free. Yet, when compulsive sexual behavior and our own reactions to it are involved, trust, respect, and caring are lost, and thoughts and behaviors become twisted by deception, power plays, manipulation, and shame. Even when physical contact is present, the results of this type of sexuality are often disconnection and loneliness.

Because of the intimate nature of sex addiction, we feel hurt at our core. We are affected where we are most vulnerable. We feel confused, unsafe, and abandoned. Many of us struggle to understand what makes the sexual acting out an addiction.

Compulsive sexual behavior is harmful to all those involved in, affected by, and reacting to it. The range of compulsive sexual behavior runs the gamut, from the compulsive avoidance of sex, to masturbation or compulsive demands for sex within the relationship, to engaging with various kinds of "love affairs" including emotional affairs, pornography, one-night stands, and prostitutes. There are many other behaviors too varied and numerous to list here. No matter what the behavior, the important thing to bear in mind is that if we believe that our lives have been affected, we have a place in COSA.

When untreated, sex addiction and the shockwaves that ripple out from it have been known to tear relationships and lives apart. In some cases, it can lead to incarceration, grave physical illnesses or accidents, mental breakdowns, violence, or suicide—involving either the addict, someone whose life has been affected by the addict, or both.

COSAs are faced with at least four major sources of pain. First, there is the pain caused by our thoughts about the sex addict's behaviors, which, by their very nature, hit us at the tender root of our human experience. For example, partners of sex addicts may interpret the other person's behavior as a deeply personal rejection. Second, there is the disorienting, corrosive pattern of lying, which many COSAs experience as being at least as painful as the acting-out behaviors themselves. This leads to further disconnection and loss of trust. Third, in realizing the full extent of the sex addiction and the destruction it has caused, COSAs often experience waves of grief related to a profound sense of loss. This loss often extends far beyond the addict and the addict's behaviors to the loss of what we thought our lives were or of what we hoped they would be. It may continue to permeate our lives well beyond the duration of time we spend with the addict. Finally, there is the pain caused by our own reactions to the compulsive sexual behavior. In our efforts to cope with the stress, many of us slip into cycles of extreme thinking and disruptive behavior that are damaging to us and those around us. With the help of COSA, we walk through the pain, and we become healed and renewed. We find a whole new way of living our lives and responding to our circumstances, and we receive the gifts of COSA recovery.

IDENTIFYING THE TRAUMA

Discovering or identifying compulsive sexual behavior can be one of the most emotionally traumatizing events in a person's life. This discovery can emerge in myriad ways. Some COSAs are completely unsuspecting and are abruptly sideswiped by indisputable evidence of someone's sexual acting out. Our lives change dramatically in that instant, and we feel emotional vertigo as we perceive that our reality is not at all what we thought it was. Many COSAs come to the discovery more slowly, as a lingering suspicion accumulates into too much evidence to refute. Or we have felt deep inside that something was wrong for a long time, and as our denial gradually dissipates, the truth of the situation emerges in vivid detail. Some of us gain general knowledge about the nature of sexual addiction, and we come to realize that we have participated willingly or unwillingly in someone else's sex addiction. Perhaps we had attempted to be "open-minded" about another person's compulsive sexual behavior even though it was against our values, was illegal, or was physically painful for us. In such cases, part of the trauma is having the blanket of our denial ripped away, or having our frozen feelings suddenly thaw and break open. Or perhaps we had been subjected to unwanted sexual advances, or someone exposing himself or herself to us. In addition to witnessing compulsive sexual activity or evidence of it, there may be legal, financial, and medical effects, and effects on our own judgment of ourselves. Regardless of how we find our way to COSA, we have trauma to work through.

 The shock of what we have seen and experienced may feel as if it is seared in our minds. Sometimes the shock feels like too much for us. Our senses shut down and we retreat to a place inside where we convince ourselves that we don't see what we see. This is a form of deep denial meant to protect us from the horror we feel at what we have witnessed or experienced. It makes us feel disconnected from reality. We walk around in a state of anxiety or stunned disorientation. We ask ourselves, "Is this really happening? Did I really see or hear that? How could I have allowed myself to participate in that?" Once we identify the trauma, COSA recovery can support us in healing from it.

In recovery, we come out of denial as gently yet as thoroughly as we can, without shame or judgment. We come to terms with the reality of our lives. Resources for help and support abound; we can reach out to our sponsors and utilize the Steps, COSA program literature, the COSA fellowship, and other resources as needed. There is power in this unflinching look at the facts, because once we're clear on the nature of our situation, we can begin to find solutions.

CONTENDING WITH DECEPTION

One of the most destructive aspects of sexually compulsive behavior is the deception often surrounding it. In fact, some COSAs find this even more of a betrayal, and more difficult to recover from, than the sexual behaviors themselves.

Sexual addiction is sustained by an intricate web of secrecy and deception. Our attempts to challenge or put a stop to sexually compulsive behavior can be disorienting because instead of our efforts being effective, we are often met with blatant lies, half-truths, or distortions. Often, when pressed to explain, a sex addict will offer rationalizations that seem to make sense. Their thinking and words twist things around, and we can end up feeling paranoid and unreasonable or like we are somehow to blame. Without recovery, sex addicts often will not admit guilt or say they are sorry. It can be "crazy making" to live with or to be around a practicing sex addict. Without *our own* recovery, we live in a state of confusion, stress, and perpetual insecurity because we don't know what is true, or whom or what to trust. When we are told over and over again that our perceptions are wrong, we come to doubt our perceptions and ourselves. We may conclude that we are being overly sensitive and overreacting. We have difficulty trusting our own sense of reality.

When trust has been repeatedly broken, we close off our hearts in an effort to protect ourselves. Without honesty, our relationships feel shallow and unsafe. We feel hopeless and disconnected.

Not only have many of us been lied to for years, most of us have been lying to ourselves. If it feels too awful to believe our suspicions, or we are trying to maintain some sense of calm, we may go along with the sex addict's distorted reasoning. In our efforts to survive, we hide from the truth, locking it away deep inside. We ignore what others may clearly see as "red flags." Our inner spirit may be screaming to us that something is wrong, yet our outer experience is blanketed in our own denial. Our attempts to adapt to the addict's alternate version of reality make us emotionally—and sometimes physically—sick.

Recovery shines a bright light on these patterns of deception. Once we are able to see the lies, we discover that the fabric of our relationships and of our lives is threadbare and full of holes. We begin to acknowledge the painful truth. Accepting our reality *as it is* doesn't mean that we have to like it or condone it. It simply means we can now make more fully informed choices. We can save our energy for making changes where we do have power: changing ourselves.

When we look at our lives and ourselves honestly, we can begin to discover our authentic selves. In COSA, we learn to trust our perceptions and intuition, and to reinforce this with the support of trusted friends in the fellowship. We develop integrity. Our thoughts, words, and actions—and thus our insides and outsides—are more often aligned and in harmony.

GRIEVING OUR LOSSES

With our experience of the effects of compulsive sexual behavior and our reactions to it, the losses are numerous. There are losses surrounding the addict and the acting out, including loss of relationships, shattered trust, compromised physical health in some cases, and loss of lifelong dreams.

There are also the losses we incurred when we turned the pain upon ourselves. Some of us adapted to the behavior of the addict or addicts to the point where we abandoned ourselves. We allowed years to go by unnoticed, without caring for our own needs; we ended up with unfulfilled wants and needs, or without even knowing what we wanted or needed. We lost precious time. Some of us acted in ways that felt humiliating and degrading. We sacrificed our values, morals, dignity, and self-respect.

Our struggles also affected others we cared about. In our own COSA disease, some of us neglected our children or failed to protect them. We distanced ourselves from other family members. We lost friends. Some of us engaged in illegal or dangerously irresponsible activities, or we lost jobs or other important opportunities that affected those who were relying on us.

Some of us discover that the grief stirred by sex addiction does not stem solely from our present circumstances. Our increasing awareness of sexually compulsive behavior may bring other truths to light, such as a dysfunctional upbringing or molestation in our childhood. We may begin to recognize how these experiences shaped our pattern of choosing people who are unavailable or dangerous. We may come to realize that we have lived through similar predicaments more than once.

The grief can feel overwhelming; it brings many of us to our knees. In COSA, though, we connect with safe, supportive people who help us summon the courage we need to face our circumstances and to feel what we need to feel in order to heal. The Twelve Steps provide a solid structure upon which to climb out of the depths, and we find a Higher Power of our own understanding on which we can rely. When we use our recovery tools to work through our grief, we find clarity and transformation. We discover the true and steady core of who we really are. We find great relief by connecting with others in COSA who understand our feelings, who have walked through similar circumstances, and who have found a way not only to survive, but to thrive.

NOTICING OUR REACTIONS

Due to the personal and sometimes extreme nature of our situations, we may find ourselves flooded with intense emotions. Without help, we find ourselves reacting in destructive ways. Some of us lash out in rage or shut down and become depressed. Some are filled with anxiety and lose hours searching for clues to the addict's activities. Others feel drawn to sleep too much. Many become consumed with hypervigilance and high-functioning perfectionism, hoping that if we just manage *well enough*, we can somehow stop the chaos in our lives. Some of us lose ourselves in hypersexuality in an effort to keep the addict's attention, or as a way to punish or retaliate. We may do sexual things in ways and with people that we never imagined we would do, and feel swallowed up by overwhelming shame. Others of us become lost in eating disorders, compulsive obsessions, or other addictions of our own. And yet, these reactions do not provide true relief. None of this means we are bad people; we are hurt people. We have been trying to cope in the only ways we know how.

Many COSAs develop symptoms akin to post-traumatic stress disorder (PTSD). We have indeed been traumatized. We are often fearful. We feel on edge most of the time. We feel as if the trauma is happening again. No amount of reason or proof can convince us it is not. We can be suddenly and intensely upset by things that another person might not think much about: a washcloth out of place, extra mileage on the car, the sound of a phone receiving text messages, a computer virus, or mysterious marks on skin or clothing. For a COSA, one tiny pebble of doubt can become an avalanche of emotions and reactions. It can take some time and work to learn how to handle triggers in a healthy way. We need to be gentle with ourselves in the process.

Often we continue to struggle with the trauma and emotional triggers regardless of whether or not the addict is still acting out, or even whether or not the person is in our lives anymore. We often suffer with all-consuming fear of the next discovery or the next betrayal. We are determined not to let ourselves be hurt or deceived again. Even if we understand rationally that this is beyond our control, it doesn't stop us from straining to predict the future, trying to build an emotional fortress around ourselves, or trying to control outcomes.

Most people would not know, and do not know, how to handle emotions and trauma this intense. Without support, we may develop or continue to use faulty coping mechanisms. In many cases, these coping behaviors can progress and intensify much like an addiction, with identifiable signs and symptoms. Without recovery, we run the risk of being swept away by the pain and our reactions to it, losing days, weeks, months, or even years of our precious lives to our own "dis-ease." The Twelve Steps of COSA and the support of the COSA fellowship provide us with the structure and support we need to work through our challenging feelings and reactive behaviors. We learn to *respond* to our feelings and to situations, rather than to react. We develop an understanding of ourselves, and we learn how to take care of ourselves in gentle, nurturing ways.

FINDING HOPE, HEALING, AND FREEDOM

We came to COSA carrying the weight of our painful, traumatic experiences. We were in crisis. Our pain drove us to seek relief.

The COSA program has helped us find solid ground on which to stand. We often look back upon the situation that brought us to COSA as an important—even crucial—turning point in our lives. For some of us, working the COSA program gives us access to our inner being, which may have been hidden away since childhood—long before we first encountered compulsive sexual behavior.

It is possible to heal from the past and find new ways to relate to ourselves, to our loved ones, and to our sexuality. We can learn how to accept our circumstances and work to change what needs to be changed in us. We can come to recognize which things cannot be changed, learn from them, and move on without staying stuck in grief and abuse from the past.

Through the Steps and with the support of the COSA program, we discover a new lightness of heart and deep serenity.

We are still human, and we may lose our serenity at times, but never as badly as in the beginning. We now have the tools of our program to work our way back to this state of mind that we have come to value so highly. We emerge from this process feeling empowered, renewed, and grateful.

Acknowledgements

While it is true that each person is responsible for their own recovery, it is also true that COSA is a WE program dependent upon the collective experience, strength, and hope of our whole fellowship. This is clearly evident in the writing process of *COSA Recovery*. At the 2014 Annual Delegate Meeting, the Literature Committee was instructed to work solely on creating a book that would not only address the Steps, Traditions, Concepts, and COSA Tools but would also be written from a perspective unique to COSA.

Upon receiving this directive from the delegates and with continuing support from the ISO of COSA Board, the Literature in Development Committee took on the task that had been started years earlier by the Book Development Committee. The Literature in Development Committee has been comprised of many different COSA members from a variety of backgrounds, skill sets, and experiences. The common denominator over the years of writing *COSA Recovery* has been the unique, highly collaborative process by which it was written. Prior to a chapter being written, the fellowship was surveyed with specific questions requesting direction for the particular Step, Tradition, Concept, or COSA Tool. Once the section was written by a primary author and editor, it was reviewed and edited by the entire Literature in Development Committee in a group editing process. When the committee reached consensus, fellowship feedback was collected for a 90-day period. This valuable feedback was reviewed and carefully considered, and was then incorporated as much as possible into the chapter. A final edit was completed by the committee to prepare the chapter for presentation to the COSA fellowship and delegates for review. Groups and meetings had an opportunity to reach a group conscience about whether or not they approved the chapter for inclusion in the book. Each year at the Annual Delegate Meeting, chapters completed that year were presented to the COSA delegates for voting and approval.

Each word has been thoughtfully crafted to reflect the voice of the entire fellowship rather than that of any one individual. The writing process for *COSA Recovery* truly exemplifies the collaborative principles of a WE program. We are grateful for and acknowledge the experience, strength, and hope of each COSA fellowship member. Thank you to all those who have contributed to the creation of this valuable asset, *COSA Recovery*.

INTRODUCTION TO THE TWELVE STEPS OF COSA

When we listen and share in COSA meetings, we feel relief that we are understood and validated. We no longer feel as if we are crazy, and we see that we are not alone in our struggles. We see evidence of real healing and growth in the lives of COSA members around us, and we are inspired by the grace with which they walk through life's challenges.

As we open ourselves up to the warm support of our newfound community and as we practice recovery principles, we begin to see new possibilities for our lives. This is just the beginning. While COSA meetings provide relief, the Twelve Steps of COSA promise true recovery. As we work through the Steps with a sponsor, we gain insights into ourselves and our lives. As we continue in the process, we begin to feel freedom, gratitude, and a newfound sense of balance.

At first, the prospect of working our own Twelve Steps seems baffling. In COSA, we learn that we only have the power to change ourselves; we cannot change another person. We also discover, in time, that in our efforts to survive the traumas and painful circumstances in our lives, we may have developed coping mechanisms that caused injury to ourselves and others. The Twelve Steps provide us with clear guidance for facing our lives honestly and finding a healthier, happier course.

Step work requires quiet time for introspection and enough courage to take certain actions; however, we are not asked to do our Step work all on our own. In fact, the first word of the Twelve Steps is "We," and this language of we, us, our, ourselves is stated or understood in every Step. This means we are no longer alone in dealing with the effects of compulsive sexual behavior on our lives. We have the guidance and support of our sponsors. We also have our community of trusted recovery allies who share their knowledge with us and encourage us along the way. We stay consistent with our COSA meetings, and we listen for experience, strength, and hope. Through this process, we tap into the transformative strength of a Power far greater than ourselves.

It can be hard work at times, yet we soon feel the positive effects of Step work. We begin to feel stronger, more peaceful, and more resilient. We come to see that we have many more choices than we thought we did. Through the Steps, we come to know ourselves with gentleness, acceptance, and compassion in a way that we may never have experienced before. We find a Higher Power of our own understanding that we can rely on. Clarity, integrity, and self-esteem become supporting pillars in the new structure of our lives.

We take the Steps in order. If we approach each Step with an open mind and an open heart, awareness and change will come, as it has for so many who have gone before us. With rigorous honesty, openness, and willingness, we can trust the process. Although the Twelve Steps may challenge us at times, they actually pave the way to true recovery and progress.

Some of us work the Steps quickly, and some more gradually. Regardless of the pace, it doesn't take long for us to realize that the Twelve Steps are the life-giving heart of COSA recovery. Many of us revisit the Steps over and over throughout our lives. The core guiding principles become second nature to us as we study and apply them. As the Twelfth Step states, "Having had a spiritual awakening as the result of these Steps, we tried to carry this message to others, and to practice these principles in all areas of our lives." These principles become the foundation on which we build serene and fulfilling lives, by living in the present moment, one day at a time.

Step One

*We admitted we were powerless over
compulsive sexual behavior—that our lives
had become unmanageable.*

In Step One, we accept the truth: we are not all-powerful. We concede that we are human, and we can't control others or our circumstances. We also see the damage and unmanageability caused by our attempts to exert power where we have none. We admit that we cannot recover from this by ourselves; we need help. We become willing. Step One is essential to our healing. When we work this Step and apply its principles in our lives, we open ourselves up to the possibility of a new way of living.

OUR POWERLESSNESS

When we heard the words of the First Step, "We admitted we were powerless over compulsive sexual behavior—that our lives had become unmanageable," many of us felt confused or even angry. Most of us did not have obvious struggles with compulsive sexual behavior and while many of us felt desperate and in great emotional pain, some of us felt our lives were completely manageable. We had kept our lives and the lives of others from falling apart. What did this Step have to do with us?

For those of us with partners or spouses who struggled with compulsive sexual behavior, our powerlessness showed up as failed efforts to get them to stop. Our attempts to be attractive enough, smart enough, loving enough, or sexual enough had not produced the results we desired. Parents, siblings, children, and friends of addicts related to this too. We had tried to be sweet and loving, indifferent and distant, or angry and punishing. We had forgiven them, or we had kicked them out. We had told them exactly how to behave or we had become extremely accepting of all behaviors. We took them to therapists, psychologists, psychiatrists, churches, Twelve Step meetings, and rehab centers. We "helped" the addict by learning about sex addiction and then relaying the information in hopes they would "get it." Our list of attempts to control the addiction was as long as the addict's. Still we were lied to and betrayed, and the acting out continued. Seeing that our efforts were so ineffective, we had to admit we were powerless over the compulsive sexual behavior and the addict.

Some of us wanted to end a relationship with a sex addict or uphold boundaries around the acting out and found we could not. When the addict acted out, we berated ourselves for putting up with it. Yet we froze at the thought of sharing how we felt, asking for a need to be met, or following through with our own boundaries. When dealing with the addict, we became confused. We found ourselves unable to distinguish truth from lies. We felt trapped and were in deep pain as we abandoned ourselves over and over again. Some of us even felt like we were addicted to the person (we needed their approval and love) and to the relationship (we needed it to feel worthy and whole). We admitted we were powerless over our addiction to both the relationship and the addict.

Many of us had been molested, raped, sexually abused, abandoned, or neglected or had witnessed these events. These episodes may have been with our partners, our parents, a family member, a friend, or a total stranger. Because of these experiences many of us developed faulty core beliefs. We often believed these behaviors of others indicated that we were not worthy of love or respect, that our worth was tied to our sexuality or to the transgressor, and that we were not safe. We developed distorted views of ourselves, love, sex, reality, feelings, and life itself. These faulty beliefs and distorted views comprised some of the ways we had been affected by compulsive sexual behavior. We recognized our powerlessness when we accepted our inability to change past events or to easily change these core beliefs.

Many of us had experienced trauma from living with those addicted to sexual behavior. At times our wounds would be triggered, and we would feel as if we were reliving the damaging experiences. It felt terrifying when it was upon us. We were hypervigilant in our search for signs of danger, or we retreated into a shell for protection. Some of us felt enraged or "crazy." We could not control the depth to which we had been affected; we could not control the things our minds interpreted as signs of danger. We realized we were powerless over our triggers and the feelings that accompanied them.

Some of us had loved ones who had recognized their addiction and had sought recovery. This was wonderful, yet it prompted us to try to control in a different way. Now we counted their meetings, and approved of or denied their choice of sponsors. We corrected them when they said or did things we deemed inappropriate, and we told them how to recover. While it was important for us to pay attention to the choices of those we were involved with and to speak our truth, we had to admit that no matter how closely we watched and no matter how good our suggestions were, we were powerless over the sobriety of our loved ones.

Once we had identified what we were trying to control, most of us were able to admit—accept as true—that we had been powerless to change it. We could not control sex addiction, compulsive sexual behavior, or the sex addicts. We had no power to change the past or our own addictive behaviors. We could not will away our trauma. As we worked this Step, we began to develop the ability to determine what we had power over and what we did not.

OUR UNMANAGEABILITY

It may have been easy for us to see the out-of-control behavior of others in our lives, but few of us wanted to admit that our efforts to control had failed and left our lives in varying degrees of chaos. While the specifics varied, we found that when we were truly honest, we could see that our attempts to control created more shame, anger, despair, desperation, and confusion. The consequences of these efforts clearly created unmanageability.

Reflecting upon our efforts to control the compulsive sexual behavior of the addict, we saw that we had developed our own unhealthy thoughts, behaviors, coping mechanisms, and beliefs. We began to realize that these effects were progressively debilitating. Some of us became clearly and obviously out of control. We suffered from serious physical or mental health problems. We placed our own lives, or those of our loved ones, in danger as we became increasingly obsessed. Some of us nearly died through continually neglecting ourselves, placing ourselves in dangerous situations, or attempting suicide. We acted out our rage and fear on our children, our families, our coworkers, and those closest to us. We turned to other addictions and compulsions to manage our pain.

Others among us became adept at living a double life, yet the cost was no less real. While we appeared to the outside world as if we "had it all together," we were slowly withering away in the prison of our own isolation and unspoken secrets. We pushed ourselves relentlessly to keep the mask of normalcy in place, while behind the façade, we became increasingly depleted. We lived in fear that the truth of what was happening in our lives would be discovered. As we worked to deny reality and our feelings, we became disconnected from ourselves, and from authentic relationships with those close to us. Our lives had become unmanageable.

MAKING THE ADMISSION

In order to let go and make the admission asked of us in the First Step, it helped to clearly understand the nature of how we had personally been affected by compulsive sexual behavior.

Some of us prepared for this Step by writing. We looked back at our histories. What had our lives looked like before we came to COSA? Before we met the sex addict? Many of us felt there was no need to look at our past; the current situation was what had brought us to COSA, and we simply wanted to focus on recovering from that. We were encouraged to explore it anyway because, after examining our past, many of us found experiences and beliefs from our childhood that greatly influenced our responses to compulsive sexual behavior. Often it gave us clues to why the drive to control was so strong, how the patterns of control had developed, and how the path to unmanageability was paved. Whether the discoveries were significant or minor we realized it was important to look.

We also looked in detail at what and whom we had tried to control and at the specific ways we had attempted to control them. How had these behaviors led to the resulting unmanageability in our lives? What did the unmanageability look like? Many of us wrote about our histories, our attempts to control, and the resulting unmanageability. We answered questions given to us by our sponsors, and some of us defined the words of the Step. Some of us worked privately and exclusively with our sponsors, while others also shared their stories with their group because saying the words out loud often helped them accept the truth on a deeper level. Some of us, without writing, simply submitted wholeheartedly to the principles of this Step.

Regardless of the specifics, with the guidance of our sponsors, we each came to the place where we could fully surrender and take the core action of Step One: we admitted our powerlessness over compulsive sexual behavior and over the people, places and events, and feelings we had so desperately tried to control. Surrender and admission of our own limitations, often on a daily basis, was necessary if we were going to fully embrace the new way of living offered to us in the Twelve Steps.

Step One brought with it a myriad of feelings. Relief poured over us when we realized that we were never the cause of another's addiction, behavior, or choices. We felt we could finally take a breath and begin to allow others to be responsible for their own actions. We felt grateful that the Steps offered us an effective way to ease our guilt, shame, fear, resentment, and remorse. We found that when we let go of focusing on the people and situations we had no power over, we were free to focus on the one person we were truly responsible for: ourself. We were empowered to turn our attention to our own change and growth.

At the same time, many of us felt anger, pain, and grief as our eyes opened. It was heart-wrenching to realize that there was not a single word we could say, nor a single action we could take, that would lead our loved ones to sobriety or that would change the past. The pain of this realization made it no less true, and hanging on to the illusion of control had created more pain. For our own well-being, we admitted the truth that we are not all-powerful, and we let go of our attempts to manage, manipulate, and control.

Regardless of our feelings, we were assured by our sponsors, our fellow COSAs, and the wisdom of those that had gone before us that this Step was only the beginning; help and healing were on the way. No matter how unpleasant the past, we were finally on the path to real change. We had only to look around at those who had worked the Steps before us to know that it could work for us too. We were ready for a true and lasting solution to our dilemma. We were ready for Step Two.

STEP ONE AFFIRMATION

Today I remind myself to let go of my desires to change the past and control the future. I am growing in acceptance of my life as it is today; thus, I make decisions and act from a balanced, well-informed place. While I see the harm that my attempts to control have caused, I am grateful that becoming aware of these truths has made me willing and teachable. I detach from others' choices and make healthy choices in my own life. I have plentiful resources in recovery and trusted COSA friends who can support me. Today I am ready for a new way.

Step Two

*Came to believe that a Power greater than
ourselves could restore us to sanity.*

Step Two is built upon the understanding we gained in Step One. Through our initial Step work we reached a crucial turning point. We saw how our lives had been affected by compulsive sexual behavior, and we felt the resulting unmanageability. We finally conceded that we simply couldn't fix our problems alone, and that continuing our course of action would be destructive and perhaps deadly. Our desperation for relief from the pain and struggle rendered us open and teachable.

We now see that while we have power over our own choices, we cannot control others or their behavior. We recognize that when we are fueled by self-will, our most earnest efforts may bring short-term relief, but they cannot restore us to balanced, sane living. In fact, in our attempts to control, we may cause harm. Once we admit that we have limited power in Step One, Step Two then leads us to a new, greater source of power than can help us return to sane, healthy living.

COMING TO BELIEVE

In Step Two, the process of coming to believe in a Power greater than ourselves was a personal one, and completely unique to each of us. For some, it happened quickly, and for others, more gradually, over months or even years.

When we were new in the COSA program, we may not have been convinced that a Power greater than ourselves could restore us to sanity. Yet one thing was overwhelmingly clear: something or someone had helped the COSA members around us. Many of those we heard sharing in meetings had somehow found a way through the pain we were experiencing.

The concept of a Power greater than ourselves was something many of us grappled with. Some of us were committed agnostics or atheists who felt a great deal of resistance to this whole line of thinking. For others, anything we perceived as even slightly religious reminded us of painful experiences from our past or conjured strong oppositional opinions. It was hard for us to trust anyone or believe in anything. We resisted this Step, and we worried we would not be able to come to a belief with which we felt comfortable.

When we struggled with these difficulties, our sponsors were invaluable guides. They explained this was not about religion, but about the spiritual principle of looking to something beyond ourselves for help. They shared their own beliefs in a Higher Power and encouraged us to reach out to other COSA members to ask about their experiences with the spiritual aspects of the program. In some cases our sponsors suggested writing assignments that helped us define a Power greater than ourselves. When applicable, some found it helpful to seek additional guidance from trusted members of our respective spiritual or religious communities.

As we began considering Step Two, we contemplated the meaning of the words. We realized we had already begun the process of coming to believe in a Power greater than ourselves. When we had initially reached out to the COSA fellowship, we had been seeking help from something outside our individual selves. By attending our first meeting, we showed our willingness to entertain new possibilities—those beyond what we alone could dream up. When we read from the COSA website and studied our first piece of COSA literature, we were admitting that we didn't have all the answers. We were willing to connect with a new body of knowledge and seek the healing power of a community. We had come to believe that this group and its Twelve Step approach might be able to help us when we couldn't seem to help ourselves.

For some of us, it helped to make a list of powers we already knew were greater than ourselves. For some, the collective knowledge and experience of our COSA group became the voice of caring, strength, and guidance that we needed, and in this way the group became our Higher Power. Nature, too, was more powerful than we were. We did not make the sun rise in the morning or set at night. We did not produce the weather nor could we change it. We did not create planets or solar systems. These forces worked without us. We saw that nature was indeed a Power greater than ourselves. This helped us to admit we were not the most powerful entity in the universe and opened the door to the possibility of believing in an infinite something rather than relying solely on our finite selves.

Our sponsors also encouraged us not to be overly concerned with arriving at a final definition at this point. They suggested that we find a concept of a Power greater than ourselves that would work for the time being. They assured us that this concept would likely change and grow as we did. We just needed to start to believe.

Some of us had a spiritual practice already, but our faith had been shaken by the traumas in our lives, and we struggled with a great deal of anger and doubt. We wondered, "If God loved me, how could this have happened?" We felt as if God had abandoned us. We felt scared to believe.

It took time for us to reconcile our difficult circumstances with our belief in a loving, caring Higher Power. It helped us to journal about our thoughts and feelings and to ask other COSAs about their experiences. Some of us wrote out specific affirmations for ourselves that reflected an acceptance of exactly where we were with our beliefs and a willingness to consider new perspectives. Many of us prayed about it. We tried to practice patience and allow the answers to come in their own time.

For those of us who had a clearly defined and steady belief in a Power greater than ourselves, the premise of Step Two was fairly comfortable. We may have been tempted to breeze right through it, yet the Second Step directed us to explore our beliefs from a new vantage point. Were we asking God to help us and guide us, or were we still trying to manage on our own? Did we believe God would help us? Were we harboring fears about being loved, guided, and accepted by this Power? Some of us discovered doubts about our worthiness, or thought others deserved help more than we did. We forgot about our own needs and the importance of spiritual guidance and replenishment. Step Two was an opportunity to deepen our understanding of our beliefs and strengthen our faith.

RESTORATION AND SANITY

Another part of our Step Two work was learning to let go of trying to restore ourselves. Most of us were accustomed to being self-sufficient and solving problems largely through our own efforts and determination. Many of us grew up in families or in circumstances in which our needs had not been met or we were criticized for needing help or for being vulnerable. We learned at an early age to be independent and to avoid relying on anyone. In fact, as children, we often took care of our siblings and even our parents. We took pride in being capable, giving, and accomplished. Nonetheless, our self-reliance had proved insufficient when dealing with the effects of compulsive sexual behavior; in fact, self-reliance was one of our greatest challenges in working Step Two. It took practice to learn how to let go of control and ask for and receive help. It took willingness and courage to believe we could and would be helped.

It was also important to consider the final word expressed in Step Two: sanity. While we admitted we had been struggling, many of us balked at the idea we might have been thinking or acting in an insane way. To some, the wording seemed extreme. Our sponsors encouraged us to examine our behaviors in response to the compulsive sexual behavior and the addict. Many of us could identify times of rage when we had screamed at or hit another person or injured ourselves. Some of us had searched for evidence of acting out and then looked the other way when we saw clear red flags. Some of us had unprotected sex with the addict although we knew they were not monogamous. We may have put ourselves and sometimes our children in unsafe situations. We made a list of our behaviors that were questionable. When we looked at them honestly, we had to admit we had acted insanely.

Certainly we had done our best to cope with the stressful and tragic circumstances, but our best effort had not resulted in our lives changing for the better. Some of the consequences that came from these acts of insanity were financial ruin, serious health problems, our own addictions, and the loss or breakdown of close relationships. In our bleakest moments, some of us believed that the only way out was death. We often feared we might be going crazy, and truth be told, in varying ways, we were.

Our lives—and as a result, the lives of our families and those who loved us—ricocheted from one drama or emergency to the next. Many of us were caught in a nearly perpetual state of drama and crisis because we simply didn't know any other way. If we thought of the often-quoted definition of insanity as doing the same thing over and over again while expecting different results, then we had clearly acted insanely.

APPLYING STEP TWO

Each day we practiced this new concept of believing. When we struggled with a person or circumstance, we reminded ourselves that we did not have power over them and focused instead on our new belief that there was a Power greater than ourselves who could help us. Sometimes we feared that there might be too much wreckage to repair, that our situation was simply irredeemable, or that somehow we deserved what we were going through. However, as we continued to practice Step Two and to enjoy the fruits of our labor, our belief in this Power grew stronger.

As time went on and we continued to work this Step, we began to look beyond our immediate calamites and instead found or rediscovered soul-nourishing activities that helped restore us to sanity. We enjoyed the simple pleasure of a pet's company, a refreshing walk, or a night at the movies. Some of us rekindled our interest in a hobby we had neglected or in our favorite sport.

As we continued to attend meetings, we saw more glimmers of hope, and our belief grew. Little by little, we saw positive changes occurring in our lives—changes we never imagined would be possible. The chaos we had described so vividly in our First Step began to fade. It was gradually replaced by a new sense of inner strength and good, orderly direction. We began to feel joy again. It became quite clear that a Power greater than ourselves was at work in our lives.

STEP TWO REFLECTION

Through Step One, we saw clear evidence that we were not all-powerful and that our repeated efforts to exert power where we had none didn't work. We began to recognize that we had tried to turn other people and our external circumstances into our sources of serenity. In our efforts to fix or change people and situations, we had also tried to be a higher power. In Step Two, we admitted to ourselves that we needed a new understanding of just who was in charge. When we worked Step Two, we realized that the solution to our problem did not need to be determined by the sheer force of our own will. We felt relieved. We were not being asked to recover all by ourselves. We were simply being asked to believe that a Power greater than ourselves could restore us. We earnestly prepared ourselves to ask for the help of that Power. Great gifts awaited us as we moved forward to Step Three.

Step Three

Made a decision to turn our will and our lives over to the care of God as we understood God.

In Step Three, we made a decision that deepens our commitment to recover and opens the door to true healing. It is an informed decision because we have closely considered the nature of our powerlessness, the insanity that comes from attempting to exert power where we have none, and the possibility of believing in a Power greater than ourselves. We have fully conceded that we cannot fix our problems by ourselves; we need help. With these first two Steps in place, we deliberately decide to trust and rely upon a Higher Power of our understanding. By taking Step Three, we experience a sense of relief and inner peace, and we develop a firm foundation upon which to build the rest of our recovery.

CONSIDERING STEP THREE

In Step Three, we are asked to purposely and consciously make a decision. This was an important decision and was challenging for many of us. It helped us to first consider the rest of the words of the Step. We were asked to turn over our will and our lives. What did that mean exactly? We thought of our will as everything that happened between our ears: our thoughts, feelings, and desires…our ambitions, goals, and dreams. Our will is what drives us to take action. What about our lives? We thought of our lives as everything that happened outside of ourselves. Our lives are our families, our careers, our homes… the dishes in the sink. They are our behaviors and the carrying out of our choices. We had used our will to manage our lives for so long. Could we now decide to trust that a Power greater than ourselves would care for us?

For COSAs who had suffered abuse or other serious violations of our personal boundaries, the concept of surrendering to any "power" felt dangerous and nearly impossible. However, when we considered the exact wording of this Step, we were able to put our minds at ease. This Step directed us to simply make a decision—no action was required at this point. In addition, we were not asked to place our faith in any one person or in a specific religious concept. Instead, we were to seek a God of our own understanding, whom we could trust. We were free to let go of any limiting ideas we had and to develop a new relationship with a gentle, compassionate Higher Power of our own choosing.

In our first attempts at working this Step, many of us did not yet have a clear conception of a Higher Power, or our faith in God had been seriously shaken. Rather than waiting until we had this completely sorted out, we started with whatever understanding we had. We gathered enough willingness to believe that our Higher Power would care for our lives, enough to make a decision. It was much like planting a small and mysterious seed. We did not know exactly what the result would be—how long it would take for the seed to sprout, or how tall the plant would be, if it would ever flower, or if it would bear fruit. Nevertheless, we decided to trust in the potential of that seed and the powerful process of growth.

STEP THREE IN ACTION

What did it look like to take Step Three? For some of us we simply made the decision to trust in the process and we continued working the rest of the Steps. We recognized the problem in Step One, acknowledged the solution in Step Two, and made a decision to trust the solution in Step Three.

For others it was a daily spiritual practice. Some of us said a simple prayer when faced with a situation that bothered us. We would say, "Whatever you want, God" or "I give it to you, God." Some prayed on their knees in the morning and asked God to care for their day, and again from their knees thanked God at night. Some used a God box: when a troubling situation presented itself, they slipped a note into the God box as a symbol of trust that it was now in God's hands. Others had only to remind themselves that they had already made the decision to turn over their will and that their lives were already in God's care. There was nothing more they needed to do.

As we worked this Step, we began to see the ways in which we had made people and situations our Higher Power. We had made our serenity and self-worth contingent upon individuals and events being a certain way and when they were not, all felt lost. Conversely, we also saw how we had attempted to be godlike in our efforts to control. Step Three helped us make more effective choices about where we placed our faith.

However, even well into recovery, we sometimes found ourselves in the midst of trying to manage outcomes or change people. Some of us tried not only to change or control the sex addict, but also our children, parents, relatives, friends, job, education, health, home, finances, or just about any situation. Often, we did not realize we were attempting to control until we felt depleted, angry, hopeless, crazy, or overwhelmed, having spent hours, days, weeks—maybe even years—trying to change someone or something over which we had no power.

With the help of this Step and our sponsors, we recognized that when we were feeling frenzied or constricted, we were not seeking our Higher Power's will for us. We were relying instead on self-will, and our serenity suffered. When we found ourselves in this situation, we asked ourselves: "What am I trying to control? What do I actually have power over?" Often, when we paused to reflect on these questions, we realized that we had decided on a desired outcome and were using our willpower to force that outcome.

We redirected our focus by asking "Am I willing to turn everything that is not in my control over to my Higher Power?" And then perhaps, "What do I need to do to take care of myself right now?" Step Three helped us to make good use of our will. Instead of using it to try to control life, we used it to align ourselves with our Higher Power. This, we found, was a much better use of our will.

We discovered that trying to control simply doesn't work. We thought it would make us feel safe, yet we discovered it led to even more fear. In Step Three, whether with willingness or out of desperation, we took small steps toward learning to trust our Higher Power. Many of us started the process of letting go by working with the situations in our lives that were the easiest to release. We could "turn over" the party we were hosting or whether or not we would find a parking spot close to the grocery store. Eventually, we grew in our ability to turn over the situations that were most important to us. We began to "let go" of situations at work, our relationships with our families, and our loved one's sobriety. As we experienced the relief of letting go and trusting a Higher Power, our willingness increased.

In surrendering the situations in our lives that we were powerless over, we found and claimed our true power and thus felt a sense of peace. The "what ifs" began to disappear, and we felt lighter and more courageous. We gradually discovered the freedom that came from being humble enough to say to ourselves that we did not have all the answers.

We also relaxed, knowing that we had the rest of our lives to practice the first Three Steps. We did not have to master letting go in one day. We grew in our understanding of a Higher Power. Over time and with practice, we learned to rely on and trust the God of our understanding. Our initial spiritual spark became a steady glow.

STEP THREE REFLECTION

The decision we make in Step Three becomes the foundation of our lifelong recovery journey. Deciding to trust in the loving care of a Higher Power provides strength and gives us the courage we need to continue our important and meaningful work in the COSA program. Through working this Step, our spirits become refreshed and revitalized. Our trust in ourselves and our hope for our lives increases. With the foundation of the first three Steps firmly in place, we are ready to gain a whole new perspective on our lives in Step Four.

Step Four

*Made a searching and fearless
moral inventory of ourselves.*

Step Four asks us to take an unflinching look at the one person we have power to change: ourselves. We make a comprehensive written inventory of our lives, both past and present. We set aside our defenses and closely examine the patterns in our thoughts, feelings, and behavior. We do this not to find fault, but to grow toward a change for the better. We begin to see the aspects of our character that have harmed us, harmed others, and stood in the way of healthy choices. Our inventory and insights during this Step Four process help us clear the way for deeper, more joyful relationships with our Higher Power, our trusted friends in recovery, and ourselves.

FOURTH STEP PRAYER

Higher Power, grant me the willingness to look carefully at all aspects of my life. Help me to be honest with myself about my strengths and weaknesses.

Please help me set aside my defenses. Relieve me of judgment and blame. Help me feel your comfort and support as I uncover the truth.

Guide me and give me courage as I walk through all the emotions this Step may stir within me. Keep me close to my trusted friends in recovery who can support me as I do this important work.

May the wisdom I gain as a result of working this Step help me make positive and lasting changes in my life. Help me share these priceless gifts of the Fourth Step with others.

CONSIDERING STEP FOUR

When we were new in COSA, many of us were confused about what a "searching and fearless moral inventory" even meant. What was a moral inventory and how would it help us? Why did it have to be fearless? Several people had hinted in meetings that it was a daunting task, but well worth the effort. We shared about the reservations we had. We asked questions. Ultimately, we trusted our sponsors and our Higher Power to guide us through the Fourth Step process.

Given the painful events that first prompted us to find the COSA program, many of us wondered why we needed to write our own inventory. Wasn't it those who had affected us with their compulsive sexual behavior who needed to look at themselves and their behavior? Weren't they clearly the ones in the wrong? Many of us saw ourselves as the innocent ones or as the responsible ones who had kept everything together as the sexual addiction caused chaos, confusion, and pain. Even those of us who went against our own values or developed our own addictions in an effort to cope often felt, at first, that it was the sex addict's fault that our lives looked the way they did. Our sponsors listened and encouraged us to continue moving forward. They knew from experience how Step Four could clarify the causes of our pain and ultimately lead to healing and freedom. Steps One, Two, and Three had proven to us that relief was available. We took a leap of faith, trusting that Step Four would help us too.

As we entered into the important work of Step Four, we called upon all that we had gained in the first three Steps. Using our newly strengthened reliance on a Power greater than ourselves, we felt ready to learn more about ourselves. We asked our Higher Power to help us let go of self-judgment and be honest about our lives, without internally berating or shaming ourselves. We set aside our desire to have this Step figured out ahead of time, or to do it perfectly. We turned the outcome over to our Higher Power and simply did as our sponsors suggested.

TAKING OUR INVENTORY

Our searching and fearless moral inventory required a great deal of writing. It would have been just as impossible for us to keep everything straight in our minds as it would be for a store owner inventorying stock. We needed it in front of us, on paper. We heard in meetings about many different types of inventories, such as resentment inventories, fear inventories, and sex inventories. We trusted our sponsors to guide us in the way they had worked their Fourth Steps.

The word "searching" guided our endeavor. We gave it everything we had. We made it as thorough and honest as we could. For some, it took weeks and for others, months. When it seemed like too much, we took breaks to nurture ourselves and have some fun. We practiced patience and gentleness with ourselves, but we did not stop altogether.

As with all the Steps, we were not alone in this venture. Once again, we had the support of our Higher Power, our sponsors, and our groups. This was incredibly important as we worked through the inventory. We did not try to figure out how to do this Step ourselves. Our sponsors gave us direction. We did not face ourselves, our past, or our feelings alone. We reached out many times during the process—to other COSAs with phone calls, and to our Higher Power with prayers. We started receiving some of the gifts of this Step right away. We were developing our ability to ask for and receive help, guidance, and loving understanding.

For some of us the word "fearless" suggested that we might encounter fear while working this Step. For others it suggested that this Step required the determination to persevere despite any inner resistance we felt. Regardless of which interpretation worked for us, we often found that this one simple word, "fearless," gave us the strength we needed to keep going. When deep feelings or resistance emerged, we summoned courage and strength. We reached out to sponsors, friends, and especially to our Higher Power during these times for support and encouragement. We learned that we were able to move through fear and take action. We didn't have to let fear paralyze us or change our course.

Lastly, this was our own inventory, not the inventory of other people. Most of us felt like victims and had a great deal of pain when we thought about the impact of compulsive sexual behavior on our lives. We were confused, hurt, angry, and scared. It was easy for us to see the wrongs others had done and were doing. It was harder for us to focus on ourselves. Our sponsors explained the gifts of this Step would come from looking at our own thoughts, feelings, and actions. When we recognized our own patterns, we could move toward real change, clarity, and choice.

We started our inventory by specifically naming who and what we resented. When had we experienced times of conflict or pain? What were the circumstances? How did we feel in relation to these people, places, and things? These were easy to answer. We wrote them down.

When that portion was complete, we reflected more deeply on the specifics. We asked ourselves: Did I feel threatened in some way? How did I act or react in these situations? Was I dishonest? Did I blame others to justify my own poor behavior? Did I rely on others to make me feel safe, loved, useful, or whole? Did I act in ways that were immoral or in ways that conflicted with my own values? Why did I act the way I did? These questions and their answers were the very heart of the inventory: we looked thoroughly at the part we played. We looked for the thoughts and behaviors that caused harm to ourselves and others, made the situations worse, or were outside our values. We wrote all of these down.

We found that our part was sometimes difficult to see. Our dishonesty could be so covert. It often showed up as being dishonest with ourselves, not speaking our truth, acting as others would have us act, believing as others would have us believe, denying reality, and creating fantasies. We blamed the addict for our unhappiness and our misery. And yet, while the addict's behavior, at times, had harmed us, weren't we the ones who denied our own feelings about it over and over again? Our dishonesty was not the addict's fault.

Some of our behaviors were not so covert. Many of us had reacted to our pain and shame with acts of rage, verbal and physical abuse, sexual revenge, and excessive use of alcohol or drugs. Our fears manifested themselves as hypervigilance, snooping, and manipulation. Sometimes, these painful feelings got acted out toward our children, our family, our friends, and our co-workers. These behaviors were ours, not the addict's.

We listed the feelings driving our undesirable behavior. Was there shame, anger, pain, guilt, or loneliness? What were our fears? We began to realize that our previously unrecognized feelings almost always drove our undesirable behavior, which harmed us and the people around us. Did we have painful shame messages echoing from our past or coming from people currently in our lives? What were the messages? How did we react to them? Gradually, we began to see the choices we had been making and the new choices we could make. We started to recognize and let go of the victim role. We began to feel the gift of hope.

We found it important to examine the effects of the compulsive sexual behavior we had witnessed. We looked closely for any unhealthy patterns in our own sexual behavior. We asked ourselves if we had used sex to gain attention, validation, approval, love, or commitment from others. Did we feel obligated to have sex when we weren't feeling open or safe? Had we participated in sex in ways that felt uncomfortable to us? Did we use sex to control or manipulate? Punish or reward? Had we been actors in bed? Were we neglectful or even unaware of our own needs? Were there times we felt shut down or avoided sex or pleasure altogether? In what circumstances had we felt sexual shame?

This was eye-opening for many of us and played a key role in bringing our sexual selves into alignment with our own values. We were growing toward a healthy sexuality. We were learning about nourishing intimacy. It felt so empowering to see how we may have harmed ourselves in the past, and to own our decisions going forward. For some, it was the first release of the shame we had carried from our sexual past. We got it out of our heads and our bodies and onto paper. Once we saw our own sexual patterns, we had the prospect of making new, healthier choices.

It was also suggested that we look for and note our assets. In this case, we saw ourselves fully, and recognized when our thoughts and actions were in line with our values. We recorded when we had spoken up for ourselves, honored our feelings, and trusted our Higher Power. We took note of when we positively impacted the people around us. One little bit at a time, we moved through our inventory. We began receiving the gift of balance.

STEP FOUR REFLECTION

By the time we reached the end of Step Four, we had learned how to look closely for our patterns and were ready for a new way of living. We started to know ourselves, to feel our feelings, and to hear our own thoughts. Our eyes were opening. We saw what was going on around us and wanted to make healthy choices instead of denying reality. We saw how we had abandoned ourselves and others. We started to recognize the terrible messages we had been telling ourselves and we longed to be free from them.

We clearly saw the shortcomings that had harmed us and kept us from healthy relationships with ourselves, our Higher Power, and others. Our new awareness could be painful, yet it was a natural and essential part of the process. We were reminded that we could not heal what we could not see. We were ready to let go of the victim identity and take responsibility for our own unhealthy and compulsive reactions to the sex addict. Through Step Four, we began experiencing the gifts of a more honest perspective. We noticed ourselves thinking differently. We were changing. We were ready to share in Step Five.

Step Five

Admitted to God, to ourselves, and to another human being the exact nature of our wrongs.

In Step Four, we worked hard and discovered much about ourselves. We felt strongly motivated to change, but the process calls for one more Step before we address our character defects directly. In Step Five, we are asked to be transparent and vulnerable with our Higher Power, ourselves, and another person. We deliberately put down our defenses, and we become accountable. As we work Step Five, we discover that owning and sharing our imperfections frees us from the weight of secrecy and shame, opens us to a deeper level of connection with ourselves and others, and gives us the strength and clarity to continue our recovery work.

APPROACHING STEP FIVE

In Step Four, we identified many of our wrongs. We looked at our sexual histories and our fears. We examined our part in situations we resented and discovered patterns of dishonesty, self-righteousness, blame, neglect, and ill treatment of ourselves and others. We realized we had been disrespectful, manipulative, critical, over- and/or under-responsible, and had acted outside of our own values. There was a lot to digest, and for Step Five, it was critically important to have an accurate account of who we were and just how we had acted.

However, some of us had a strong reaction to the word "wrongs." Many of us had badgered ourselves relentlessly throughout our lives or had been criticized or shamed by others. When we heard the word "wrongs," we cringed or felt defensive. Some of us even shut down completely. It was difficult to work this Step when we resisted the words used in it.

Some of us found it helpful to replace the word "wrongs" or define it differently. Instead, we referred to them as destructive behaviors, unhealthy or faulty coping mechanisms, old habits, unhelpful or self-defeating choices, ineffective strategies, flaws, or simply "our part." Our sponsors suggested a balanced perspective. The point of Step Five was not to criticize or berate ourselves. This was not helpful, and it was not the goal.

In our childhoods, many of us developed the belief that we had to be perfect in order to be worthy of love. The message that we must be flawless seemed prevalent in books, magazines, movies, TV shows, songs, advertisements, and almost anywhere we looked. For some of us, this message was reinforced by the words and behaviors of family members, peers, teachers, and even religious leaders. Many of us developed a sense that we were just not good enough. It was this faulty belief that fueled our resistance to acknowledging our wrongdoings and kept us hiding in shame.

We had learned to avoid connection and manage the pain of rejection by disguising and guarding our true selves with people pleasing and perfectionism, or on the opposite end of the spectrum, self-righteousness and rage. How could we now lower our shields of protection and admit our mistakes, our wrongs, our harms, and our sexual indiscretions? Some of us felt we would die of shame if we had to go through with it. Some of us told ourselves, "I don't need to take this Step. I will just skip it, or I will only share some of it."

The problem with this thinking was that by working Step Five partially or not at all, we would rob ourselves of the gifts of this Step. As long as we kept our flaws secret, we could not be free from our shame, we could not make lasting changes, and we could not genuinely connect with others. It kept us running and we could never get away because we were running from ourselves—from our own internal judgments of who we were and how we had behaved. What we didn't know and couldn't truly feel and experience until after we completed Step Five was the relief, freedom, and recovery that resulted from coming out of hiding.

SHARING OUR STORIES

Fortunately, we did not have to share our most vulnerable selves with anyone and everyone. This Step called for a safe person and helped us practice the skill of developing relationships with trustworthy people. It was up to us whom we shared our Fifth Steps with and why.

An important consideration was who not to choose. Our partners, family members, and our friends outside of recovery were not ideal choices. While many of us shared the insights we were learning about ourselves with our loved ones as we worked through our Steps, we opted not to select them to complete this Step. We needed to be able to share freely. If we had planned to share our Step work with a loved one, it would have been difficult for us to be completely honest. It was also important that the person we appointed be unaffected by the situations we were sharing about and have no investment in the outcome of our work or our decisions.

We thought carefully when selecting the person with whom we would share our story. We looked for someone who did not shame or judge, someone we trusted to provide acceptance, perspective, and guidance. We chose someone who listened and who showed signs of a strong relationship with their Higher Power. We sought a person who was safe, honest, and compassionate.

For most of us, our sponsors were the natural choice. They had knowledge of working this Step and we had already grown to trust them. When we had relayed our troubles to them in the past they listened, were understanding, and were able to relate to us and share their own experiences. They offered insight and direction on how we might use the program tools to navigate through our tough situations. They kept the details of our shares confidential. They were safe.

For others, another choice was necessary or preferable. Some chose therapists with Twelve Step backgrounds, and others had religious practices that encouraged consulting a duly appointed spiritual advisor. What was important was choosing someone with whom we could share the most vulnerable parts of ourselves.

Step Five called not only for acknowledging our wrongs to another person, but to God and ourselves as well. Before sharing our Fifth Step with another person, some of us said a prayer asking our Higher Power to be present, while others took time alone in quiet reflection, composed letters to our Higher Power, or prayed about each of the wrongs we had uncovered. Some of us wrote in a journal about what we had discovered or read our stories out loud to ourselves. It was important during these practices that we were our own safe, compassionate, and loving friend.

When we were ready to share our work, our sponsors guided us to arrange a location that felt comfortable to us. They suggested somewhere quiet, a peaceful place that might help us feel safe and had little or no possibility of interruption. It could be a spot in nature or a cozy living room. We had not realized how important this was. A safe place meant we could be more open and expressive about our past.

We took our time. Some of us shared the details of our Fourth Step as we worked through it, while others waited until after they were finished and shared it all at once. A one-on-one, face-to-face conversation was ideal. However, some of us shared over the phone, at our local meetings, or in Step groups.

It wasn't easy to admit that we were not perfect and had harmed ourselves and others. Many of us found we had tremendous shame and grief as we acknowledged these patterns. We felt pain when we realized we had subjected ourselves to mistreatment. We felt ashamed when we acknowledged how we had hurt people with whom we were close. But this is when Step Five really called for change. Instead of hiding, denying, avoiding, blaming, minimizing, or justifying our actions, we allowed ourselves to acknowledge the truth and feel our feelings, and then we shared our discoveries with another.

Each confidante was a little different. Some made a special effort to ease our minds before we began by sharing how they felt when they took their Fifth Step. Some just listened. Others offered their own experiences that related to what they were hearing. Some offered feedback, mentioning or taking notes about character defects or assets as they listened. Some helped us explore whether we were taking too much (or not enough) responsibility for a situation. Many of them gave us encouragement and guidance and offered different perspectives. They were honest, respectful, balanced, and gentle. For some of us, this was the first time we felt completely accepted by someone.

It was this experience of being vulnerable, of sharing our mistakes and our feelings, which was truly transformative. For some of us, it felt like we were hearing our own stories told in their entirety for the first time. We had been running from ourselves all our lives, afraid that someone would find out the truth about who we really were. We had thought if anyone found out about our lies, our behavior, or our thinking, then surely they would run from us. We would be abandoned, rejected, exposed, and ashamed. We would be alone. The paradox of this Step was that when we shared our imperfect selves with a safe person, we actually felt better about ourselves and more connected with others.

A level of forgiveness and compassion started to creep in. We had made mistakes, we had messed up, and we had acted badly, but we began to understand the truth that everyone is flawed—yet worthy of love. Embracing our imperfections and taking responsibility for our actions led us to feel at peace with ourselves and connected with the human race. We were not better than or less than other people; we were simply equal to them. Our shame and unworthiness loosened their grip and were replaced with a humble and open heart.

MOVING FORWARD

After we completed our sharing, our sponsors recommended taking time to reflect on all that we had uncovered. They suggested quiet meditation and self-care. The work we did in

Steps One through Five had laid the foundation for our recovery. Had we been honest, courageous, willing, humble, trusting? Had we been thorough? While we chose not to pick up the perfectionistic magnifying glass, we asked ourselves if we had done our best. We had come so far from that first COSA meeting. We felt joyful at the comparison and hopeful for the future. We felt confident, loved, and accepted. With our strengthened connection to our Higher Power, a better understanding of ourselves, and the support of others, we were ready for change. We were ready for Step Six.

Step Six

*Were entirely ready to have God remove
all these defects of character.*

Through our work in Steps Four and Five, we became aware of behaviors that had created problems for us. To prepare for Step Six, if we had not done so already, we worked to name the characteristics driving our choices and leading to the development of troublesome behavior patterns. This we called our list of character defects. Now Step Six asks us to achieve a state of being—readiness. There are two aspects to this readiness. First, we become ready to let go of our character defects. Second, we become ready to have God remove them.

APPROACHING STEP SIX

Upon first hearing Step Six as newcomers to COSA, many of us winced, imagining rounds of self-shaming. It sounded dreadful. We soon found that this was not the case. Our sponsors told us this Step was to be used to help us grow and heal, not as a way to beat ourselves up. We were working to achieve a willing and humble state, not perfection. As we listed our character defects, it was important for us to avoid slipping into any past habits of self-criticism or self-loathing. A gentle and loving approach would prove to be the most helpful and successful way to navigate this Step.

We achieved a neutral state of mind, neither coddling nor condemning ourselves, by looking more carefully at our problematic characteristics and how they had served us. Often, they appeared to have protected us or helped us survive. For example, our aggressive reactions told people to back off. Our people-pleasing was a way to garner love and acceptance. Our perfectionism and self-criticism were attempts to shield ourselves from others' judgment. Our criticism of others helped us deny our own feelings of low self-worth. As we looked at each of our troublesome behaviors, we saw how these coping mechanisms had sustained us and even helped us survive difficult situations. Sometimes we developed these techniques when we were young and had few available ways of taking care of ourselves.

We came to see our defects of character as a kind of distorted self-care. The circumstances some of us were facing caused these old survival techniques to flare up. This set off our instinct to fight, flee, or freeze, and we reacted. These were natural human responses to trauma. Few of us had the knowledge and training to respond any other way. We needed help and support to move past these protective, instinctive reactions. We kept this in mind as we looked at our list. We might appreciate how our coping mechanisms had served us in the past, yet we could acknowledge their destructiveness in our present circumstances and feel a desire to let them go.

Our sponsors pointed out that some of our character defects, if brought into balance, could become assets. We saw that instead of conjuring up fear-filled stories, we could apply our creativity to healthy problem-solving. When examining our caretaking behavior, we realized that the amount of focus and energy we devoted to caring for others would be a wonderful gift if turned toward ourselves. Even our perfectionism, when dialed down a few notches, could play out as concentration and determination.

We did not use this new way of thinking to minimize or negate the difficulties and harm created by our character defects. Instead, we used it to understand that, although we had acted out our character defects, they were separate from our core and were not definitions of our true selves. We could love ourselves, accept our humanness, and be ready and willing to move away from the painful and destructive patterns on which we had come to rely.

It was important to note that feelings themselves did not belong on our list of character defects. Many times, feelings such as fear, anger, pain, or shame had driven our behaviors. However, it was not the feelings themselves that had caused problems—it was our reactions to those feelings.

BECOMING READY

Many of us arrived at Step Six ready to have our defects of character removed. We had experienced the destruction, despair, frustration, and grief they had created. We were ready to be free of them. In fact, we couldn't wait to be rid of them! As we became aware of our character defects, they seemed to become magnified: each time we acted in accordance with a character defect, we became more aware of our feelings and of the consequences of our actions. For those of us in this state, we focused on becoming ready and willing to have *God* remove these defects from us.

If we did not arrive at Step Six with this readiness, we worked to achieve it. Our sponsors encouraged us and suggested ways that would help us become ready. Some of us listed our character defects and, alongside each one, the percentage of willingness we had to let go of it. If we were not 100 percent willing, we did some work around it.

We talked to our sponsors and other COSA members. We heard other COSA members share the gifts they had received from working this Step. They recounted how their lives used to be and how they had been changed by this Step. They described how they had become ready and how they let go.

At the suggestion of our sponsors, many of us wrote about our character defects. We reflected on how they had affected our lives. How had we acted them out? In what situations had they come up? Had they brought joy, peace, and clarity? Did these ways of behaving make us feel better or worse? Had the situations improved? How did our defects of character affect others?

We also wrote about how our lives might look without our character defects. While we did not get attached to our visions, we imagined the possibility of a better life without our negative character traits. We asked our Higher Power for insight, guidance, and willingness to let go of a character defect. If we needed to, we would pray for the *willingness to be willing* to let it go.

Even after understanding the consequences of our character defects, some of us still wanted or thought we needed to hold on to a few of these well-honed tools. After all, they had helped us survive for a long time.

We might have thought, "If I am honest now, people won't like me, or I will face consequences. I might be rejected and abandoned." In the past, our defects seemed to give us power: "You'd better not mess with me. I will put you in your place!" Some of us might have concluded, "If I let go of these characteristics, I will have no power! I will get abused. I will feel worthless. I need them." Who would we be and what would our lives look like if we gave up these tactics? Sometimes we felt like these traits were part of us: "I take care of people; that is who I am." When we looked at our defects of character, we could see how they had served us. What we could not see clearly was what would happen to us if they were gone.

This seemed like a dead end, until our sponsors guided us to look again at the most important part of the Step: being entirely ready to *"have God...."* We discovered that the heart of Step Six is taking a leap of faith—achieving an internal state of willingness and trust. While we received direction and support, we alone had to let go and trust God. No one could do this for us. We didn't know what we would become. We didn't know what life would look like without our defects of character but when we took our leap of faith, we were able to trust God with that.

We found Step Six was asking us to surrender again to our Higher Power. This surrender seemed like a tall order, but when we examined the word *remove* in this Step, we began to think it was reasonable. We learned that the word *remove* was an action word that meant "to distance from." This aided our understanding of just what we were trying to believe God could and would do for us. We were coming to believe that God could distance us from our defects of character. We were not expecting that God would eradicate these characteristics, but simply that God would move them away from us or us away from them.

We realized that our surrender was part of the Step Six process. When we were able to achieve this surrender, this faith, we actually felt different. There was a sense of relief and hope. Our lives changed in that moment. With this action came the gifts of the Step.

It was important for us to let go of perfectionism. There were some character defects we were just not ready to let go of, and that was okay. We could continue working the Steps, and when and if we became ready, God and this Step would be there.

THE GIFTS OF STEP SIX

As we work with our defects of character, our understanding of ourselves grows. We feel amazed at how much room there is for change that will affect our lives in a positive way. We become aware of our wounds and the defense mechanisms we have used to protect them. We feel a sprinkling of forgiveness and compassion towards ourselves and others, and we feel hope. We learn in this Step to be willing to trust the recovery process and to trust in a Power greater than ourselves. In this humble and ready state, we look to Step Seven.

Step Seven

*Humbly asked God to remove
our shortcomings.*

In Step Seven we stand at the confluence of considerable recovery work. We have walked through Steps of honest self-discovery; acceptance; a commitment to new, healthy behaviors; and a heartfelt willingness to let go of our shortcomings. Through our diligent work in Steps Four and Five, we discovered and accepted how our behaviors had made our lives unmanageable, causing harm to ourselves and others. In Step Six we prepared ourselves by becoming ready to let go of our shortcomings and willing to let God remove them. Throughout these previous Steps, we have honestly and rigorously done our part. Now in Step Seven, it is time to ask God to remove the character defects that block us from God's will for us. It is time to step into the joy of living lives that release us from the restrictions of our shortcomings.

HUMBLY ASKED

The kind of humility asked of us in Step Seven was a conscious spiritual surrender. It was not based on feelings of unworthiness, desperation, or defeat. Humility was not humiliation. As we began to experience the grace and gifts we had received by working the previous Steps, we came to trust that our Higher Power cared about us and was working on our behalf. This warmed our hearts and softened us. Knowing our Higher Power was on our side helped our humility grow from a place of love, gratitude, and respect. Our faith and trust grew as we saw changes in ourselves and transformations in others. Humility, born of trust and faith in our Higher Power, readied us to willingly ask our Higher Power for help.

Initially, asking for what we wanted and needed was challenging. Previous experience with asking for what we wanted may have led to disappointments or even humiliation. But we were reminded that we were not in charge of when and how our defects would be lifted. We let go of our idea that we knew what was best for ourselves, and we trusted our Higher Power to determine when and how the defects would be lifted. By doing this, we asked for help from a spiritual place, aligned with our Higher Power's will for us. We were asking the right source, our Higher Power, and we asked with the knowledge that what came next might not be what we expected or understood in the moment. Yearning to move forward, we allowed ourselves to be vulnerable and took a leap of faith.

Some of us resisted or resented the very idea of having to ask for our shortcomings to be removed. Early in recovery, when our own shortcomings were pointed out, we sometimes felt angry or ambivalent. In our pain, we tended to see only the shortcomings of those who had wronged us. Perhaps we eventually recognized some of our own shortcomings and tried to remove them through self-discipline or sheer willpower, only to find that our efforts failed. It was a painful realization that we could not do this work alone.

To move forward, we focused on the growth and freedom we had gained through our previous Step work. We considered what life could be like if we were relieved of our shortcomings. This exercise of reflection brought us back to gratitude, trust, and humility. We felt more able to let go of our fears and resentments related to asking for our Higher Power's help. We began to feel safe in the knowledge that in Step Seven, what we were asking for was in line with God's will for us.

Some of us were overwhelmed by the mistaken idea that we had to change ourselves, and we found the prospect of removing our defects of character daunting. We were grateful to be reminded that our part of Step Seven was merely to "humbly ask." It was our Higher Power who would lift our defects and heal us. Our part was to remain willing, trust our Higher Power, and allow the process to unfold in accordance with our Higher Power's will for us.

As we took time to reflect on this Step, we examined the evidence of God's love for us. We worked with our sponsors. We prayed and meditated to recognize old feelings and the unmet needs beneath them. We let go of the untruths that we were unlovable or unworthy.

With those stumbling blocks out of the way, we could sharpen our focus and see the ways our Higher Power expressed love and care for us. We thought back to times when our Higher Power had given us just what we needed, when we needed it. These may have manifested as a sudden sense of peace in a painful situation or as a moment of clarity and detachment in the midst of turmoil. Perhaps it came in the form of a welcomed and unexpected answer. In reflecting on these experiences with an open heart, we were amazed at the number of ways our Higher Power had acted on our behalf.

MANY WAYS TO ASK

As we began planning our approach to asking for our Higher Power's help, we shared with our sponsors and asked for their feedback and guidance. Our sponsors helped us see that there were many ways to prepare our Seventh Step prayer. We were free to choose what worked best for us. Many of us, using our list of character defects from our Fourth and Fifth Steps, prepared a list of what we wanted God to remove. Some of us wrote one prayer containing all our shortcomings. Some wrote separate prayers, one for each shortcoming. We may have chosen to put our shortcomings in order from our highest to lowest priorities. We may have included our hopes for what our lives would be like after our most pain-inducing shortcomings were removed. For example, we asked for controlling behaviors to be removed so that freedom and detachment could take their place. We may have confided in our Higher Power that we weren't sure we had uncovered all of our character defects, and we asked for the rest to be revealed to us. Some of us simply asked God to reveal and remove our shortcomings. While God may not have removed our shortcomings in our preferred order, we turned them over and trusted they would be removed according to God's timing and unique plan for us.

Some of us felt confusion or fear return when we wrote about the specific shortcomings we wished to have removed. Our shortcomings had been such an ingrained part of our survival, we wondered what we might be like without them. For instance, if we let go of controlling behaviors, would we be left dangerously vulnerable? If we stopped caretaking, would people still love us? As much as we wanted to be rid of our shortcomings, some of these old behaviors had been our early coping skills. We were advised to take our time and be gentle with ourselves.

We looked back at the pain and harm our character defects had caused us and those around us. The behaviors that were once our survival mechanisms were now destructively turning against us. They stood in the way of our new-found strengths and assets. We meditated on the gifts and joy that could be possible in our lives once our character defects were no longer haunting us. We sought encouragement from our sponsors, who reminded us that our best selves were ready to shine through once our shortcomings were removed.

When we felt that our request was aligned with our heartfelt recovery goals, we were ready to approach our Higher Power. If we chose to write a prayer, we may have read the final version to our sponsor first before praying privately later. Or we may have asked our sponsors to be present with us as we spoke aloud to God our heartfelt request to have our shortcomings removed. Some completed Step Seven in other ways that were personally meaningful, such as lighting a candle or sitting outside in nature while reviewing our defects and sincerely asking our Higher Power to remove them. With our humble request now entrusted to God's care, we opened our hearts to a new way of living!

THE GIFTS OF STEP SEVEN

One of the immediate benefits of working Step Seven is a new hope and optimism that we can truly be changed. We also feel a closer and more personal relationship with our Higher Power.

In the process of removing our shortcomings, God creates spiritual space for our healthy recovery behaviors to flourish. With the awareness and perspective gained from all our recovery gifts, and with a new sense of humility and trust in our COSA program and our Higher Power, we are ready for Step Eight.

Step Eight

Made a list of all persons we had harmed, and became willing to make amends to them all.

Each of the previous Steps asked us to look within ourselves. Step Eight asks us to look outside ourselves, specifically toward the people we have harmed. With a humble heart and the recovery tools of the last seven Steps to aid us, we begin the process of seeking willingness to make amends. There is great wisdom in amends being a two-step process in which we first identify the amends and then develop the willingness to act. Step Eight provides us with time to contemplate the harms we have done to others along with space for a change of heart, thoughts, and behaviors. We ask our Higher Power to remove obstacles to willingness, such as resentments, fears, rationalization, and justification. Doing the work of this Step softens our hearts and makes space for forgiving ourselves and others.

MAKING THE LIST

Our work in Step Four gave us the first glimpse of those we may have harmed. Many of us chose to use our Step Four findings as the starting point for our Step Eight list. We applied ourselves with honesty and humility as we added each name to our list. Having seen the healing changes this Step made in the lives of others who worked it before us, we felt encouraged. We had seen their attitudes and behaviors change. We had heard them share their lightness of spirit and the improvement in their relationships with others. We moved forward with the hope that we could also be restored to sanity.

There were many ways to create the list. For some, it was simply handwritten. For others, it was a detailed spreadsheet with rows for people's names, a column for harm we had done to them, and a column for our level of willingness to make amends (e.g., now, someday, or not yet willing). Some of us asked our sponsors or others who had worked this Step for input on what had worked for them. With this wealth of information, we created a method that worked best for us.

No matter how we constructed the list, it became a powerful tool. As we looked at each name, our Higher Power helped us become conscious of the harm our actions, thoughts, and behaviors had caused ourselves and others. Perhaps by being dishonest, selfish, self-seeking, and frightened, our boundaries had become weak or non-existent. We may have become enmeshed in a victim, rescuer, and perpetrator dynamic that was addictive, compulsive, and out of control. Whether we caused harm inadvertently or purposefully, we acknowledged that our choices and behaviors had hurt others and ourselves.

Although Step Eight asks us to do the difficult work of accepting responsibility for our harmful actions and behaviors, we heard that one of the great purposes of this Step was to free ourselves from the guilt and shame we carried about our mistreatment of others and ourselves. With this in mind, we endeavored to be gentle and to exercise compassionate accountability for ourselves.

Prior to recovery we may not have been aware of how our character defects manifested in our relationships and dealings with others. What we thought were tools, options, or solutions may actually have been our faulty coping skills. Lashing out or retaliating may have been all we were capable of in certain situations. Punishing ourselves for this would actually work against the purpose of this Step. Instead, with the support of our sponsor, this Step brings us the opportunity to be accountable for our past and present actions and to free ourselves from the burdens of guilt, shame, and regret.

BECOMING WILLING

One of the biggest challenges many of us faced was being willing to make amends to those who had harmed us—especially if the harm to us felt far greater than the harm to them. Defensiveness, pain, wounded pride, judgment, and resentment toward such people blocked our willingness and stood in the way of our spiritual growth. Justification, rationalization, and minimizing came into play.

We recognized that these faulty defense mechanisms diverted our attention away from healthy remorse and from humbly seeking the spiritual gifts that willingness and acceptance bring to us. We realized that Step Eight is about healing ourselves, not exonerating others from their part. In our effort to move forward, we sought to detach from the other party's harm and focus on our part. Our part may have been a small portion of the overall harm that occurred in our interaction, but it was still our responsibility. By focusing on our part, we found healing and freedom from the impediments of anger, blame, and resentment.

Uncomfortable feelings and fears may have caused us to hesitate in taking this Step. Some of us were tempted to stray out of the present into futurizing or "what if" territory. We reminded ourselves to stay within the scope of what was asked: to make a list and become willing. All this Step required of us was that we *become willing*; no further action was asked. We set aside concerns about outcomes or the possibility of facing the persons to whom we needed to make amends and kept our focus on the current Step. With our Higher Power's help, we faced any mental or emotional blocks as they arose. We trusted the process and had faith we'd be provided with all we needed as we prepared for Step Nine.

A BALANCED APPROACH

Sponsors played a crucial role in helping us discern where we had been overly responsible for others by taking on unearned guilt or responsibility for harms we didn't cause. They helped us right-size our part and let go of issues that didn't belong to us. Sponsors also helped us to recognize where we had avoided mentioning an issue or person to whom we may owe amends.

Our list would not be complete without adding ourselves to it. Our Fourth Step revealed how we had harmed ourselves. For many of us, acknowledging and accepting this was harder than facing the harm we had caused others. We may have neglected ourselves, put ourselves in harm's way, ignored our needs, or acted against our values. We may have blamed and shamed ourselves for things we did not have control over, such as abuse or harms that were done to us when we were children. We may have ignored our Higher Power's will for us. Our health, peace of mind, and self-respect may have been harmed. We accepted that it was appropriate and in fact vital to add ourselves to our Eighth Step list.

As we looked at our self-harm, we tried to be gentle. We stayed focused on self-acceptance, compassion, and forgiveness. If we were to free ourselves from the weight of our past behaviors, we had to accept and forgive our shortcomings and character defects. We also kept our eyes on the mental, emotional, and spiritual freedom this work could bring.

IT IS A PROCESS

The wording in the Step, "became willing," indicated a *process* in which a spiritual surrender or change of heart was needed. *Willingness* would lead us to detachment from the other party's injustice or wrongs toward us. We would move towards acceptance of their humanness and imperfections, releasing our resentments and pain.

We recalled times when we'd made amends unwillingly, out of obligation or to keep the peace, but it wasn't heartfelt or genuine. Such amends gave us no relief. Sometimes, we even felt worse, and resentment and anger grew. We compared that to a time when we'd made heartfelt amends and considered how that felt. We realized that a willing heart unencumbered by anger and resentment could give true, genuine amends. We sought to find that place within us for each person on our list.

We asked our Higher Power for help with willingness. Perhaps there were people on our list to whom we were already willing and eager to make amends. Yet there were others with whom we still struggled, so we asked our Higher Power simply for the willingness *to be* willing. In such instances, some of us found it helpful to look with fresh eyes at those more challenging people on our list and to see things from their perspective. We sought to accept them as they were. We began to feel compassion and empathy toward them. Those feelings were indications that we were becoming willing. From this place we could feel resentment toward them slip away, and peace and forgiveness take its place. We felt a weight lifted from us.

As a result of our work, we experienced the change of heart we would need in order to make true amends. The priceless wisdom of this process became clear as we prepared to reach out and make reparations to those we had harmed.

THE GIFTS OF STEP EIGHT

Our work in Step Eight gave us hope that we could shed our old resentments, heal old wounds, and lead an intentional life—one in which we avoid harming others or creating new resentments. We were confident that we had prepared ourselves to set matters right and make amends to all those we had harmed, including ourselves. We were ready for Step Nine.

Step Nine

*Made direct amends to such people
wherever possible, except when to do so
would injure them or others.*

Our journey to Step Nine has included a lot of challenging spiritual work. This process has been introspective: inside ourselves, with our Higher Power, and with our sponsor. Then Step Eight directed us to look outwardly at amending our relationships. Now, in Step Nine, we take this work out into the world. We seek to set right the harms we have caused in the past, and we focus on living one day at a time with new, healthy relationship behaviors. We experience a greater sense of peace.

APPROACHING STEP NINE

As with learning anything new, we were humbled by how much we didn't know and were required to learn when beginning to work this Step. We learned that our sponsor's guidance was essential to help us plan our amends. Some of us may have felt frustrated that we couldn't just do this on our own without help. It was humbling to realize we perhaps needed as much support from our sponsors, co-sponsors, Step group, or other COSA friends as when we were newcomers.

With our sponsors, we discussed our relationships, the harms we had done, and the past situations where we wished we had been able to respond with healthier behaviors. In practical terms, our sponsors recommended straightforward and specific amends. If we became stuck or unsure, we asked for help in finding the words and avoided justifying our behaviors.

We were gentle with ourselves, since our previous Step work had given us insight that many of our original coping mechanisms were misguided. We came to realize that we were no longer victims—we were adults who could take responsibility for the harm we had caused others and ourselves.

MANY WAYS TO MAKE AMENDS

With our Step Eight list and a willingness to move forward, we developed a plan for our amends in Step Nine. We walked closely with our Higher Power and sought to act from a spirit of accountability, kindness, humility, forgiveness, and tolerance.

We began Step Nine with the amends that felt the easiest, the ones we felt most willing to make, or those which we felt our Higher Power was calling us to make. These amends started our path toward freedom and serenity.

We came to understand that, if at all possible, the best way of making amends directly to a person we had harmed was face-to-face. When the time came, we made appointments with each person on our list if we could. This may have been challenging or even terrifying for those of us who had learned to fear direct communication. We discussed each amends with our sponsors first.

We sincerely apologized for harm done, we accepted responsibility, and in some cases, we asked whether we had done other harms of which we weren't aware. We honored the other person as worthy of respect and kind treatment. We made reasonable restitution by taking actions such as repayment, spending time listening or helping, minding our own business, and being honest. We did our best to practice new, healthy behaviors thereafter.

When past harms could not be amended directly, we could still make things better spiritually and symbolically. We considered many ways to accomplish indirect amends and sought guidance and examples from our sponsors. Some of us took on service commitments in COSA or in our communities. Others made a monetary donation to an organization related to the amends. Some of us planted a tree or wrote a poem to honor a person for whom direct amends would be injurious to them or to ourselves. Or we wrote an amends letter but just read it to our sponsor, placed it in a box as a symbolic way of turning it over to our Higher Power, or disposed of it. We may have even found we needed to make amends to animals, organizations, employers, or institutions.

Some of our amends may have felt uncomfortable or forced us to face consequences we would have previously avoided. We continued to check in with our sponsors, especially if we found ourselves beginning to spiral downward into shame or fear. We honored ourselves by acting with the humility we had learned in Step Seven.

LIVING OUR AMENDS

At the heart of our recovery was living our amends—changing our behavior in the present and trying to be of service moving forward. We could generously express gratitude in relationships. The combination of a sincere apology and changed behavior was a powerful demonstration of our new recovery mindset.

Some of us found that our Higher Power presented us with opportunities for further amends we had not anticipated. For example, we may have suddenly remembered the names of people we had forgotten, or we unexpectedly encountered someone we had no idea how to find. Perhaps our Higher Power put something in our heart that we had not even written about in Step Eight, or we suddenly thought of a way to amend something grievous.

In prayer, we asked our Higher Power to guide us as we humbly shared our amends with those on our list. We listened to the other person's response, but we did not approach our amends with expectations of forgiveness or a particular response from the other person. We let go of outcomes and remembered that each amends we made was to set things right and to free ourselves. We approached others with kindness and did what we could reasonably do, keeping in mind not to cause further injury. We recalled that our role was not to rescue others or resolve their problems, pain, or challenges. We owned our part only, and we did not take on responsibility for things that were not ours.

We were grateful when the outcome of an amends provided healing in a relationship. If the outcome did not match our desires, we sought support and comfort from our Higher Power, sponsor, and COSA friends. We practiced surrender as we recognized that our Higher Power's will was being done.

EXCEPT WHEN TO DO SO WOULD INJURE THEM OR OTHERS

Our sponsors were especially helpful with complex amends. Before taking action, we discussed with our sponsors complicated amends and situations in which making amends might cause further injury to ourselves or others. Examples included those to whom making amends would expose damaging information, or, as part of an amends, revealing (to a person we had gossiped about) what we had said about them to someone else. Our sponsors cautioned us never to take action when our own motives were suspect, or we could cause further damage. For instance, we would not use our amends as an attempt to manipulate someone else into making amends to us.

Other complicated amends included people who were abusive or who had caused us a great deal of harm through compulsive sexual behavior. Some people might have been so unhealthy in their own diseases that they were either unsafe for us to meet directly, or they would not show up for an amends meeting. We did not take it personally; we endeavored to identify what we needed to do to move forward with amends that could still free us from the burdens we were carrying.

We treated those to whom we made amends with compassion, since they had their own histories and injuries that might have been unknown to us. In some cases, we discovered that people to whom we made amends had also been affected by compulsive sexual behavior and had suffered their own pain. We remembered that the other person, place, institution, or animal, is also a reflection of a Higher Power, and just like us, has a right to serenity, respect, and safety.

We were thorough, thoughtful, and patient as we worked through these amends. We considered indirect, symbolic, or living amends. We prayed and meditated and sometimes wrote and rewrote amends for the more difficult and challenging situations. We found creative but honest ways to make amends to those who had died or those who we could not find or reach. Throughout this process, we kept asking for feedback from our sponsors, turning over the outcome to our Higher Power, and staying connected to our COSA program.

RESPONSES TO OUR AMENDS

Many of us were grateful to find most people were kind, generous, and gracious toward us when we made amends. Some people had little to say; others had a lot to share. Some people were stoic, while others caught us off guard by jumping at the opportunity to make their own amends to us. Some situations took time to process, and others were so miraculous that we were moved to tears of joy. We did not seek any specific outcome or expect anything in return. Whatever the outcome, we were grateful to have taken responsibility for our past behaviors and cleaned up our own side of the street.

Sometimes the response we received was negative. When this occurred, we employed our recovery tools and slogans, and we reached out for support. We practiced the principles of the program while using our own boundaries and detachment to prevent injury to ourselves. We kept ourselves physically safe, nurtured ourselves, and sought emotional support from our trusted program friends and our Higher Power.

When working Step Nine, many of us "bookended" each amend, contacting our sponsors or others in our program before and after making the amends. We shared the outcome with our sponsors. This process helped us accept any result an amends might bring and allowed us to discuss new insights. The support and encouragement helped many of us find the courage to make difficult amends that we might otherwise have continued to avoid.

We took any feedback or information we received through our Ninth Step amends and looked for what our Higher Power was gently trying to teach us. This spiritual process opened our hearts to receive new insights, and we reflected on the lessons we were learning. We tried to follow our Higher Power's will and let our Higher Power carry us through this Step.

STAYING WITH THE PROCESS

Step work requires thoroughness and courage. Especially as we began to deal with more complicated amends, some of us experienced resistance within ourselves. At times we found willingness was starting to fall away. Fear and anger arose. Some of us minimized the need for the amends or rationalized that we had already done enough. At times, we procrastinated. All the seemingly justifiable reasons for not making these amends suddenly became louder than the still and soft voice of our Higher Power, nudging us to clean up the past.

At times we may have had to begin all over again, to become willing to make an amends. Sometimes we were so filled with fury that we had to go back and do some additional Step Four and Five work before we could continue. Some of us benefited from outside help to deal with trauma, shame, or unhealthy coping mechanisms that emerged.

If we started to become overwhelmed or stuck, we reached out to our sponsors and program friends. We shared about our Step work in meetings. We talked with other COSAs who had completed this Step and asked them to share their experience, strength, and hope. We continued to be inspired by the lightness we heard in others and the improvements in their relationships. We noticed those who had worked this Step sounded more at ease in their relationships and their lives.

Some of us moved quickly through our amends. For others, the amends process was slower, perhaps excruciatingly so. In either case, we tried to keep moving forward, taking it one amends at a time. We came to understand that we could trust our Higher Power to set the pace for us. We continued to make progress by focusing on the freedom and joy we desired.

AMENDS TO OURSELVES

Perhaps most importantly, we made amends to ourselves. Many of us had harmed ourselves the most. We had blamed ourselves for the effects of compulsive sexual behavior on our lives and the lives of those around us. Often we still carried the shame and pain we had suffered.

Our sponsors and COSA fellows shared their experience, strength, and hope about their own amends to self. Examples of the types of amends we made to ourselves included: encouraging ourselves to have fun by taking up a hobby, expressing daily self-compassion and love or affirmations, eating healthy meals, taking ourselves for medical care, changing our boundaries and choices in relationships, honoring our sexuality, and celebrating recovery milestones and other successes. Some of us wrote amends letters to our "child" selves. We shared our self-amends with our sponsors, and some of us, in order to support our self-amends process and celebrate together, also chose to share these amends with our meeting groups.

THE GIFTS OF STEP NINE

Through this healing process, we were astounded by the trust, honesty, confidence, and self-respect we gained. Having now attained a deeper understanding of how our words and actions had impacted others, we found respect for ourselves and a profound sense of maturity. We also felt an incredible sense of relief. Our guilt and shame were dramatically reduced. We felt calmer, more serene, and more comfortable in our own skin. We felt a deeper connection to our Higher Power. We found love and self-forgiveness. If we experienced the forgiveness of others, it brought additional peace and reconciliation.

Our relationships began to look healthier. We were able to acknowledge our imperfections and be vulnerable with others. Through the process of making amends, we became less reactive and more able to respond to others with curiosity and kindness. We developed a better understanding of how to take responsibility for our own actions, while not taking on others' responsibilities. We no longer had to hide ourselves or who we were in the moment. We felt closer to people, and we could feel an ease and a freedom we had never before experienced.

Having received all these gifts, we were sure we did not want to return to life as it had been before Step Nine. We wanted to keep our behaviors aligned with recovery and to maintain our freedom, ease, and serenity. We were ready for Step Ten.

Step Ten

Continued to take personal inventory and when we were wrong promptly admitted it.

In Steps One through Nine, we become honest with our Higher Power, ourselves, and another human being; face our character flaws; and set right our past errors. With Step Ten, we commit to examining our assets and shortcomings regularly and to taking responsibility for our mistakes as soon as possible. This clears the way for us to continue to learn, grow, and live in serenity.

Steps Ten, Eleven, and Twelve help us maintain our new spiritual way of life. When we veer off course, Step Ten helps us right our ship, and Steps Eleven and Twelve help us navigate in alignment with our Higher Power's will for us. We can become introspective and take responsibility for our behavior, deepen our spirituality, and provide service at any point in our recovery.

APPROACHING STEP TEN

Before recovery, many of us felt like victims, subject to a stormy sea of emotions. We often reacted compulsively to feelings and situations. Our rash responses and behaviors hurt others and left us feeling emotionally, and sometimes physically, distressed. Or we hid in fear, avoided necessary action, and harmed ourselves in the process.

In COSA recovery, we defined our sobriety in terms of behaviors that were healthy for us—those we wanted to continue or begin. We also identified behaviors from which we wished to abstain—those that were not sober. As we worked the Steps with this clear understanding, we began to experience emotional balance and gain perspective on the past. In many cases, we came to recognize how living in fear, assuming the worst, and acting on hasty judgments had damaged our lives and relationships. We noticed how behaviors such as overanalysis, rigid perfectionism, and enmeshment with others had created a false sense of control, which eventually left us feeling empty and alone.

We soon realized we never wanted to return to the powerlessness and unmanageability that came from our old way of living. We were no longer willing to be tossed around by the tides of emotions and reactions. Instead, we wanted to maintain the steadiness of our sobriety. We learned that continuing to take personal inventory, as Step Ten recommends, could help.

The thirteen short words of this Step do not specify exactly how we should continue to take personal inventory. To get started, we discussed with our sponsors and other COSA members how they worked this Step. We read Twelve Step literature and considered the variety of tools and approaches available. Ultimately, we each decided which method or combination worked best for us. Over time, our Step Ten practices evolved, and we made adjustments to keep things fresh and aligned with our continuing personal growth.

Some practices adopted by COSA members are passed down from the founders of Alcoholics Anonymous (A.A.), who gave us the Twelve Steps. A.A. described three types of inventories: (1) a spot-check inventory that may be done whenever needed, (2) a daily review with credits (things done well) and debits (things for which we may owe amends), and (3) annual or semiannual "housecleanings" or opportunities to check our overall progress. These three types of inventories were first described in the book *Twelve Steps and Twelve Traditions*, originally published by the A.A. Grapevine, Inc., in 1953.

ANYTIME INVENTORY

The spot-check inventory helped us deal with life on life's terms each day. Whenever we felt emotionally unbalanced or noticed ourselves beginning to lose serenity, we learned to take a spiritual pause—to step back, breathe, and connect with our Higher Power. We learned to take a quick inventory of our feelings, thoughts, and options before acting.

We sought to recognize thoughts and actions that were based in dishonesty, fear, resentment, or self-seeking motives. Emotional pain, shame, self-pity, and fear were often at the root of our agitation.

We practiced identifying our feelings and needs without judgment so that we could take care of ourselves. Recalling the acronym "HALT" helped us consider whether we might be hungry, angry, lonely, or tired. Sometimes, we realized that we had not honored our boundaries.

As recovering members of COSA, we turned to the Twelve Steps and COSA tools. We prayed for guidance from our Higher Power, asking that we be inspired with thoughts and actions that aligned with our Higher Power's will. We reminded ourselves of the decision we made in Step Three. Sometimes, tools such as writing in a journal and practicing self-care helped restore the serenity and emotional balance we needed to clearly see the right actions to take.

We also learned that overthinking, obsessing, and sulking were not healthy behaviors because they concealed our Higher Power's message and kept us in a self-centered place. Instead, we reached out to our sponsors and trusted COSA friends. If we needed to discuss a situation with another person or make amends, we did so as soon as possible.

Many times, this saved us from emotional traps, such as pride, vengefulness, and the desire to control, that otherwise could have led to self-righteous criticism or argument. Whether we used it several times a day or just occasionally, we found that the spot-check inventory allowed us to successfully avoid behaviors such as manipulating and raging. Instead, we learned to surrender the feelings, along with the related people and situations, to a Power greater than ourselves. In this way, we continued to replace unwanted reactions with healthier behaviors.

DAILY INVENTORY

Many of us adopted the practice of taking a daily inventory. For some, this was simply a mental review during which we considered what we did well and what we could have done better. Or we incorporated a self-review into an evening prayer and meditation ritual or used tools such as journals and apps that made the process easier. Discussing our inventory with sponsors or other COSA members helped some of us develop good habits and accountability. Participating in a meeting dedicated to Step Ten was another choice.

The daily inventory gave us the opportunity to acknowledge our positive thoughts, intentions, efforts, and actions. Some of us assessed how we felt throughout the day and how we had taken care of ourselves. We thought about how we treated others, considering whether we had been kind and loving toward everyone. Thanking our Higher Power daily and reflecting on gratitude helped many of us center ourselves spiritually.

We also considered where we may have made poor choices or acted from dishonest, self-centered, or unloving motives based on feelings such as anger, jealousy, pride, resentment, and fear. We thought about whether our actions had caused harm to anyone, including ourselves.

As we reviewed our behavior honestly and objectively, we asked ourselves whether we had rationalized unhealthy behavior, which we knew to be denial. Conversely, had we judged ourselves too harshly, perhaps taking on criticisms or blame for things that were not our responsibility? We considered our motives for wanting to make amends. Were we taking responsibility for our actions, or were we acting from an unhealthy place, such as trying to please or save others? Were we rushing to make peace in order to eliminate uncomfortable feelings? Discussing our inventory with our sponsors often helped us learn how to distinguish our personal responsibility in a situation from someone else's responsibility.

When reviewing our behavior, we sometimes noticed our character defects. We tried not to shame or berate ourselves. Instead, we prayed, expressing gratitude to our Higher Power for the new awareness. We asked our Higher Power to remove our defects, guide us toward healthier new behaviors, and help us change. We thought about how we might act differently in the future. We also prayed for the insight, willingness, and courage to make any necessary amends. Practicing patience and gratitude for our progress, rather than expecting perfection, was essential to our emotional and spiritual healing.

We turned our focus toward the new behaviors that could replace those we wished to surrender. Visualizing ourselves making better choices in the future often facilitated real change. Some of us found ideas for new behaviors in COSA literature. We also reflected on our previous work, such as our sobriety circles or the list of behaviors we may have created during Steps Six and Seven to replace our old, unwanted behaviors.

With our Higher Power's guidance and support, we resolved to make amends for our mistakes and put new behaviors into action. As we worked towards positive change, we embraced the notion that COSA is a program of spiritual help and healing. We gratefully accepted our Higher Power's love, forgiveness, and assistance. Our daily review often concluded with humbly thanking our Higher Power for our progress.

ANNUAL OR SEMIANNUAL INVENTORIES

After some time in recovery, many of us looked for an opportunity to evaluate how far we had come and to celebrate our successes and overall progress. Annual or semiannual inventories presented opportunities to consider our behavior over time and to revisit our definition of sobriety. As we advanced in our Step work, we opened ourselves to acknowledging character defects that we may not have been able or ready to see previously. We valued the chance to set new intentions and goals for our spiritual, emotional, and interpersonal development. Reviewing our progress with our sponsors, trusted COSA friends, or others helped us recognize our growth and see where we could continue to improve.

PROGRESS, NOT PERFECTION

When we first started looking at Step Ten, many of us worried that we did not have the time and could not keep up this new routine. Some of us felt intimidated or struggled to find a process that worked for us. With the help of our sponsors and other COSA members, we established a realistic and achievable approach and celebrated our progress. We felt inspired and grateful as we noticed the continuing improvements in our lives.

No matter which method or combination of approaches we chose, we found a way to honestly reflect on our thoughts, feelings, and behaviors. We were not able to do this perfectly, and occasionally we slipped into old, unhealthy behaviors. When that happened, we owned up to it, humbly asked for help to change, and committed to do better next time. We reminded ourselves that we sought progress not perfection.

As we acknowledged our shortcomings and loved ourselves anyway, we surrendered our tendency to fight and struggle. Forgiving ourselves with love and kindness brought welcome relief and a deeper sense of self-acceptance. As we accepted our own fallibility, our empathy and compassion for others grew as well. From that place of compassion, our capacity to accept and forgive others increased. This depth of understanding and emotional maturity helped us carry the message to those who still suffer.

THE GIFTS OF STEP TEN

Step Ten helps us continue the work accomplished in Steps One through Nine. It calls on us to be mindful, humble, and accountable for our behavior on an ongoing basis. By regularly assessing our behavior, we can quickly evaluate which behaviors align with our Higher Power's will for us; then, we can choose wisely and with intention. If we owe amends, we admit it and move forward without delay.

Steps Ten, Eleven, and Twelve go hand in hand. In Step Ten, we reflect humbly and communicate honestly. When we routinely check our motives and take responsibility for our behaviors, we free ourselves from the burden of fear and resentment. Clearing our minds and hearts creates space for our growth in Steps Eleven and Twelve, where we deepen our spirituality and give to others what we have received. With gratitude, we recognize that the COSA promises are coming true in our lives.

Step Eleven

Sought through prayer and meditation to improve our conscious contact with God as we understood God, praying only for knowledge of God's will for us and the power to carry that out.

Faith and humility converge in Step Eleven as our relationship with God deepens and strengthens. We work to improve our conscious contact with our Higher Power through prayer and meditation, as we seek our Higher Power's will for us. Practicing Step Eleven is a continual process that requires commitment, practice, and patience. We open ourselves to profound spiritual growth as we work this Step.

APPROACHING STEP ELEVEN

As we reflected back on the prior ten Steps, many of us recognized that a Higher Power had been with us. In Step Two, a Power greater than ourselves became a tangible concept. Our trust in that Power grew as we worked Step Three and decided to turn our wills and our lives over to God's care. Based on the foundation of Steps Two and Three, many of us sensed that our Higher Power was by our side, and we moved trustingly forward through the next Steps. With our Higher Power's guidance, and that of our sponsors, co-sponsors, Step study groups, and wise COSA friends, we continued to grow in recovery. Little by little, as we put our trust in our Higher Power, many of us witnessed miracles that helped our faith blossom.

The words of Step Three were echoed in Step Eleven: "God as we understood God." Steps Two and Three invited us to come to know and trust in a Higher Power of our own understanding. Step Eleven offered us the opportunity to revisit our perception of our Higher Power and deepen our connection. Some of us held tightly to our initial understanding of a Higher Power, while others noticed that the concept of a Higher Power changed and evolved as we worked the Steps and became more aware of the spiritual gifts we had received. However we approached it, Step Eleven gave us the spiritual freedom to follow our hearts and our intuitive wisdom as we determined what worked for us individually.

IMPROVING OUR CONSCIOUS CONTACT

In Step Eleven, we opened ourselves to connecting with our Higher Power through prayer and meditation. Some of us saw prayer and meditation as a single action; others saw them as two separate exercises. Many conceptualized prayer as talking to God and meditation as listening to God.

Determining how to pray was a very personal choice for each of us, and the way we approached prayer may have unfolded over time. For some of us, our religious practices and places of worship were a haven where we could sing or chant our prayers together in community. Others were uncomfortable with or never identified with formalized religious practices. We may have experienced religious or spiritual traumas or received shaming messages—from religious institutions and even our families of origin—about "God" and our place in the universe. Our sponsors were there to remind us that COSA is not a religious program but a spiritual one, and that we had the freedom to develop our own individual spirituality.

We may have searched for new practices of our own, expressing ourselves very personally to our Higher Power. Some of us experienced spiritual connection through journaling, reading, spending time in nature, or finding a sense of true belonging in our COSA groups. We may have read or recited prayers that touched us. Or we prayed wordlessly, connecting to our Higher Power through our innermost thoughts and feelings.

As with prayer, we also found that there was no right or wrong way to meditate. Some of us created space in our lives for tranquil time to sit in stillness and listen. Letting go of outside distractions, we looked deep inside ourselves and quieted our thoughts. Focusing on our breath, we may have achieved a state of quiet calmness within which we strengthened our connection with our Higher Power.

If one meditation practice did not work for us, we tried another way, maybe several, until we found something that allowed us to comfortably clear our minds and calm our hearts. Some of us meditated by holding a sacred object, lighting a candle, or listening to music. Concentrating on the experience, strength, and hope being shared in the serenity of a COSA room or spending time in contemplative reading or writing were other choices. We may have experimented with active forms of meditation such as walking in nature, practicing yoga, running, or even connecting with our pets. The options were endless. Most of us found that our preferred methods ebbed, flowed, and changed as we grew in recovery.

SEEKING GOD'S WILL

While Step Eleven gave us room to decide how to pray and meditate, this Step advised us to pray only for knowledge of God's will for us and for the power to carry that out. We had to practice letting go of our self-will and asking instead for the courage and wisdom to know and carry out God's intention. Some of us asked for clarity in distinguishing God's will from our own will. While sometimes God's will was immediately clear to us, at other times we needed to wait patiently to receive the message.

In the past we might have been tempted, when praying, to ask for specific solutions to specific problems. We may have asked our Higher Power to do things our way, to give us what we needed, or at least what we thought we needed. We may have even bargained with our Higher Power, saying things like, "If You change the behavior of my loved one, I promise to be a better person." But we were learning that attempting to force solutions or figure everything out on our own are actually forms of self-will.

Some of us experienced our work in Step Eleven as the ultimate surrender, which in turn opened us to our Higher Power's gifts of ease, grace, joy, and abundance as we had never before experienced them. When we surrendered our will to our Higher Power, we often found that we were provided with everything our hearts could want and need. By letting go of what we thought we wanted and becoming open to God's will for us, we discovered new possibilities and choices and a sense of peace. Step Eleven led us to paths that we might not have otherwise considered. Often, we received more wisdom than we thought possible and more strength than we could have mustered when left to our own devices.

This kind of surrender required immense trust. In truth, trust was hard for many of us. In the past, and perhaps even in our current relationships, our trust had been violated. The thought of trusting our Higher Power may have brought up familiar feelings of fear and wanting to control. We were gentle with ourselves as we wrestled with our faith and tried to trust the process anyway. We realized we did not have to do it alone nor did we have to do it perfectly. For those of us with past religious traumas, the idea of "God's will" may have felt punishing or frightening. We reminded ourselves that Higher Power was a loving presence in our lives that had our best interests at heart.

Our sponsors were there by our side, guiding us and sharing their experience, strength, and hope. They listened to us express our fears and doubts, and they encouraged us to reach out to our Higher Power for guidance when we felt stuck or unsure. We were inspired by our sponsors and fellow COSA members when we heard them speak of their connection with their own Higher Power. We noticed their serenity and we felt hopeful.

Even if we concluded that there were spiritual mysteries that we might never fully comprehend, we became more comfortable with not having all the answers. We began to trust implicitly. As we let go of the responsibility of having to figure everything out, we happily became the passenger and let our Higher Power take the wheel.

In seeking God's guidance, we asked questions such as: "What is your will for me?" "How can I be the best version of myself?" "How can I best serve today?" "How can I carry out my purpose?" "What is my next step?" Or we simply prayed, "Your will, not mine, be done." As we worked this Step, many of us found that the answers to these questions emerged and transformed over time, sometimes daily or even by the hour.

Many of us established regular rituals to improve our conscious contact with God. Some created a spiritual routine to connect with God first thing in the morning. We may have paused to pray and meditate at specific times throughout our day, or used a routine behavior, such as passing through a doorway or starting our car, as a Step Eleven reminder. Some of us set an alarm to remind ourselves to check in spiritually or attended a COSA meeting to help us focus on Step Eleven. Many of us needed these consistent, humble reminders that it was our Higher Power running the show, not us.

LISTENING AND RECEIVING

Some of us received clear messages we recognized as being from our Higher Power. As we continued to practice Step Eleven, our awareness grew and our intuition became more finely tuned. Many of us began to experience a feeling of being in sync and in step with God.

By listening to our Higher Power, we learned to hear our own truths. Before recovery, many of us felt disconnected from ourselves. Practicing the Eleventh Step brought us home to ourselves. We became aware of the inner voice of our deepest self, which knew instinctively what to do.

In addition to seeking God's will for us through prayer and meditation, we also sought the power to carry out that will. While we began Step One acknowledging our powerlessness, by the time we reached Step Eleven, many of us felt empowered to act from a place of spiritual centeredness and well-being. Whatever our Higher Power guided us to do, we began to feel both the clarity and courage to follow through. Action and empowerment were priceless gifts of our Step Eleven work.

THE GIFTS OF STEP ELEVEN

The Eleventh Step offered deepening spiritual connection, love, and grace. This Step brought us closer to God and helped us let go of our own will. We opened up to God's will and to the miracles of who we are on this Earth. We turned our faces toward a Higher Power and eagerly received the miraculous gifts of recovery.

Many of us experienced a deep sense of joy, peace, and freedom. We felt a calm growing within us, a sense that all would be well when we connected with our Higher Power's will for us. We experienced a new and deepened feeling of confidence, trust, and faith, knowing we were making decisions led by our Higher Power. When we trusted that things would work out, even when we did not see how, we felt peace. We confidently leaned into our Higher Power's strength and knew that we did not have to do it alone. We rested in the care of our Higher Power and in the loving fellowship of COSA.

As we continued to practice Steps Ten and Eleven in our own recovery, we strengthened our ability to offer hope to others in need of the COSA message. We were ready for Step Twelve.

Step Twelve

Having had a spiritual awakening as the result of these steps, we tried to carry this message to others, and to practice these principles in all areas of our lives.

Through our personal experience, we COSA members have confirmed that we maintain and grow our recovery by sharing it with others. Step Twelve is essential to each individual's progress and also sustains the COSA fellowship as a whole. The principles of Step Twelve include joyful living in emotional sobriety and outward action in the form of giving without expectations. The strength, hope, and joy we have gained by working the Steps bring us to a new state of consciousness. From this state of sanity and serenity, we are able to give freely to those who still suffer from the effects of compulsive sexual behavior.

HAVING HAD A SPIRITUAL AWAKENING AS THE RESULT OF THESE STEPS

At this point in our Step work, many of us are able to look back and realize that admitting our powerlessness and the unmanageability of our lives led us to precious gifts. Working the

Twelve Steps allowed us to heal, learn, and grow in ways that we had never before imagined. We gained the ability to recognize our strengths and weaknesses, to view them with a balanced perspective, to admit our mistakes, and to make amends. We cultivated a strong connection with a Higher Power, which enabled us to take responsibility for our lives. With the help of our Higher Power, our sponsors, and other COSA members, we learned how to find and maintain serenity one moment at a time. We came to accept and love ourselves and others.

As we approached Step Twelve, some of us were perplexed about the definition of a spiritual awakening. Through our work in COSA, we developed a personal relationship with a Higher Power and moved beyond our past beliefs. Some of us were expecting a grand spiritual awakening, something akin to a bright light breaking through clouds over a mountain top. Some wondered whether an inner voice would proclaim clearly that we had attained an awakening or whether we would notice a physical sensation, such as levitation or a heart opening or expansion.

While some of us recall a distinct memory or feeling, most of us experienced the spiritual awakening as a gradual process, unfolding incrementally as we worked each Step. Our practice of the Twelve Steps made us ready to receive the gifts of sanity, emotional sobriety, and serenity. It was through our daily choices, decisions, and disciplined practice of new behaviors that our awareness expanded, and we awakened to new possibilities. Over time, we developed spiritual and emotional maturity, which enhanced our ability to carry the message to others. We experienced many qualities described in the Promises, which we had heard and read in COSA meetings. We noticed the gifts of COSA in our lives. We recognized this as the spiritual awakening we sought.

WE TRIED TO CARRY THIS MESSAGE TO OTHERS

Steps One through Eleven kept us accountable to our recovery program and prepared us to deepen our service. Step Twelve directly calls us to carry the COSA message to others who still suffer. By working this Step, we demonstrate our commitment and accountability to the COSA fellowship as a whole. Step Twelve also brings to mind the slogan, "We have to give it away to keep it." In other words, sharing freely what we have gained is how we continue to heal and grow.

As we navigated through the Steps, our sponsors encouraged us to embrace opportunities to serve the COSA fellowship. Early in recovery, carrying the message was sometimes as simple as being present in meetings and listening attentively to someone who was still suffering. Because our lives had also been affected by compulsive sexual behavior, we were able to provide empathy to a newcomer in a way that few others could. We shared the experience, strength, and hope we had gained as we worked the COSA program.

Some sponsors encouraged sponsees to do specific tasks for the fellowship, to participate in business meetings, or to fill service positions. Serving the fellowship helped to ensure we regularly attended meetings. We found that service enhanced our level of participation and the depth of our interaction with other COSA members. Additionally, service contributed to our sense of purpose and belonging in our COSA group and in the fellowship as a whole.

By the time we reached Step Twelve, we felt immense gratitude for those who had passed along COSA's wisdom through countless acts of service: sponsorship, speaking, leading meetings and workshops, and serving as intergroup representatives and as delegates. We gained strength and hope from long-time

COSA members who had maintained recovery and continued to practice the COSA principles in their lives. Their shared experience and support helped deliver us from desperation and hopelessness to serenity, joy, and freedom.

For many of us, Step Twelve presented an opportunity to give back by becoming sponsors ourselves. We recognized that sponsorship played a key role in COSA's ability to be fully self-supporting and self-sustaining. Freely giving to others what had been so generously given to us fulfilled COSA's primary purpose of carrying the message to those who still suffer.

At first, some of us were intimidated by the idea of sponsoring others. We worried that when a sponsee had questions or needed help, we would not know what to say or would say the wrong thing. Perhaps we did not feel confident that our experience, strength, and hope would be sufficient. Some members worried about past tendencies to overcommit or "people-please." Our sponsors and those in long-term recovery helped us navigate such dilemmas and self-doubt. As our personal healing progressed, we spent less time thinking about ourselves and more time considering how we could be useful to those who still suffer. We found balance and confidence. Many of us came to realize that our Higher Power was working through us to carry the message to others. When we focused on the guidance we received from our Higher Power, our sponsors, and other experienced COSA members, our worries subsided.

Some of us started meetings, including groups to study and work through COSA's Twelve Steps. Some of us volunteered at levels beyond our individual meetings, such as serving on the International Service Organization's board or committees. We found increasing joy in our contribution, learning, and self-development. Serving others and the fellowship in these ways became a part of our living spiritual practice.

WE TRIED TO PRACTICE THESE PRINCIPLES
IN ALL AREAS OF OUR LIVES

Before recovery, many of us had persistently repeated unworkable behaviors in our relationships. For example, some of us depended too much on ourselves and tried to arrange life to be the way we thought it should be, instead of seeking direction from our Higher Power. At times, this led us to disregard other people's boundaries, needs, and wishes. Some of us avoided taking personal responsibility, neglected ourselves, and became overly focused on other people or unhealthy sources of emotional comfort and security.

By working the Twelve Steps, we developed spiritually and gained a right-sized sense of self in relation to those around us. Working our COSA program and deepening our relationship with our Higher Power helped us develop a stronger foundation of emotional stability, no matter what challenges we faced.

This part of Step Twelve invited us to take the principles of the program beyond the fellowship and live them daily in the greater world; that is, it asked us to embody COSA's Steps, Traditions, and Concepts and to use COSA's tools in our approach to everything in our lives. Step Twelve asked us to carry our awakened spirit into every situation, whether we were doing simple daily tasks, dealing with a difficult person, or facing a crisis or traumatic experience. We were encouraged to find love, tolerance, faith, and purpose in all circumstances.

Many of us recognized that remaining fit to practice Step Twelve involved practicing the other Steps and a daily recovery routine. This included making conscious contact with a Higher Power, attending meetings regularly, and connecting with a sponsor and/or other COSA members, as well as reflecting on our feelings and reviewing our behaviors (Step Ten), and applying the Steps and Traditions to specific situations. This regular practice helped us to recognize moments of insanity or instability more quickly and more consistently. We surrendered our struggles to our Higher Power more readily, while fairly considering how our behavior ("character defects") may have contributed. We shared our self-reflections with someone else and humbly asked our Higher Power for help to let go of unproductive approaches. We sought the willingness to take the next right action, which sometimes included making amends. As we practiced the principles, we gained the courage to take those actions, using recovery principles to make healthier choices.

Step Twelve is dynamic and continuous. It calls on us to practice the program's principles in all areas of our lives, even when we experience difficult moments and find ourselves anxious or agitated. We pause to reflect mindfully and listen for an intuitive voice of wisdom. We wait until clear guidance emerges before making a decision or taking action. Many of us recall helpful program slogans like "Easy does it," "One day at a time," or "Do the next right thing." We often recite the Serenity Prayer, mindfully seeking the wisdom to distinguish that which we can control from that which we cannot, the courage to take necessary action, and the serenity to accept things beyond our control. We practice the principle of humility by regularly reaching out to our Higher Power, sponsors, and other COSA members. We express willingness by diligently applying the Twelve Steps and other COSA tools to maintain emotional sobriety. We manifest patience and love by taking the time to respond with respect and thoughtful intention to ourselves and others. We practice honesty and integrity by "saying what we mean and meaning what we say."

Working the Twelve Steps in all areas of our lives on a daily basis transformed—and continues to transform—our outlook on life. Our inner peace, strength, and ability to be happy and useful have increased. We have begun to approach our personal and professional endeavors from a perspective of humble, spiritual service rather than from a motive of needing to please others, receive praise and attention, or gain status or material wealth. Humble dependence upon a Higher Power enables us to serve others in a healthy, balanced way. Love, acceptance, and hope replace bitterness, intolerance, and regret. We find we spend less time in conflict and distress and more time being useful to our Higher Power and those around us.

THE GIFTS OF STEP TWELVE

Step Twelve reconnects us with the world in an authentic way. It encourages us to share the joy of living rather than keeping the gifts of recovery to ourselves. Carrying the message grounds us in humility and steers us away from self-centeredness. Practicing the principles helps direct us along a spiritual path. Step Twelve gives us the opportunity to give back to the COSA fellowship and to our Higher Power in gratitude for all that we have received in recovery. And it is in giving that we receive even more. By trying to carry the message to those who still suffer and by practicing the COSA principles in all areas of our lives, our own recovery is reinforced and deepened. We recognize that our Higher Power is doing through us more than we ever thought possible.

INTRODUCTION TO THE TWELVE TRADITIONS OF COSA

While the Steps support our individual recovery, the Twelve Traditions of COSA provide a spiritual framework for healthy interactions at the group and fellowship levels. Our Traditions serve to unite our fellowship in its common purpose, yet also encourage COSA groups' autonomy, so that each group develops its own unique flavor: unity not uniformity.

With its Twelve Traditions as guidelines and suggestions rather than rules, COSA is a loosely structured organization. It does not monitor its groups or provide oversight, and it is fueled almost exclusively by its members' voluntary service. One would most likely expect utter chaos when people who are suffering from the effects of compulsive sexual behavior join together. But with the wisdom of our Traditions guiding our interactions, we find a calming, healing environment in which we can help others as we find our own path to recovery.

Unlike working the Steps, which are usually approached in a systematic order, the Traditions do not need to be studied in a particular order and can help us at any point in our recovery. Many of us have found that studying and applying the Traditions can provide valuable insights and relief in our recovery journeys as well as in our day-to-day relationships and experiences outside of COSA.

COSA's very survival and growth are protected by the Traditions. They guide our fellowship, our groups, and individual COSA members in ways that keep our program secure and unencumbered from outside distractions. The Twelve Traditions support the health and safety of our COSA recovery spaces, thus providing fertile ground for us to cultivate our own recovery.

Tradition One

Our common welfare should come first; personal recovery depends upon COSA unity.

Tradition One contains several key concepts: common welfare, personal recovery, unity, and priorities. The phrase "common welfare" refers to the well-being, comfort, safety, and protection of our fellowship as a whole and of the groups within it—including our local meetings, intergroup meetings, the Annual Delegate Meeting, the Board of Trustees, and service committees. When COSA is strong and healthy, it supports our individual recovery. So, this Tradition urges us to make the welfare of the group a priority of our own recovery. It tells us we can support the well-being of the group by thinking and acting in ways that promote unity.

The strength of the fellowship comes from the collective wisdom and accumulated efforts of all the COSAs who have come before us. This is a rich resource, available to us now because COSA members of the past have been willing to sustain the fellowship and maintain its focus. Now, by using Tradition One to guide us, we do our part to assure that COSA will continue to grow into the future. We stay united with a caring and respectful attitude toward our community and a focus on our common unified goal: to use the Twelve Steps to recover from the effects of compulsive sexual behavior.

From the moment we read our first piece of COSA literature or join our first COSA meeting, we begin to recognize the power of a unified recovery community. It is easier, and more joyful, to recover together. We give and receive acceptance and understanding. We celebrate and gain hope from each other's successes, and we relate to and support each other through our sorrows. When one of us is going through a rough spot, there are others who feel grounded and strong who can offer support. They share their experience, strength, and hope; encourage us to use recovery tools; and offer a calm, listening ear and an open heart. When we regain our footing, we can offer these gifts to others.

Whether we are giving or receiving support, there is something in the collective will-to-heal that lifts us up. It gives us the courage and strength to walk through our challenges. We bear witness to each other's growth.

Considering all of this, it is clear that our personal recovery and our common welfare are directly connected. They are interwoven like threads of fabric; each strengthens and supports the other. We come to see that tending to our common welfare is part of the self-care we learn to practice for ourselves.

There are many ways, from simple to more extensive, that we can contribute to our common welfare. One of the best ways is to diligently work our own COSA programs, studying and applying the principles in the Steps, Traditions, and Concepts. As we grow, we develop useful understandings we can share. The peace of mind and fulfilling life we gain from recovery provide inspiration to newcomers and long timers alike.

As Tradition One points out, unity is essential to our common welfare. One way we can support our common welfare and promote unity is by respectfully interacting with other COSAs. When we work the Steps in our COSA program, we become aware of times when we have acted out of self-seeking or fear (or both) or have thought of ourselves as either superior or inferior to others. In recovery we grow into a more moderate approach, honoring others and ourselves from a right-sized perspective. We come to realize that there is a direct link between how we treat others and how we treat ourselves.

With unity in mind, we work to achieve these ideals: We treat each other with kindness and consideration, and we engage as equals. We do not let differences in personality or opinions divert us from recovering and helping others to recover. We rotate service positions so that no one person is thought of as an authority over others. In our words and actions, we aim to refrain from gossip, criticism, and judgment. We strive to be kind, accepting, and inclusive rather than cliquish. When we practice Tradition One in these ways, we keep the group safe and therefore united.

Another way to support our common purpose and unite is by welcoming anyone who identifies as having been affected by compulsive sexual behavior, as expressed in Tradition Three. Not every COSA will be just like we are. Our COSA Diversity Statement makes it clear that we welcome "all genders, all varieties of relationship to the addict, all religious and spiritual preferences, all employment statuses, all marital statuses, and all ethnicities, cultures, and languages. COSA does not discriminate on the basis of class, sexual orientation or gender identification, physical or mental challenges, race, or national origins." This means that anyone who identifies as having been affected by compulsive sexual behavior can join the COSA fellowship.

This does not necessarily mean that we will feel equally comfortable with all COSA members. We may have personal preferences or perspectives that are challenged from time to time. Our sponsor can be a great resource for guidance and direction at these times. As we navigate our way through discomfort and set boundaries as needed, we learn to take care of ourselves while at the same time safeguarding unity. We honor ourselves by making individual choices that work for us, and we balance this with honoring the principles of the fellowship. As we do this, we grow spiritually and learn new things about ourselves and others.

Tradition One reminds us that it is important to maintain a unified recovery focus. Other recovery resources of many types are available to all of us—in person, online, and in print. Many of these are useful and life-enhancing; they can certainly complement what COSA Twelve Step recovery has to offer. We COSAs are, of course, welcome to participate in any of these other recovery options as we see fit. It is also inevitable that current psychological theories and social, economic, and political events will influence our thinking. The COSA fellowship, however, has no opinion on any of this. It focuses simply on utilizing the Twelve Steps to recover and heal from the effects of compulsive sexual behavior. We honor ourselves by deciding whether COSA's Twelve Step approach is for us and by pursuing any additional resources we desire, and we support COSA unity by leaving outside resources outside.

What would happen to our program if we started to incorporate expensive therapies, religious practices, reading materials from other fellowships, political discussions, exercise regimes, nutritional guidelines, or medical theories into our meetings or literature? Our unity would be compromised. The clarity and message of the COSA program would become diluted, confusing, and divisive. Some of our members might feel excluded, alienated, or unsafe. Staying within the parameters of COSA Twelve Step recovery keeps our program simple, unified, and attainable by all.

Finally, we uphold Tradition One and create unity in how we conduct decision-making, whether at the meeting level, regionally, or within the International Service Organization (ISO). We aim to let go of the need to "be right" or feel "in charge." Safe communication and respectful, attentive listening help us carefully consider differences of perspective or opinion. All those present are encouraged to speak for an equal amount of time, and all viewpoints, including those of the minority, are equally valued. We strive for unanimity whenever possible, as we work together to determine the collaborative decision of the group, known as the "group conscience."

This does not mean that we withhold our opinions or abandon ourselves in an attempt to please others and achieve unity. On the contrary, we value ourselves as we value every member of the group. It is important that we express our ideas, beliefs, concerns, and points of view. Diversity can create strength and richness in a group. We show up and speak up in a respectful way, and then we trust the process of the group conscience. In this way we honor ourselves while at the same time valuing and protecting the unity of the group.

Tradition One tells us it is in our own best interest to value and tend to the well-being of the group. It indicates that the best way to maintain the well-being of the group is to unite. If we are good stewards of the COSA fellowship in this way, we are best able to accomplish what we, as individuals and as a fellowship, have set out to do: to recover and to help others do the same.

One of the benefits of learning about the Twelve Traditions of COSA is the opportunity it gives us to practice the principles of the Traditions in other groups to which we belong. For example, we may consider how the concepts presented in Tradition One apply to our families, our workplaces, our religious or spiritual groups, our communities, our country, or even the world. When we apply Tradition One, we can recognize and appreciate how each group benefits us and how prioritizing unity can protect and nurture those groups.

Tradition Two

For our group purpose there is but one ultimate authority—a loving God as expressed in our group conscience. Our leaders are but trusted servants; they do not govern.

Tradition Two supports the principle we established with Tradition One: putting our common welfare first. It also clarifies our approach to leadership and decision-making. Simply put, our common welfare is strengthened when we approach each other as equals. We don't place any one person in a position of ultimate authority; instead, we seek our Higher Power's guidance, both individually and as a group.

The first sentence of this Tradition mentions our group purpose, which is recovering from the effects of compulsive sexual behavior and carrying the message to those that seek help. In some areas of our lives we may need to answer to other authorities, but for decision-making and direction within our COSA groups and fellowship, we have one ultimate authority: a loving God. This loving Higher Power guides and resides in the wisdom of the group.

Accepting our Higher Power as our ultimate authority helps us refrain from unsolicited advice-giving or the temptation to "teach" others. Our groups thrive when our trusted servants understand that they do not govern. Honoring the group conscience as expressing the will of our Higher Power brings unity, prevents discord, and allows the group to survive.

Of course, we value the wisdom that some members have gained from working the Steps, honoring the Traditions, and studying the Concepts. We also appreciate the historical knowledge of the fellowship that some long timers have. These precious people can be quite helpful in our journey of healing. At the same time, it is always important to remember that neither our individual recovery nor our group's welfare rest in the hands of any one person—regardless of how wise, experienced, or caring they may be. We seek support and input, yes. But ultimately, we trust our Higher Power's guidance within us and within the democratic wisdom of the group.

The words "loving God" are important to contemplate. Whether or not this matches our childhood experience of a Higher Power, Tradition Two tells us that a loving God is the ultimate authority for our COSA fellowship. The word "loving" is usually associated with being caring and accepting, and our Higher Power guides us as we learn to love and accept ourselves and others. We begin to recognize that embodying this love, care, and acceptance is not passive. Sometimes following our Higher Power's direction requires courageous honesty and firm resolve. Honoring our loving God in any relationship—whether between two people, within our group, or at the international level—means speaking up for ourselves, listening attentively to others, working with others to make the best decisions for all involved, and finding the serenity to accept outcomes.

Individually, we may seek guidance from our Higher Power through a variety of activities: sharing in meetings, listening as other COSAs share, reading COSA recovery materials, talking with our sponsor and other recovery friends, and doing our Step work. We pray and meditate, and we carefully consider our options. Then we make our decisions based upon what we determine to be our Higher Power's will for us. The Traditions point to this same kind of thoughtful and unhurried solution-seeking for our groups.

The word "conscience" is specific and important to this Tradition. According to several dictionaries, this word refers to inner knowledge, a sense of fairness, justice, and integrity. Acting with a clear conscience implies acting based upon what we consider to be right or good.

The "group conscience" idea is a direct way in which Tradition Two upholds the principle described in Tradition One. Even if we as individuals have strong opinions or desires, we do not act on self-will or impulse where COSA is concerned. Instead, we seek to determine the group's conscience. We keep our common welfare foremost in our minds.

Determining our group conscience is an ongoing activity. Most groups hold monthly group conscience meetings to discuss decisions that need to be made. Although one person may be a facilitator, each group member has an equal right and opportunity to weigh in on a given issue before a vote is conducted. Often, group conscience meetings will begin and end with the "we" version of the Serenity Prayer. This helps us align with the loving God mentioned in the wording of Tradition Two.

Group conscience meetings are a great place to practice attentive listening, safe communication skills, and open-mindedness. Any time a challenging issue comes up, group members can aim to be patient and respectful. We learn the benefits of engaging in discernment rather than grasping for a quick fix.

The Steps, Traditions, and Concepts are useful resources for clarification and direction. In a healthy group conscience meeting, we witness the principles of the program in action. For some, this may be the first time we've seen this type of calm, clear communication applied to topics that might otherwise be contentious.

Sometimes the conscience of the group is not readily apparent, or an issue is complex. As we do in our individual recovery, we seek guidance from respected sources and trust our Higher Power's timing. We make the best decisions we can, based upon what we know today, and if the way is not clear, sometimes the best option is to wait.

To do every single group-related task by consensus would obviously be awkward and inefficient, so we elect leaders to help. We trust that these generous volunteers will fulfill their commitments to the best of their ability and will ask for support when they need it. While our leaders may be wise, talented, and charismatic, it would be against the Traditions for them to control or dominate. Instead, they approach their roles with humility, as servants rather than authority figures. Each member of COSA is valued equally.

One of the reasons we rotate service positions is so that no group or leadership role becomes directly associated with a specific individual. The Program is based upon both timeless principles and a relationship with a Higher Power of our understanding. It does not depend on any one person, no matter how admirable. As Tradition Twelve reminds us, "we place principles before personalities."

On a personal level, we can honor Tradition Two in all of our relationships—in COSA and beyond—by aiming to be fair and unassuming in our words and actions. Instead of engaging in our old habit of advice-giving or getting stuck in our old patterns of caretaking or enmeshment, we can cultivate skillful listening habits. We can pay attention to—and be realistic about—our motives in any negotiation. We can be considerate of others, weighing their opinions equally and respectfully with our own, even as we honor feedback from long timers. Traditions One and Two remind us to aim for balance, honoring our own wants and needs along with the wants and needs of others. We don't dictate and we don't grovel. We relax the constrictions of fear and let go of the desire to be in control. Instead, we grow into the openness of faith and the spirit of collaboration.

Whether in the COSA group context or in other areas of our lives such as work, family, and friendship, Tradition Two reminds us to listen for our Higher Power's guidance. Even when collaborating with others and seeking their input, we can slowly and meditatively find the loving direction we need to move forward. Through practicing Tradition Two, we can have better relationships and reach the best decisions for all involved.

Tradition Three

The only requirement for COSA membership is that our lives have been affected by compulsive sexual behavior. The members may call themselves a COSA group, provided that, as a group, they have no other affiliation.

The first sentence of this Tradition describes our welcoming attitude toward anyone whose life has been affected by compulsive sexual behavior. The second sentence clarifies the sole focus of COSA. We are a fellowship of diverse individuals, yet when we gather for COSA recovery, we set aside all other affiliations and stay attuned to our shared purpose.

The intention of this Tradition is to ensure that the COSA recovery program is available to anyone—absolutely anyone—who wants it. This means that COSA ought to be accessible for those of any race, ethnicity, age, gender or gender identity, sexual orientation, religious or spiritual affiliation or non-affiliation, economic or financial status, profession, political stance, or life experience, including those who belong to other Twelve Step programs or support groups. COSA has no attendance requirements; we are all welcome, whether it is our first meeting or we have been attending for years. While we strive to be self-supporting through our own contributions, there are no membership dues. We belong, regardless of our ability to pay. Our meetings provide a place for each of us to feel safe and free from judgment.

We are also diverse in the ways in which our lives have been affected by compulsive sexual behavior. We may or may not currently be in a relationship with a person who has engaged in such behavior. The behavior that affected our lives may be that of a spouse, a partner, another family member, a friend, a teacher or spiritual leader, or a coworker. We may have been victims of sexual abuse or experienced the trauma of growing up with a sexually addicted parent or in a sexualized home environment. We may have been affected by compulsive sexual behavior we have witnessed or experienced in our culture or in the media, or we may have been affected by such behavior at work or in a school group or religious organization. The ways in which we react to the effects of compulsive sexual behavior will vary. Most of us experience some level of grief and trauma, and we have differing abilities for managing our distress in a healthy way.

Some of us have engaged in compulsive sexual behavior ourselves, in an attempt to satisfy the cravings of another person in our lives, to retaliate, or to cope with our own emotional pain. Anyone recovering from the effects of compulsive sexual behavior in others is welcome in COSA. Those who *also* struggle with their own compulsive sexual behavior are welcome as well, and these COSAs may choose to seek additional help in other programs designed to address those issues specifically. Regardless of how we've been affected by compulsive sexual behavior, COSA is here for each of us.

The first sentence of Tradition Three can be perceived as a reassuring expression of acceptance, a scary idea, or maybe a bit of both. It is a relief to know that we belong, no matter who we are or what we have experienced. At the same time, of course, sharing a COSA meeting with those who are quite different from us can challenge us and push us out of our comfort zone. We may discover hidden fears, biases, or triggers that we didn't realize we had.

We may be tempted to avoid meetings where the COSAs are "different" than we are, or to restrict who can join COSA. However, part of our recovery is learning how to apply the Twelve Traditions so that we can successfully face and handle challenges that may arise from diversity in our meetings. Remembering Tradition Five, that our primary purpose is to carry the message to those who still suffer, we seek to incorporate welcoming wording into our meeting formats and implement meeting practices that help everyone feel welcome, safe, and supported.

Given the nature of our life experiences, some of the sharing in meetings and between members will inevitably touch upon disturbing situations. Sometimes hearing another COSA member share their experiences may bring up our own wounds from the past and set off emotional triggers. Since we are affected by compulsive sexual behavior in a variety of ways, hearing this information will affect each of us differently.

Even though we in the fellowship aim to be sensitive in our sharing, if emotional triggers arise, we can reach out to our sponsors and to other trusted COSAs for support and guidance. These are opportunities to learn how to set emotional boundaries for ourselves. Sometimes this means changing external circumstances. Often, though, it means making adjustments within ourselves. With the help of our sponsors, our Step work, and our Higher Power, we learn new emotional and spiritual skills. If we open our minds and hearts to our similarities rather than constricting around differences, we may gain a new perspective and grow in compassion for ourselves and others. We come to understand that discomfort can actually be a catalyst to strengthen our recovery and our connection to a Higher Power.

The second sentence of Tradition Three builds upon the inclusive approach introduced in the first sentence. As individuals in our lives outside the COSA program, we have diverse affiliations and beliefs which may contradict those of other fellowship members. And yet, we want COSA to be here for everyone who wants it. Therefore, we endeavor to keep our COSA program separate from our outside interests or beliefs. With this mindset, we keep COSA recovery available and welcoming for everyone.

For example, consider a group that combines COSA recovery with an expensive therapeutic treatment. While this type of group may indeed help people heal, it would not be considered a COSA group because of its potential exclusion of those who cannot afford it or who disagree with the therapeutic approach.

In another instance, if a group studies specific religious or philosophical teachings alongside the COSA literature, this may benefit some members, but it would not be considered a COSA group either. The reasoning is this: while a religion or philosophy may be helpful for some, affiliating with a specific belief system would exclude those who practice other religions and forms of spirituality as well as those who practice none at all.

There is an abundance of psychological, spiritual, and self-help literature available that addresses the issues many COSAs face. Other Twelve-Step programs may also be helpful for some COSAs. Individual COSA members are certainly free to use any and all of these resources. However, as members of the COSA fellowship, we need to clearly differentiate these "outside" resources from our COSA literature offerings. The use or provision of such resources is up to an individual meeting's group conscience, but the group should make clear that the resources are not affiliated with COSA.

Some COSA members in their professional lives sell products or services that help with healing from trauma. They may want to share their resources with members of the COSA fellowship. As well-intentioned as these members may be, the boundary between the COSA group and everything else must be clearly defined. There is no place for commerce within the COSA fellowship, and members need to keep business and recovery separate. If services, products, or therapies are mentioned within the COSA meeting, it could give members the impression that COSA is endorsing them as part of the COSA program, and Tradition Six cautions us that COSA ought not endorse any outside enterprise. We don't want any COSA member to form the misguided belief that they need to buy something in order to recover, belong, or be accepted. It is natural for COSA members to develop relationships beyond COSA and to offer helpful suggestions to each other, but this type of interaction should be approached with the utmost care and take place outside of our COSA meetings and gatherings.

We may not feel equally comfortable and safe with every COSA member we meet, but we want the COSA program to be available to all. Upholding Tradition Three means we listen for similarities rather than judging or excluding differences. We keep our meetings safe by honoring the Traditions and Concepts. We practice boundary-setting and self-care. In doing these things, we assure that the tools and gifts of recovery are available to each and every person who reaches out to COSA for help.

Tradition Four

*Each group should be autonomous
except in matters affecting other groups
or COSA as a whole.*

Tradition Four empowers each group to choose how to support its members. We balance this freedom with responsibility to the COSA fellowship as a whole.

Having autonomy means we have the independence to craft our meetings in a way that meets the needs of local members. This applies to everything from where and when we meet, to our meeting format, to which COSA readings we use. One group may prefer open sharing while another may prefer sharing on specific, scheduled recovery topics. A group may host a series of speakers or allow time for COSA literature study, journaling, or presentation of Step work. We have the autonomy to customize our meeting formats, workshops, and retreats. Each of these may have a unique character. We can be playful, we can experiment—there are many possibilities!

Tradition Four reminds us that with this freedom we also have the responsibility to consider the welfare of our fellowship. In the context of our COSA groups, we do this by staying true to COSA's Steps, Traditions, and Concepts. If we stray from these, we run the risk of diluting or distorting the COSA message of recovery, thereby harming COSA as a whole.

It may seem obvious not to stray from these principles, but sometimes in our enthusiasm to share the things that help us, we veer off the mark. For example, a COSA member may promote a specific therapeutic approach or religious practice that has helped them. As well-intentioned as these suggestions may be, recommending these practices in a COSA meeting is not in keeping with our COSA Traditions (especially Traditions Three, Six, and Ten).

Tradition Four advises us to consider how promoting outside (non-COSA) resources during a meeting could affect COSA as a whole and interfere with our ability to fulfill our primary purpose. As individuals, we are free to take advantage of any and every resource that helps us heal. If another person is interested in our experiences with non-COSA resources and is asking for input, we are free to discuss this in conversations outside of the group context (such as one-on-one fellowship before or after the meeting, or phone conversations separate from the meeting).

Using our abundant COSA literature during meetings—*COSA Recovery*, booklets, and our *Balance* newsletter—is an effective way to ensure that our fellowship transmits a consistent, unified message. While there is non-COSA recovery literature that many have found helpful, we take special care in selecting which literature to use and make available at our meetings, as we want to maintain our focus on COSA recovery.

According to Tradition Four, it is the individual group's choice and decision as to what literature to use in meetings, as long as it does not affect other groups or COSA as a whole. It is wise to clearly identify the source of any literature we use, and to conduct regular business meetings to assess whether the group's choice still meets the needs of its members and furthers the COSA message. Tradition Four encourages us to make an informed choice about this and any other questions or issues that come up in our groups.

In some cases, the effects of a group's decision on COSA as a whole might be apparent in a particular geographical area. For example, if all the meetings in a particular region were women-only meetings, that would pose a problem for male COSAs in that area, and this would impede reaching out or carrying the message to those who are still suffering. Some regions (and also telemeetings and online groups) have intergroups that may help bring awareness to these and other considerations that affect all of their constituent groups. When groups and intergroups make decisions by considering the Traditions and how the fellowship may be affected, then the groups and the fellowship are strong, unified, and healthy, and we have more to offer to all who want the gifts of recovery.

Regarding small decisions we make as a group, it is not necessary to consult our International Service Organization (ISO). We do, however, use the principles of the program to guide us in making any decision that may impact other groups or the fellowship as a whole. If we cannot resolve an issue at the group level, or if it is not appropriate to do so, we can ask our delegate to contact the delegate liaison, who can consult with the ISO board. Our ISO board has experience with exploring such matters and with considering the effects on the COSA fellowship worldwide. Alternatively, if we have an intergroup, we can first ask our intergroup representative to bring a question or concern to our intergroup.

In our groups, we enjoy tremendous freedom in the way we fulfill our primary purpose of carrying the message of hope and recovery to those who still suffer. We balance self-direction with consideration for others and healthy interdependence, just as we do in our individual recovery. In this way, each group can function in the manner best suited for its specific members, while the integrity of the larger COSA fellowship is respected and maintained.

Tradition Five

Each group has but one primary purpose—to carry its message to those who still suffer. We do this by practicing the Twelve Steps ourselves.

As individuals, our purposes are as diverse as we are. As COSA members, we are unified by a single purpose: carrying the COSA message to those still suffering. As a fellowship, COSA addresses one issue: the effects of compulsive sexual behavior on our lives. COSA provides safe haven, support, information, and open hearts and minds. We carry the message by sustaining our own recovery, doing service work, and focusing on our primary purpose.

This Tradition is about love and compassion for ourselves and those around us, especially those whose lives have been affected by compulsive sexual behavior. At the core of the Fifth Tradition is the fundamental reminder that we must love and care for ourselves first before we can love and care for another.

While COSA's Twelve Steps and Traditions are based upon those of Alcoholics Anonymous, COSA's Fifth Tradition adds the concept that we carry the message by practicing the Twelve Steps ourselves. As COSAs, we often need the reminder—or for some, the permission—to keep the focus on ourselves. By practicing the Twelve Steps ourselves, we find recovery. By taking care of ourselves, we model recovery and carry the message to others. As our recovery grows, we offer hope, and we light the way for those who are still suffering. Working together, focused on one primary purpose, we ensure COSA endures. It makes so much sense!

Prior to recovery, many of us were accomplished helpers, trying hard to take care of everyone else at the expense of our own sanity. We neglected ourselves and sometimes felt like martyrs. Through the wisdom that we gain in recovery, we realize that we do not know what is best for another person. In fact, when we try to fix things for others, we may be acting in ways that actually disrespect their dignity, disempower them to find their own solutions, and interfere with their opportunities to grow in relationship to themselves and their Higher Power. Tradition Five gives us the opportunity to learn how to help others while remaining true to our COSA sobriety.

We carry the message by "staying on our side of the street" and "living in the solution," which means practicing the Twelve Steps in all areas of our lives. Our spiritual transformation in recovery is attractive and inspiring to others, both within and outside COSA meetings.

We may also carry the message when we perform acts of service. Service as a spiritual practice is offering our love and support to others and passing along the gifts that we have received in the program. Service also helps us to maintain and strengthen our own recovery; many believe that the person offering service benefits even more than the receiver. Service opportunities include leading a meeting or maintaining outreach tools, such as our website, lists of area meetings, literature libraries, and phone or email lists. Helping with COSA retreats and conventions are additional ways of carrying the message.

Carrying the message through service does not have to be a huge undertaking to be significant. Small gestures can make a world of difference for a COSA member who is suffering. We carry the message when we offer support to a sponsee or when we answer a call or text from another member. We carry the message when we share at COSA meetings. We remember how we felt when we attended our first meeting, whether face-to-face, by phone, or online. Many of us were petrified. Yet we discovered we were no longer alone. COSA members offered friendly greetings and shared their experience, strength, and hope. We received a departing gift of a list of first names and phone numbers, which at times became a lifeline to serenity. This sparked the beginning of our COSA recovery program.

By opening our meetings with the Serenity Prayer, we invite ourselves to open our hearts so that we can feel the constant presence of a Power greater than ourselves. When we welcome our Higher Power to oversee our meetings and then share vulnerably from the heart, we often give encouragement, hope, or ideas to another COSA member. And although we may not know it, our sharing may have a lasting effect on that COSA member. When we are spiritually present and receptive, we are open to receive exactly what we need. In the same regard, many of us use the Serenity Prayer to invoke such openness prior to our Step work.

Tradition Five serves as a beacon that lights the way to our primary purpose: carrying the message to those who still suffer. We get there by practicing the Twelve Steps ourselves. This Tradition encourages us to cultivate our recovery and model experience, strength, and hope for others. And the gifts keep multiplying!

Tradition Six

A COSA group ought never endorse, finance, or lend the COSA name to any related facility or outside enterprise, lest problems of money, property, and prestige divert us from our primary purpose.

Our primary purpose is defined in Tradition Five: carrying the message to COSAs who are still suffering. Tradition Six establishes boundaries to protect this purpose. It instructs COSA not to endorse, give money to, or associate its name with outside enterprises, as doing so might cause distractions or conflicts of interest.

Because we deeply believe in the COSA program and have experienced firsthand its gifts and miracles, we may be tempted to promote COSA on a larger scale. We might wish to see COSA carry its message far and wide by partnering with counseling facilities, marketing outlets, or other entities that offer help to those whose lives have been affected by compulsive sexual behavior. With the best of intentions, we might feel that COSA should use extra funds to financially support organizations with similar missions.

Tradition Six reminds us that to remain focused on our primary purpose, COSA must remain completely autonomous.

Money in a COSA group's treasury should be used only for COSA. Clean and clear boundaries between the COSA program and other facilities and enterprises are essential to COSA's survival.

Of course, as individuals, we each may decide to use our own money and resources to support any entities we choose. If a COSA group or the fellowship as a whole, however, were to become financially intertwined with outside enterprises, the group's purpose could easily become complicated and muddied.

Because COSA does not align itself with outside organizations, therapies, religions, or political parties, all members are equally welcome, without regard to personal affiliations. Hence, COSA provides a safe haven where anyone can experience healing through genuine acceptance with no hint of commercialism, coercion, or inequality. In the outside world, people typically see each other through lenses of age, gender, class, profession, level of education, and the like. In COSA, many of us feel we have found one of the few places, or perhaps the only place, where we can set aside such roles and labels and just experience each other as human beings sharing a spiritual journey together. Tradition Six protects this safe haven and helps groups maintain their integrity and spiritual aim without dilution or misdirection of our message.

While Tradition Six is intended to help COSA groups maintain healthy boundaries, we also may study the wisdom of this Tradition as it applies in our personal lives. A key recovery tool is learning to set healthy boundaries, not only to ensure our safety, but also to find dignity and honor in who we are. Without appropriate boundaries, we may be diverted from our personal "primary purpose," which may be to nurture our own emotional, mental, physical, and spiritual well-being. When we prioritize the needs of others over our own, we may become disconnected from ourselves and our own needs and desires. We may ignore the internal compass that keeps us on the spiritual course of being true to ourselves and aligned with our Higher Power's will for us.

When we set clear boundaries, we respect ourselves. This may be a new concept for many of us. Before recovery, we may have allowed others to control and manipulate us. Many of us had limited love and regard for ourselves, and this often affected how others perceived and treated us. Boundaries are empowering tools that lead us to loving self-care and serenity. Tradition Six reminds us that setting and maintaining healthy boundaries, whether in our groups or as part of our individual recovery programs, keeps us focused on our spiritual aim and connected with our Higher Power.

Tradition Six cautions that problems of money, property, and prestige—in other words, material concerns—may distract a COSA group from its primary purpose. We may find that the same consideration has held true for us individually in the past. Material preoccupations may have stood in the way of our personal primary purpose in COSA: spiritual recovery.

Before recovery, some of us tried to use money or material possessions to hide our insecurities, inflate our sense of self, or fill an empty hole deep within our souls. We focused on material concerns to distract ourselves from our own painful reality.

As our lives became more and more unmanageable, we may have tried using money, property, and prestige to show the outside world that we were successful, worthy, perfect, or maybe even just OK. We may have fooled ourselves into thinking that symbols of outward success could help us attract the right mate, keep our partner happy, or gain the approval of others. Feeling unworthy at our core, we went to great lengths to earn love from others so that we could find value in ourselves.

Now in recovery, we recognize that our egos were running the show. With self-will in the way, even if it appeared as self-deprivation and shame, we could not have a real connection with our Higher Power. If we wanted to follow our Higher Power's will for us, we needed to set aside our own will. Through working the Twelve Steps of COSA, we learned to humbly ask our Higher Power for guidance, and that led us to *spiritual* wealth and fulfillment. We became ready to let go of material concerns, and we found serenity.

Tradition Six works by providing boundaries to ensure that COSA will maintain its unity and focus on achieving its primary purpose. It also provides a model for establishing boundaries in our personal recovery and for guiding our lives with a spiritual, rather than material, aim. Tradition Six ensures that the COSA fellowship will continue to be a place where all are welcome to experience the wondrous, healing gifts of recovery.

Tradition Seven

Every COSA group ought to be fully self-supporting, declining outside contributions.

Tradition Seven, in conjunction with Tradition Six, acts as a protective shell, ensuring that COSA is not compromised by outside interests. The Sixth Tradition dissuades COSA from supporting or giving resources to outside groups. Tradition Seven recommends that COSA rely solely on its members and accept no support from outside sources. Together, these two traditions help COSA remain independent, autonomous, and focused on our primary purpose, helping those who still suffer from the effects of compulsive sexual behavior.

Even when outside funds or resources are given with the best of intentions, accepting them puts COSA at risk of diluting its primary purpose. A COSA group that accepts a contribution from an outside entity may experience a sense of indebtedness, even if the giver asks for nothing in return.

For example, a small COSA group was meeting at a religious facility. The facility offered to let the group use the meeting room rent-free. Led by the principles of the Seventh Tradition, the COSA group members decided by group conscience that they would pay rent, even though it was not requested.

They perceived the rent-free space to be an outside donation, one that may have resulted in a sense of indebtedness to the church or in the appearance of a religious affiliation. Had the church requested that the group make religious materials available during the meeting, the group members or the church may have felt that the group was obligated to comply because the meeting room had been gifted. Tradition Seven holds sacred the priority to maintain COSA's autonomy. By refusing the offer, the group was confident that it was free from outside influences.

COSA is sustained solely by voluntary member contributions, financial and otherwise. Tradition Seven offers us opportunities to support COSA every time a meeting basket is passed. Additionally, nonfinancial contributions—such as participating in meetings, working the Twelve Steps, serving as a sponsor, and volunteering for service positions—ensure that COSA can continue to carry the message to those who still suffer. These contributions secure COSA's independence and sustainability. In fact, COSA's very existence rests in the hands of its members.

When we give to COSA, we not only help it flourish, we also develop a sense of purpose and connection to our COSA community. By supporting COSA, we invest in our collective well-being. Tradition Seven's direction to be self-supporting is both unifying and empowering.

Groups may decide how to use financial contributions from members. The funds may be used to pay rent and website fees, purchase literature and materials, and help delegates attend the annual COSA convention. In addition, local groups are responsible for supporting and sustaining COSA's International Service Organization (ISO), ensuring that it also remains self-supporting. Money donated to ISO is used to pay for office rent and supplies, compensate the administrative assistant(s), maintain the website, publish materials, and help finance the annual COSA convention.

Through Tradition Seven, COSA members work together to ensure that COSA maintains a prudent fiscal reserve and has adequate resources to continue to carry the message. Each group is free to determine the amount needed in reserve. COSA groups and ISO strive to have sufficient funds not only to pay current expenses, but also to support lasting continuity.

At the same time, COSA remains humble and free of entanglements by avoiding excessive stockpiles of financial resources. Without financial distractions, COSA is better able to remain focused on helping those whose lives have been affected by compulsive sexual behavior.

At times, individuals may be unable to contribute financially. Even so, everyone is welcomed into COSA, and each member is embraced and valued equally. As some meeting scripts state, "We have no dues or fees. We need you more than we need your money." We give only what we can.

While Tradition Seven is intended to guide COSA groups to remain self-supporting, we may also apply the principle in our lives and individual recovery journeys. Some of us have found that when we are dependent on someone else, we sacrifice our autonomy and lose our sense of self-worth and capability. We often fail to take care of ourselves and instead focus on others.

In the past, we may have relied upon others to support us even when it did not feel safe or right. Perhaps we have had unrealistic expectations or hopes that someone else could take care of our needs, and inevitably we were left feeling disappointed, resentful, or victimized. When we set ourselves up to feel beholden to someone else, we often ignore our own needs and wants.

As we work the Twelve Steps of recovery and begin to trust our Higher Power, we learn to care for and trust ourselves. From this place of groundedness and connection, we regain our sense of self-worth and discernment. When we take responsibility for our own lives, we experience a feeling of empowerment, well-being, and completeness. As COSA members in recovery, we are learning to hear our authentic voices and gain the courage to follow our truth. We no longer work so hard to try to please others or to let them determine what is best for us.

Tradition Seven both secures COSA's path to its primary purpose and offers us the meaningful and often life changing opportunity to contribute to our beloved fellowship. The Tradition's lesson, that of taking responsibility for ourselves and for COSA, is key to sustaining COSA's integrity and supporting our ability to carry the message to others who still suffer.

Tradition Eight

*COSA should remain forever
non-professional, but our service centers
may employ special workers.*

Tradition Eight reminds us that recovery is never for sale. We are not paid to carry the message to those who still suffer. We freely give what was so generously given to us. We enthusiastically carry the message from a place of gratitude, not from a desire for monetary rewards. When we work for financial gain, we may lose sight of our spiritual focus. Money as a motivator might interfere with our connection with fellow COSA members, our COSA program, and our Higher Power. Tradition Eight directs COSA to remain unencumbered by financial interests.

What we have to offer others is our own experience, strength, and hope: what our lives were like before recovery, where we are now, how we got here, and where we are heading. COSA's foundation is built on the generous and free-flowing sharing of our stories and our spiritual journeys. A wonderful, nurturing atmosphere is created when we each share from the heart.

This humble and genuine sharing is the fabric of COSA. Spirituality enters in between the threads of our shares when we set aside our egos and make room to receive grace and wisdom from our Higher Power and from other COSA members. Every day in recovery is a brand new one; that is one reason we keep coming back. When we admit our powerlessness and become willing to surrender our will and our lives to our Higher Power, we experience the opportunity to touch a sense of the sacred.

We learn early on that COSA is not a therapy group. We do not give advice or try to fix one another. Some of us did not understand this at first. We attended our first meeting hoping to get easy answers. We looked to the more seasoned members to tell us what we needed to do to escape our pain. Some of us left our first meeting surprised that the COSA members in attendance did not give us any advice at all, but instead focused on their own recovery. Nevertheless, their shares helped us feel that we were no longer alone with dark secrets. Seeing their serenity and hearing them articulate feelings that we never expected anyone else to understand, we left with a glimmer of relief and hope. We gained comfort and insight that many of us could not find any other way.

Our program is a spiritual program as opposed to a professional one. When we serve in a professional capacity, we may work to find solutions for others. However, in recovery we acknowledge that we do not have all the answers. This leaves room for the guidance of a Higher Power.

There is no such job position as a professional COSA. Professionals are specifically trained to provide a service, and typically they are paid for that service. In COSA, the only "training" we receive is through the work we do in our own recovery. With the support from our program and the guidance from our Higher Power, our individual experience, strength, and hope are our unique offerings.

COSA is a fellowship of equals, whether we are newcomers or long-term members. There is no hierarchy of membership.

There are no leaders. No person is more or less valuable than another. We are all human beings. The only one with more knowledge than the rest is our Higher Power.

Some of us seek help from professionals in addition to working the COSA program. Some COSA members are themselves professional therapists, doctors, social workers, and the like. But when we enter a COSA meeting, we leave our professional hats at the door. We are all equals in COSA recovery, all here for healing. We may volunteer our talents in service to COSA, but we are not paid to perform any roles.

However, Tradition Eight states that COSA's service centers may employ special workers. It is unrealistic to expect a large international organization to run solely on volunteer power if it is to remain sustainable for years to come. COSA may employ special workers to keep things running smoothly. Without this work, the administrative services of COSA would very likely grind to a halt.

The duties performed by COSA's special workers may include such things as managing its office, monitoring the mail, sending out COSA literature, working to ensure that COSA is in compliance with not-for-profit standards, entering data for COSA's tax returns, and providing monthly reports to the board. The special workers communicate directly with the board's chair and treasurer and are accountable to the board as well as to the fellowship. At times, COSA contracts with professionals who have other specific skills that COSA needs to grow. For example, COSA may hire an expert web designer to work on its website.

Importantly, special workers are never paid to do Twelve Step work or carry the COSA message of recovery. All the tasks they perform support the program administratively so that those in recovery can continue to share their experience, strength, and hope, thus carrying COSA's message with integrity.

COSA is not a business, and recovery is not for sale. COSA is fueled by volunteer members who serve with honest, heartfelt enthusiasm rather than from a sense of obligation or a desire to profit. By freely giving service to our recovery program and offering our experience, strength, and hope to other COSA members, we honor the Twelfth Step and practice these principles in all areas of our lives. In order to keep recovery, we must give it away—not sell it, but give it. Our recovery in COSA depends upon a Power greater than ourselves, and that cannot be bought. It is always freely available to us if we are willing to do our part.

Tradition Nine

> *COSA, as such, ought never be organized; but we may create service boards or committees directly responsible to those they serve.*

Tradition Nine may sound confusing, especially to COSA newcomers. What does it mean that COSA is never organized? It may feel like a scary idea that the entirety of our fellowship would be "dis-organized." Having been deeply affected by compulsive sexual behavior, we may believe we have had enough chaos in our lives. We may feel compelled to take charge or want the comfort of having someone else in charge.

In our personal lives, we may have received positive feedback and validation—or felt a sense of power and control—from organizing things at work, at home, or in our communities. Before recovery, many of us tried to rigidly organize and structure our lives, often in an attempt to feel safe and guard against triggers. We often did more than our share of creating and enforcing rules, snooping, and supervising. Although we may not have been consciously aware of it at the time, we came to realize in recovery that we may have been attempting to gain a sense of control, to eliminate chaos, and/or to prevent compulsive sexual behavior from harming us.

Yet, coming into COSA, many of us were exhausted or resentful from feeling obliged to manage everything. We wanted someone else, like an authority figure or institution, to take charge.

So how does COSA function without organization? As Tradition Nine states, COSA operates through a structure of service boards or committees that answer to the COSA fellowship as a whole. There is no chief officer or president in COSA. There are no supervisors, managers, or other authorities. COSA members fill positions or roles with titles like "chair" or "secretary," but they are "trusted servants" who "do not govern," as Tradition Two tells us.

COSA has no directives, rules, or enforcement measures. Instead, our fellowship has suggested Steps, Traditions, and Concepts based on spiritual principles. Some meetings, including those of the International Service Organization (ISO) and the Annual Delegate Meeting, have established suggested safe communication guidelines to help members feel confident that meetings will be safe, sober, and productive. COSA members adhere to this guidance because it works. Following this guidance has helped COSA members recover and continue to carry the message to others who still suffer from the effects of compulsive sexual behavior.

For those of us who had been accustomed to caretaking, controlling, running, managing, and being in charge, this Tradition sometimes seemed difficult to follow. Serving on a committee or board felt more challenging than just doing all the work ourselves. Having more than our share of power was comfortably familiar to us, while being responsible or accountable to others required more effort emotionally. When we committed to serve on a committee in COSA, we worked alongside other recovering individuals who sought to put their will aside and give selfless, humble service. We began to learn how to right-size our relationship to power. Adhering to the guidance of COSA's Steps and Traditions helps us avoid falling into old behavior patterns when we act in service to COSA.

In recovery, when we serve our fellow COSAs, we do so with humility. Tradition Two also tells us COSA has "but one ultimate authority—a loving God as expressed in our group conscience." Individual members in service positions are encouraged to rotate regularly so that no single personality dominates, as we are guided to "put principles before personalities" in Tradition Twelve. When volunteering to serve, COSA members align our roles with our responsibilities to the other COSA members we serve. We listen to feedback and practice patience and humility when making decisions. We set aside our individual wills and egos and work together under the guidance of our Higher Power for the common welfare.

In COSA, we do not need to be organized into a hierarchy of rank. We are all equal members. Newcomers and old-timers are equals in COSA. As perfectly imperfect humans, we bring our assets and our liabilities to our COSA service work. If we are serving, it is important that we are working the Steps with our sponsors, taking our own inventory, and listening to our Higher Power's will for us. We demonstrate gratitude, respect, and grace to each other when we recognize that we are all doing the best we can.

Members of a committee or group may decide by group conscience that they would like to take a group inventory. For example, the board of COSA has taken a board inventory to determine its health and effectiveness as a board and to identify its strengths and weaknesses. Similarly, individual meeting groups may take time to assess if their meetings are healthy, functioning in line with the Traditions and Concepts, and welcoming to all who attend.

COSA as a whole works using the model of an upside-down triangle. The COSA fellowship directs the board and committees through the fellowship's group conscience. Information is passed from individuals and meeting groups through intergroups and delegates to the board chair, who is at the point representing the bottom of the inverted triangle. This differs from a top-down business model where a director or small group of directors at the top make decisions and dictate them to the rest of the group.

Local groups, intergroups, and delegates attending the Annual Delegate Meeting make decisions for which they are responsible to the COSA fellowship they serve, such as "Let's plan a retreat," or "Let's write a COSA book." Then COSA members volunteer for committees or service roles. Committees and individuals in service roles can manage planning an event, developing new literature, and distributing information to the public on behalf of the group. In each case, the service committees and roles are directly responsible to the group they serve. As trusted servants, they are responsible for carrying out the group's decisions.

Writing *COSA Recovery* for our fellowship provides an example of trusted servants at the level of the ISO being responsive to the fellowship. During the composition process, the Literature Committee asked for and incorporated feedback from the entire fellowship. Through responsible service to the fellowship as a whole, the book was written by COSA members for COSA members and reflects the entire fellowship.

Tradition Nine ensures that the ISO of COSA, by means of the board and committees, is able to function effectively and with care and responsiveness to the fellowship itself. In COSA we learn to serve with care and respect for ourselves, each other, and the group and fellowship we serve. The lessons from Tradition Nine may teach us how to cultivate equality and healthy responsiveness in our personal relationships as well.

Tradition Ten

*COSA has no opinion on outside issues;
hence the COSA name ought never be drawn
into public controversy.*

The simple, yet powerful wisdom of Tradition Ten helps us keep our mission and message clear, and our reputation clean. It supports Tradition One by guiding us to stay focused on our primary purpose of carrying our message to those who still suffer.

Tradition Ten cautions us to steer clear from issues and subjects that could divert us from, or cause controversy regarding, COSA's purpose. In doing so it promotes COSA unity and protects the health and integrity of COSA as a whole. We can also see the complementary principles from Traditions Five, Six, and Eight at work in Tradition Ten.

Outside issues such as money, politics, race, and religion can be especially controversial and divisive. They can cause rifts and damage to relationships. COSA does not offer opinions regarding political candidates or policies or address public issues on race, religion, or sexual misconduct. In COSA we seek inclusivity. This is evident in our Diversity Statement. Without any biases, we invite all people whose lives have been affected by compulsive sexual behavior into our fellowship. The gifts of our invitation come to life when such a varied group of individuals come together as equals in the safety of an anonymous gathering for the sole purpose of seeking recovery.

Tradition Ten draws from the principle of remaining nonprofessional found in Tradition Eight. This provides clear guidance to the trustees of the International Service Organization of COSA. Therefore, COSA does not give advice, recommend, or endorse any legal, medical, therapeutic, political, or other viewpoints outside of COSA. Nor does COSA partner with outside entities. The trustees focus on the welfare of the fellowship using only the principles and ideals of the COSA Twelve Steps, Traditions, and Concepts, thus ensuring that our message and reputation remain untarnished.

On the local level of our meetings, how do we know if something is an outside issue? We can simply ask: does this *carry* the COSA message, or *confuse* it?

When newcomers attend our meetings they are thirsting for our life-changing message. Imagine us extending our COSA message to them in the metaphor of a glass of clean, clear water. If something outside the COSA message is introduced to their glass, *no matter how helpful it may seem*, it clouds the water, dilutes our message, and confuses our purpose. Such outside issues may include literature or quotes from other Twelve Step programs or helping professions, recommendations on types of therapy, financial or legal strategies, or religious and political convictions. The newcomer may feel confused. They may be intimidated by strong or willful opinions. Even discussing our business titles or educational credentials during our meetings can be an outside issue and may not honor our tradition of anonymity and our principle of equality. A newcomer may assume someone is an "expert" and follow the *person* rather than the COSA *principles*. We provide the best support for our newcomers, our individual recoveries, and the health and unity of our group by keeping our message focused on COSA.

This Tradition keeps our meetings safe and sober in other ways, too. Our members do not solicit for personal business, fundraisers, or other well-meaning outside endeavors during our meeting. Such offerings are not in keeping with the principles and spirit of Tradition Ten and can be awkward when presented in our meetings.

Tradition Ten serves our personal lives well, too. We avoid the pitfalls of hard feelings and potentially damaging relationships by choosing to stay on "our side of the street" when faced with controversial subjects or situations. We wisely refrain from stoking these tensions. We can also ask ourselves if our recovery will benefit or suffer if we wade into controversial or triggering topics. Will gossiping, commenting on the latest trend, or offering unsolicited feedback or advice harm or help in our recovery and our relationship with others?

In recovery, we seek to have healthy relationships with ourselves and others. We actively endeavor to accept ourselves and others, flaws and all; we allow for each person's unique humanness and personality traits. We are all entitled to our opinions, beliefs, and convictions on outside issues regardless of whether or not we agree. Recovery allows us to detach in love and not to try to mount a campaign to convince anyone that our way of thinking is the right or only way. We find our voice and truth through recovery. We balance our voice with the wisdom to exercise constraint when warranted.

Tradition Ten ensures that the COSA purpose will remain consistent and clear, both inside and outside of COSA. Its gifts and wisdom apply from the individual level to the international level, safeguarding COSA's integrity and avoiding public controversy.

Tradition Eleven

Our public relations policy is based on attraction rather than promotion; we need always maintain personal anonymity at the level of press, radio, films, television, and other public media of communication. We need guard with special care the anonymity of all Program members.

COSA is a bountiful source of support, freely available to anyone and everyone who seeks relief from the effects of compulsive sexual behavior. In order to spread information about our resources, we must engage in various means of public relations. We approach this with care; the well-being of our fellowship depends on it.

Some of us have been tempted to share the gift of recovery by trying to convince people of COSA's potential usefulness in their lives. We can let go of this caretaking approach. There is no need to promote, recruit, chase, or coax. The outward signs of our inner transformations are persuasive enough for anyone seeking relief.

If the word attraction indicates evoking interest in or drawing attention to, what is attractive about COSA recovery? Each member of the fellowship may answer this differently. Here are some examples of what we have experienced in COSA or seen in others who have worked the COSA Twelve Steps:

- The feeling of relief upon finding a community of people who can relate to our experiences and who do not shame or judge us nor tell us what to do;
- A sense of empowerment and serenity that comes from our learning to let go of what we cannot control and from making life-nourishing choices for ourselves;
- The newly found self-awareness and self-compassion that develop with Step work;
- A growing ability to set appropriate boundaries around our sexuality and to make progress toward achieving healthy sexual intimacy;
- A way of honoring self-care and speaking our truth to others, giving rise to mutual respect and healthier personal relationships;
- The feeling of usefulness and purpose that stems from respectfully serving others in a way that supports healthy boundaries and connection to a Higher Power.

None of us needs to point out or promote the gifts of recovery; they are unquestionably present. Recovery is naturally noticeable, modeled by us in the way we live our lives. As we trust the process and work the Steps, the COSA program of recovery materializes in a unique way for each of us. The concept of "attraction rather than promotion" reminds us that we reveal the gifts of COSA to others by simply continuing to work on our own recovery.

What we have learned in our interpersonal relationships is also true in our public relations: no amount of effort on our part will spur change in others, unless and until they are ready.

Change for each of us comes from within, with the help of a Higher Power.

While we do not promote COSA, we do have gratitude for what COSA has done for us, and we wish to share with others that COSA is here for them as well. We desire to carry the message about COSA, to make the abundance of the fellowship available to those who want it. The key words here are "those who want it."

It is not our place to convince anyone that they need the COSA program. Instead, we trust our Higher Power's plan and timing, and when others do reach out, we can then actively provide support. If someone brings us their issue about being affected by compulsive sexual behavior, we can choose to share with them how we have been greatly helped through COSA. We can give them information on the program and meetings, and perhaps offer to go with them to a meeting.

The fellowship's presence is made known when we do our part, such as when we ensure our meeting's listing on the COSA website is up to date or obtain permission to leave COSA materials in our doctor's or therapist's office. Providing information about the program—by way of pamphlets, articles, books, public listings, or the website—is not "promoting." We are not forcing anyone to do or give anything. We are simply offering a connection to recovery resources.

COSA may use public message boards and social media pages to raise awareness about the fellowship and share information on the benefits of recovery. COSA's Outreach Committee seeks ways to reach the diverse population of individuals who are suffering from the effects of compulsive sexual behavior. However, the use of public platforms for outreach or any public media of communication is to be treated with great caution. Tradition Eleven reminds us that COSA is an anonymous fellowship. Anonymity plays a significant role in both our personal and public interactions.

When we protect the anonymity of others and ourselves and honor principles before personalities, it helps to ensure a clear separation between our participation in COSA and any personal or professional roles we play outside of COSA. Anonymity allows us to be our authentic selves without concern that people will judge us or interact with us based on our titles, jobs, roles, or professions. There are no COSA experts or teachers; we simply have trusted servants, who are themselves in the process of recovering. We carefully maintain anonymity for all COSA members to ensure that participation in COSA does not disrupt our public lives.

Perhaps most obvious is the sensitivity of the issues surrounding compulsive sexual behavior. Anonymity means that at no time should we ever expose another member of our fellowship. This seems straightforward, but we must remain mindful of our everyday actions that could inadvertently call public attention to our recovery friends. For example, we refrain from making COSA-related phone calls in public places or acknowledging COSA members when we are out in public with others who are not in the program. We also practice caution and consideration when placing photos and videos on social media because these platforms are not anonymous.

We also exercise restraint in personally publicizing our own recovery, such as when writing a book, lecturing to groups, or participating in media coverage of COSA. We wish to make COSA known as a fellowship but maintain personal anonymity as COSA members. Tradition Twelve urges us to ensure that personalities do not overtake principles. We serve the fellowship and our own recovery by carrying the recovery message humbly, freely, and without personal tribute or celebrity. We recognize this as integral to upholding Traditions Six and Eleven.

In addition to our own anonymity and that of other COSA members, we consider how our public interactions may affect those close to us. Given that it is often family members or friends who are struggling with sexual compulsions, our connection with COSA has the potential to implicate them by association. When we choose to break our own anonymity, even if it might be appropriate and helpful to do so, we may also be breaking the anonymity of those close to us. This could cause damage. It is important to have thorough communication with and consideration for others who may be affected, especially when we serve COSA in a public capacity.

Each time we interact publicly, we aim to keep the COSA Traditions in mind. They guide our one-on-one dialogues with people, such as in conversations with acquaintances or with a contact person for a potential meeting site. The Traditions also guide us when we represent the fellowship in a public capacity, such as when writing a public service announcement or making a flyer for a local retreat. In such instances, we are trusted servants of the fellowship, and we strive to embody the Traditions as best we can. We endeavor to protect the anonymity of our COSA fellows at all times.

When we honor anonymity, we foster an environment that allows us to safely share our experience, strength, and hope without fear of judgment or criticism. Tradition Eleven reminds us not to recruit, advise, or promote. We simply work our recovery program and uphold the Traditions to ensure that the fellowship is available to all who want recovery, while maintaining anonymity at all times. We trust our Higher Power to do the rest.

Tradition Twelve

Anonymity is the spiritual foundation of all our traditions, ever reminding us to place principles before personalities.

Before recovery, our understanding of anonymity may have been limited to the dictionary's definition: "unnamed," "unknown" or "name not made public." In recovery, anonymity takes on a deeper, spiritual meaning. Practicing Tradition Twelve ensures that the COSA message, not the messenger, will always be our focus.

Tradition Eleven emphasizes the importance of remaining anonymous at all levels of press, radio, films, television, and other public media of communication as well as preserving anonymity in public relations. Here, in Tradition Twelve, anonymity is applied personally in meetings as well as all areas of our lives. Remaining anonymous, particularly in COSA, and safeguarding all members' identities, is of the utmost importance. Tradition Twelve's spiritual significance is central to keeping the COSA fellowship intact and it is a foundational component to individual recovery.

When we are newcomers to COSA, there is great relief in knowing that our privacy will be respected through anonymity. Discovering that our lives have been affected by compulsive sexual behavior, we feel devastated, in pain, and likely full of shame. Without the protection anonymity offers, many of us would have hesitated to share our experiences for fear that our information would be exposed and that we would suffer further harm. This practical aspect of anonymity creates a safe space to listen, share, feel heard and understood, and begin our healing journey.

In addition to the practical benefits of anonymity, Tradition Twelve offers a spiritual aspect in which we trust a Power greater than ourselves and leave our social and professional labels and roles outside the doors of our meetings. We enter as equals. From this place of equality, we can experience one another free from the influences of worldly identities. We come to see that we are all the same in the eyes of our respective God or Higher Power, and we can embrace one another in unity and equality.

The environment created by anonymity in our recovery meetings is not to *hide* us, but to help *free* us. Anonymity in our meetings actually fosters greater intimacy among members. We can share our true selves safely, freely, and without fear of judgment. The trust generated, and the resulting ability to be vulnerable, brings us great relief and help to lift the burden of our isolation and pain. Sharing honestly with our sponsors and fellow members promotes healing. We become open to receiving compassion and acceptance. This nourishes our healing in a way that we have never experienced before. Because of Tradition Twelve, we are able to freely "carry the message to those who still suffer" as stated in Tradition Five, as well as receive the COSA message of hope and recovery that supports us in our healing journey.

Tradition One (Our common welfare should come first; personal recovery depends upon COSA unity.) offers an example of anonymity's spiritual influence on our Traditions. Without the equality offered through an avenue of spiritual anonymity, members with many years in recovery might be looked to as "COSA experts." Seen in that light, their singular input could sway or replace the group conscience. Without practicing spiritual anonymity, we might look upon members known to have certain professional credentials or wealthy financial status with higher regard than others in the group. Newcomers or other members might defer to them rather than develop their own voice. Situations like these could lead to a hierarchy or cause personalities to overshadow vital recovery principles. The common welfare of the group, the group conscience, and COSA unity would be harmed. Personal recovery would suffer in such an environment. Without the bedrock of anonymity, Tradition One would collapse.

The COSA Diversity Statement provides additional insight into the unifying power of anonymity. All who identify as having been affected by compulsive sexual behavior are welcomed equally in COSA. We embrace one another with understanding and compassion for the experiences that brought each of us to COSA. The Diversity Statement helps us to look beyond the ways in which we may be different from our fellows and to seek out and accept the commonalities that unite us. Diversity gives us the opportunity to learn from people of all kinds and it gives COSA a richer, more widely relatable message to share.

Tradition Twelve also helps us maintain a sense of equality in relation to others in recovery. We receive invaluable encouragement and inspiration from the experience, strength, and hope of others. By keeping principles before personalities, we can have a healthy admiration for others without putting any individual on a pedestal or readily dismissing others.

We may share and learn personal information about each other. In the spirit of anonymity, we do not pass along personal details that other members shared with us at a meeting or privately. That would be a breach of anonymity, as well as confidentiality and trust. This is an opportunity to improve our humility. We ask our Higher Power to remove any shortcomings such as gossiping or sharing personal information about another person. Part of our recovery may be that we learn what our underlying character defects are that drove us to break another's anonymity. As we gain more understanding of the principle of anonymity, we are able to practice more humility and to recognize it as a foundational spiritual principle to our entire recovery process.

The principles in Tradition Twelve are applicable to all relationships. They help us keep our friendships balanced, healthy, and reciprocal through mutual respect. Placing principles before personalities also serves us well in our homes and families. Tradition Twelve reminds us that each member of the family is valuable and is an integral part of the whole. We recognize that each of us is a precious individual, entitled to our own decisions regarding personal privacy, boundaries, and the way we express our personalities. We build good relations when we treat everyone fairly and respectfully. When difficulties arise, practicing Tradition Twelve helps us stay focused on the greater good of our family.

In places where there are established hierarchies, such as the workplace, putting principles before personalities is especially helpful. Putting principles first guides us away from aligning with cliques or gossip circles. Instead, we keep our focus on the work our employer hired us to do. When working in a team environment, we become valuable contributors if we stay detached from dominant personalities or ego-driven issues and simply focus on the assignment. No matter where we are in the workplace hierarchy, practicing these principles can help us demonstrate our integrity and earn the respect and trust of others.

As we contemplate Tradition Twelve, we see why anonymity is *the* vital spiritual underpinning of all our Traditions. The safety and spiritual growth of each COSA member and of the whole COSA fellowship depend upon anonymity, and the respect and equality that come with it.

INTRODUCTION TO THE TWELVE CONCEPTS OF COSA

As the Steps guide our personal recovery journey and the Traditions encourage healthy relationships and interactions, the Twelve Concepts of COSA guide the infrastructure and service required to support the fellowship. The Concepts affirm that the fellowship as a whole has ultimate authority over itself; it is not run by a few select members in leadership roles. We channel our collective voices through delegates who in turn communicate with the board. Rights of participation and appeal are established, and each service responsibility is matched with an equal measure of authority, so that our trusted servants are prepared to fulfill their service roles. The importance of carefully selecting and equipping those who serve the fellowship, and of rotating service positions, is made clear through these Concepts.

While the language of COSA's Concepts was adapted from the Concepts of Alcoholics Anonymous, the structure of our fellowship was only loosely based on that of AA. This can sometimes lead to confusion. One example is in Concept Twelve where AA's "Conference" was replaced with COSA's "Annual Meeting." The AA Conference is not defined as an event like our Annual Delegate Meeting but rather as a group of committees, subcommittees, and workers. Accepting these differences and concentrating on the principles of effective and sober service illustrated in the Twelve Concepts helps us avoid distraction as we carry out COSA's primary purpose.

We can apply the principles of the Twelve Concepts in our personal and professional lives as well to help ensure that we carry the peace of the program with us beyond the rooms of COSA. When we study the Concepts, we remain mindful of the way they were adapted many years ago and keep our focus on the principles expressed.

Concept One

Final responsibility and ultimate authority for COSA world services should always reside in the collective conscience of our whole Fellowship.

When we are new to COSA, it may seem as if there are others in positions of authority all around us. In our meetings we have delegates, secretaries, and treasurers. We may hear of the Board of Trustees. Surely, some of us thought, this board effectively "ran" COSA; certainly they had authority over the fellowship.

When we read and study Concept One, our understanding changes. Yes, we have many trusted servants within our meetings and fellowship. Yet Concept One proposes something radical. There are no "bosses"; in COSA we are all equals. The final authority for the COSA fellowship always belongs to the collective conscience of the entire fellowship. In effect, we learn that any power or authority comes from us, the members of the fellowship. *All* the members of the fellowship, from the newest member to the longtime member with years of recovery or service experience, have a voice. We might have elected individuals to represent us, at the meeting, committee, or board level, but we learn that these individuals derive any authority they have from each of us, acting through the group conscience.

We learn that this Concept and Tradition Two are inseparable principles. Tradition Two states, "For our group purpose there is but one ultimate authority—a loving God as expressed in our group conscience. Our leaders are but trusted servants; they do not govern." At every level of the fellowship, we practice this Tradition, and Concept One shows us an example of how to accomplish this.

In our individual meetings and groups, we are to be guided in our decision-making by a loving Higher Power as discussed in Tradition Two. By extension, Concept One tells us that it is the collective conscience of the entire fellowship, as expressed by the individual COSA groups, which has final responsibility and authority for determining the direction of the COSA fellowship as a whole.

Understanding Concept One clarifies our personal responsibilities. We have both the right and the responsibility to speak up, set boundaries, seek solutions, and carefully consider to whom we entrust roles and responsibilities. No one can do this for us. Our participation is crucial to the health of our fellowship. If we abdicate our responsibility, the meeting loses perspective, experience, strength, hope, and wisdom.

With regard to the COSA fellowship, all COSA members and home groups are responsible for being informed, discussing matters, and then relaying their group conscience to their chosen delegate who votes at the Annual Delegate Meeting. The delegates vote on policies, procedures, and changes to the bylaws of the fellowship, among other things, and they elect members to the ISO Board, entrusting them to carry out certain responsibilities on behalf of the fellowship. For this to happen effectively, our participation is essential.

One opportunity we have to see this Concept at work is in preparation for the Annual Delegate Meeting—a once-yearly gathering of the delegates and the ISO Board of Trustees, where important decisions are made on behalf of the COSA fellowship for the upcoming service year.

As a group, we elect a member of our meeting to represent our collective voice in decision-making. We discuss various items such as proposals from the board, new literature, and filling board positions, so that our delegate can best represent our meeting's group conscience. At the Annual Delegate Meeting, those members whom we elected to represent us carry our thoughts and wishes to the meeting on our behalf. Informed by the group, they cast their votes on important issues that affect the fellowship. Collectively, they represent the will of the fellowship as a whole. These delegates then carry the decisions that are made back to their meetings.

Concept One helps us to better understand our right relationship to our fellow members: one of absolute equality. It is important to listen, engage in diversity of thought and ideas, be open to change, and be willing to approach things in new ways. We learn how to practice the Second Tradition at meetings and at the fellowship level. Our Higher Power guides our decisions as a group, and subsequently the collective conscience of all COSA groups can be enacted at the fellowship level. Further, we learn to be informed, thoughtful, guided, and willing to speak our truths so that we can constructively participate in making the necessary decisions to guide our beloved fellowship. Perhaps most surprising of all, in Concept One we learn that in fact our leaders are there to serve us.

Concept One teaches us who has ultimate authority for the COSA fellowship: the right to have the final say belongs to COSA members and groups. Once we firmly understand this, we have a foundation upon which we can build our understanding of the other eleven Concepts.

Concept Two

The Annual Meeting of Delegates and the ISO Board of COSA has become, for nearly every practical purpose, the active voice and the effective conscience of our whole Society in its world affairs.

In Concept One we learn that the ultimate authority and final responsibility for the COSA fellowship is the collective conscience of its groups. The next logical question is, "How will the groups manage COSA's service affairs nationally or even worldwide?" Concept Two informs us we are to do this by means of delegated authority, a principle which appears consistently throughout the remaining Concepts.

When reading Concept Two we take note of the words "active voice and effective conscience" as they relate to the International Service Organization (ISO) Board and the Annual Delegate Meeting. We can understand our active voice to be the responsibility to act, speak, and represent the fellowship in administrative and operational matters that arise throughout the service year. Effective conscience can be understood as the group conscience of our elected trusted servants on these same matters. Just as we learn to exercise decision-making by group conscience in our meetings, we delegate the responsibility to make group conscience decisions on behalf of the COSA fellowship to the Annual Delegate Meeting and the ISO Board.

Over time, as we participate in our local meetings, we gain a better understanding of the larger service structure of COSA, starting with the Annual Delegate Meeting. Each registered COSA meeting has the opportunity to elect a delegate to represent its group. At the Annual Delegate Meeting, together with the Board, these delegates vote on issues that require group conscience and make decisions that determine the direction the fellowship will take.

The input of these delegates, sent by individual groups, is indispensable to the COSA fellowship. It ensures that the people and policies entrusted to carry the COSA message are reflective of what we, the group members, believe is best for the fellowship as a whole. When the delegates elect members to the ISO Board, they are effectively empowering those members to carry out the day-to-day work of the fellowship. The board and its committees then have the authority to make operational decisions and carry out other tasks that need to be completed on a national or worldwide scale on the fellowship's behalf.

We may wonder why such delegation is needed. It is a matter of practicality and efficiency. In order to fulfill our primary purpose, to recover and to carry the message of COSA's Twelve Steps to others, in a way that goes beyond the group level, it is essential to have a service structure beyond that group level. Given that each group operates autonomously, it would be difficult and maybe even impossible for our individual meetings to carry out the many necessary and important functions of the whole fellowship. When we imagine hundreds of groups trying to create and maintain a yearly budget, provide information to the public, create new literature, organize an annual convention, maintain a website, and handle administrative and legal tasks, the need for delegation is clear.

It is not that our groups lack people with the capacity to do these things. In fact, all of our trusted servants, delegates and board members alike, are first and foremost recovering COSA members. Rather, we realize there are some tasks that cannot be completed in an effective and timely way without this delegation. Concept Two frees our individual groups to focus on creating safe and sustainable meetings so that they can better carry the message of experience, strength, and hope to newcomers.

Thus Concept Two builds on the foundation of Concept One, which tells us that final responsibility and ultimate authority for COSA rests with the collective conscience of the fellowship as a whole. In Concept Two we learn that the COSA fellowship fulfills this responsibility through delegation: by charging the Annual Delegate Meeting with making significant policy and procedural decisions and with electing the ISO Board members. The fellowship then entrusts the ISO Board with the authority to carry out these delegate decisions and to make necessary administrative and operational decisions throughout the year. In this way, the Annual Delegate Meeting and the ISO Board become "the active voice and the effective conscience of our whole society in its world affairs."

Concept Three

To insure effective leadership, we should endow each element of COSA, "the Annual Meeting," the International Service Organization of COSA and its service committees, contracted worker, and executives with a traditional Right of Decision.

Concept One gives us clarity about the ultimate authority of the COSA fellowship. Other Concepts provide further guidance about how that authority is delegated throughout the rest of our service structure. As we grow in our understanding of how to balance the ultimate authority of the fellowship with the authority that is delegated to other parts of our service structure, we can turn for guidance to the time-tested wisdom of our Traditions, as well as to the specific guidance in Concept Three.

The purpose of Concept Three is embodied in its first words: "to insure effective leadership." Without the Third Concept, COSA would be unable to accomplish many things. What would happen if every decision had to be brought back to all of the COSA groups for approval? Decision making would become tedious and ineffective, time-sensitive decisions might never be reached, and crucial opportunities would be missed. Convention planning, website updates, outreach efforts, and literature-in-development projects would falter and halt. With Concept Three in place, all these things move forward more easily. At the same time, we free our groups from having to ratify decisions made at every level of service. They can devote full attention to the crucial task of carrying the life-saving message of COSA recovery in their meetings.

Concept Three tells us effective leadership is ensured by endowing each trusted servant, board member, delegate, committee member, meeting contact, and employee with "a traditional Right of Decision." In effect this means that when considering a matter within the scope of their defined service role, they have a right to decide whether they will handle it themselves, consult with others, entrust it to another, or seek a group conscience.

Understanding the appropriate use of Right of Decision within the COSA fellowship requires us to deepen our understanding of Tradition Two, and in particular, our understanding of the term "trusted servant." When we give responsibility to the International Service Organization (ISO) Board, the Annual Delegate Meeting, service committees, contracted workers, and delegates, we also must give them the commensurate authority to carry out those responsibilities. If we are unable to do this, we are failing to treat them as trusted servants; instead, we are treating them as messengers or puppets. It would be demoralizing to ask trusted servants to take on the responsibility of reaching out to the public and then give them a script and request that they not deviate from it.

As a fellowship, we clearly describe each task we want accomplished, and the kind of authority we are delegating to those who will fulfill that task. Our trusted servants will serve us to their potential when we grant them the freedom to exercise their best judgment in fulfilling the responsibilities we assign to them. Our servants must remain directly accountable to those they serve, yet they must also be given discretion in fulfilling their responsibilities.

We can see an essential example of Concept Three in action at the Annual Delegate Meeting. Before the meeting, local groups are presented with items for discussion and voting, giving delegates the opportunity to thoroughly discuss business items with their home groups. This allows our delegates to come to the Annual Delegate Meeting informed of the questions, concerns, and group conscience of those they have been elected to represent. We trust our delegates to balance the needs of the group they were elected to represent with the new information, discussions, and points of view they will encounter at the Annual Delegate Meeting. The groups inform their delegates but then endow them with the responsibility to cast the vote they think best serves the fellowship. Ultimately, we trust them to vote according to their conscience after considering all of the information presented at the Annual Delegate Meeting.

Suppose delegates come to the Annual Meeting with "instructions" to vote a certain way, rather than being trusted by their group to listen to ideas, suggestions, and concerns, and then act upon their conscience when it was time to make a decision. With discussion and new information coming to light, some delegates might feel that a decision different than the one they were given by their home group would be appropriate. Without Right of Decision, casting votes at the Annual Delegate Meeting could be deeply problematic for the delegate and the fellowship. If we do not allow delegates to vote their conscience, COSA as a whole might effectively be hamstrung in its ability to make or implement important decisions. Furthermore, we would not be treating our delegates as trusted servants, but rather simply as messengers for their groups. Instead, by trusting delegates to take into consideration their group's concerns and balance those with appropriate Right of Decision, effective decision-making becomes possible. It is important to note that rights in COSA are always balanced by responsibilities. Our delegates' Right of Decision does not negate their responsibility to fairly, transparently, and accurately report back to their groups or meetings.

If we think of each element of our service structure, it becomes clear how the right of decision endowed to each trusted servant helps us to accomplish the work we need to fulfill our primary purpose as a fellowship at every level of our service structure.

Concept Three also offers us spiritual guidance in our individual recoveries and our interactions with others. We are asked to trust, to let go of controlling and thinking we "know it all," and shrinking away from taking initiative. We are called upon to practice the spiritual principle of this Concept, trust: trust in our Higher Power, the group conscience, the fellowship, its principles, and ultimately, trust in ourselves and one another.

Concept Four

At all responsible levels, we ought to maintain a traditional "Right of Participation" allowing a voting representation in reasonable proportion to the responsibility that each must discharge.

Concept Four teaches that we all have a voice in COSA and a basic right to be heard. We can be assured that we are all equal and no one person is more important than another. It is essential for our unity as a fellowship that each member feels respected, that their voice counts, and that each belongs. Concept Four gives us a way for all members to speak their minds, to be active participants in the decisions that affect them, and even disagree if necessary, while doing all we can to protect the common welfare of all our members.

"Right of Participation" can be clearly seen in reference to board members' voting rights at the Annual Delegate Meeting. Some members may wonder whether it is prudent to allow our board members a voice and a vote at the Annual Delegate Meeting when they already have so much responsibility for carrying out decisions made at this meeting, and for dealing with day-to-day operations of the fellowship. Would it perhaps better serve us to simply have them facilitate the decision-making of the delegates, entrusting voting responsibility at the Annual Delegate Meeting solely to the delegates? By giving board members voting rights, we ensure that their votes will sometimes reflect their *own* service activities and proposals. It might appear to better serve us to have the delegates be the sole decision-makers, asking our board and their committees to simply carry out those decisions. Concept Four tells us that preserving the "Right of Participation" of both the board and the delegates better aligns with our fellowship's purposes.

The COSA board and its service workers have familiarity, experience, and knowledge of the many matters before the fellowship because they deal with these issues on a daily basis. They can give us tremendous practical insight into those issues precisely because of this knowledge. They may see potential pitfalls of a plan, or have practical or historical insight into the ideas being discussed. Their voices and votes are important contributions to our decision-making.

Allowing a voting representation in reasonable proportion to the responsibility that each must discharge gives us further assurance that we need not be concerned that the votes of the trustees could have the ability to override the voices and votes of our delegates. At the Annual Delegate Meeting, the delegates always substantially outnumber the board members. Since we make decisions by unanimity whenever possible, and failing that, by substantial majority, the delegates will always have a greater say in decision-making. The discussion and voting structure assures participation by all, and that the delegates will always be able to express the conscience of the groups they represent.

Assigning the sole authority for decision-making to one group and the responsibility for carrying out those decisions to another group could compromise our efficiency, and simply put, it does not support the common welfare. Concept Four provides specifically for participation among all levels of the service structure. All the various groups involved in the International Service Organization, be they board members or delegates, have a voice and a vote at the Annual Delegate Meeting. Thus, those who make the policies and those entrusted to carry them out throughout the year meet at the Annual Delegate Meeting and make decisions together.

The lessons of this Concept apply to every level of the COSA fellowship, from our home groups' business meetings to our volunteers and service committees. The Fourth Concept is one way of putting the principle of group conscience to work in any service structure. We should encourage all group members to participate in the decision-making process. By bringing different perspectives together, we create an opportunity to develop an informed and balanced group conscience, one that leads to sound decisions guided by a Higher Power. Individual conscience freely expressed is an essential element in group conscience at any level.

As recovering COSA members, we bear in mind that participation is not a one-way street. Just as we hope that when we speak, others will hear us out and sincerely consider our point of view, we must also be willing to extend this same courtesy to others. Our experience teaches us that when we participate in good faith, considering all opinions expressed, we are more likely to be guided towards decisions that benefit the whole. Furthermore, when we are truly allowed full Right of Participation, and thus feel heard, we are more likely to be able to cheerfully support the group's decision, even if it is not the one we might choose individually.

Concept Four offers an invitation to members who may fear speaking up or lack confidence in expressing their point of view. We need *every* voice to be a part of the group conscience.

When we have an opinion but fail to express it, we deprive the group of something truly valuable: our perspective and our unique voice.

Concept Four promotes harmony, good faith, belonging, and unity. When we listen to and carefully consider each voice, we allow every member to be fully heard and we treat them as who they are: valued members of the COSA fellowship.

Concept Five

> *Throughout our structure, a traditional "Right of Appeal" ought to prevail, so that minority opinion will be heard, and personal grievances receive careful consideration.*

Concept Four reminds us that fellowship voting privileges are allowed in proportion to each individual's or group's level of responsibility. Individuals vote in their group meetings, delegates vote in the Annual Delegate Meeting, committee members vote in their committee meetings, and board members vote on board-level issues. Although we always seek unanimity, even the most diligent and respectful decision-making process will sometimes yield a result with which some members disagree. Concept Five ensures that members and groups have the right to request reconsideration of a decision they do not agree with and, further, to request that those who participated in making the decision listen to, and carefully consider, the opinions expressed. This Concept serves to protect us from the harm that an uninformed or misinformed majority may cause.

The words "throughout our structure" indicate that the request to appeal a decision may come from any level of our fellowship: an individual, a group, an Intergroup, a committee member, or a board member. "Minority opinion" and "personal grievances" encourage us to remember that each of our voices is important and worthy of being heard, even when those voices are speaking alone. For many of us, the COSA fellowship is the first place we dared to speak up, even if we still felt fear. For others, it may be the place where we developed and practiced the willingness and ability to truly listen without judgment. When we give "careful consideration" to an appeal, we dedicate thought and reflection to it, and we do so with the same sincere interest and attention we would want given to our own plea.

By honoring Concept Five and respecting the opinions and voices of those appealing a decision, we give the fellowship another opportunity for increased certainty and agreement in reaching a group conscience. We strive to avoid making easy choices today that may turn out to be problematic in the future. Even when the minority voice does not change a majority's decision, those few who spoke out will know that they were not overlooked or cast aside. Whether we are approving new literature, amending our bylaws, or voting on the purchase of medallions in a small meeting, Concept Five gives every minority, be it an individual or a group, the means of participating with confidence they will be heard, and without any shame.

Those members or groups who believe an error in judgment has been committed or a mistake has been made have a right, and perhaps a duty, to share their views. In the same way that we practice rigorous honesty with ourselves as we work the Twelve Steps, our service to the COSA fellowship will be most impactful when we employ the same principles of clear, truthful communication. Neglecting to exercise our right of appeal may end up depriving the fellowship of an opportunity to better carry the message to those who still suffer. While it may be difficult for some of us to share our opinions, especially if we are new to the fellowship, our moment of struggle in speaking out may be the start of a lifetime of peace for someone else and it may encourage our own growth, serenity, and sense of freedom to speak up in the world.

When we allow Concept Five to influence our service to the COSA fellowship, our families, and our work, the gifts of the program will spring to life not only for us but for those around us. Our active consideration of perspectives other than our own is living proof of our willingness to grow and collaborate for the greater good. We owe it to ourselves and each other to encourage sharing opinions that differ from what is most popular or widely believed. We must also remain accountable for thoroughly examining those other viewpoints and inviting discussion when required for complete understanding. When considering whether or not to reverse a decision, our human desire to be right should always yield to our spiritual need to do the right thing, according to our Higher Power's will for us.

As we reflect on Concept Five's importance in our service to the COSA fellowship, we also see how it can be applied to our families and our work. It may be helpful to ask the following questions: Do I encourage the sharing of opinions that differ from the majority? Do I go along with the majority even when it bothers my conscience? Do I gloss over minority opinions, giving them no more than an obligatory consideration? Do I understand why it can be difficult for someone to speak up when they have an opinion different from that of the majority?

The Fifth Concept suggests that we surrender fear and use our right of appeal to stand up to a majority when we have a different opinion. It also suggests that we stand down and listen to the minorities in our midst to achieve true unity in our fellowship. Once an appeal has been heard, the final decision rests with our Higher Power's will as expressed in our group conscience.

Concept Six

The Annual Meeting of the board and delegates recognizes that the chief initiative and active responsibility in most International service matters should be exercised by the trustee members of the Annual Meeting, acting as the International Service Organization.

The first five Concepts of COSA give us clear guidance about how individuals and groups may participate in the process of managing COSA's business. Concept One states that "final authority for COSA world services should always reside in the collective conscience of our whole Fellowship." Concepts Two through Five guide our decision-making process, including the way we manage differences of opinion. A shift occurs as Concept Six places responsibility for managing the overarching business of the entire international fellowship squarely on the shoulders of the board members. While our primary purpose of carrying the message to those who still suffer is spiritual in nature, accomplishing that purpose requires tangible human efforts. Concept Six tells us that the responsibility for those efforts lies with the International Service Organization (ISO) board.

In Concept Six, "chief initiative" refers to a primary and important right to initiate action. "Active responsibility" denotes an accountability or duty that is characterized by action rather than by contemplation. We are reminded here that the ISO board is charged with overseeing the practical implementation of most service-related matters. Those matters include but are not limited to literature development, web services, management of the operating funds, and public communication.

Once each year, COSA delegates gather together with the ISO board for the Annual Delegate Meeting. This meeting provides an opportunity for discussion, collaboration, and voting which establishes a group conscience on issues that affect the worldwide fellowship. In the months preceding the Annual Delegate Meeting, delegates each discern their home meeting's group conscience regarding the business items on which they will vote. After the delegate meeting, the ISO board members continue to meet monthly and communicate frequently, maintaining the momentum required to carry out the plans that were established during the meeting with the delegates. As a smaller group, the board is able to more quickly take action and make swift progress toward the fellowship's goals than a larger group would be.

It is important for us to understand that Concept Six does not give the ISO board ultimate authority over the fellowship or its daily business. It simply states that when the time comes for action to be taken regarding matters of worldwide service, the board is responsible for doing so. They are not entirely responsible for making the decisions that determine what that action should be. Once the delegates who represent the whole fellowship have reached consensus with the board on a desired plan of action, they wisely turn over the implementation of that plan to the board. The board members are then accountable to the fellowship for exercising their chief initiative and putting plans into action. In recent times, there has been increased communication during the year between the board and the delegates and their groups due to weekly fellowship emails, video conferencing, and a greater reliance on electronic communication. In this way, feedback can be exchanged during the year when necessary.

The first word of Step One is "We" because this is a program based on working together, interdependently striving to accomplish our primary purpose through various actions. The services provided through the board's activities are the very components that enable our local groups and meetings to be there when we need them: online meeting facilities, literature, the COSA website, and more. Our inverted triangle of leadership puts the many individual voices of COSA members around the world at the top, and the ISO board at the bottom as our servant leaders charged with accomplishing the plans of the fellowship.

We see Concept Six at work all around us in healthy group dynamics. Some examples are: When the fellowship votes to approve new literature, the publication of that literature is facilitated by a small committee under the direction of a board member. Once a local meeting decides through group conscience to purchase medallions or literature, responsibility for placing the order and bringing the materials to the meeting is given to just one or two people. Large corporations are often run by small boards which take direction from proxy holders who represent their stockholders. A family may work together to decide on their next vacation destination, but the arrangements are made by just one or two people who are authorized to act on everyone's behalf. In most cases, practical action can be accomplished more quickly by a small, nimble group than by a large one.

Ultimately, Concept Six is a reflection of our willingness to trust the process and turn over control of outcomes to our Higher Power. COSA as a whole makes decisions through our network of individuals, local meetings, Intergroups, delegates, and board members. When it comes to taking decisive action toward practical results around our world service matters, we turn to the ISO board for initiative and accountability.

Concept Seven

The Charter and Bylaws of the International Service Board are legal instruments, empowering the trustees to manage and conduct international service affairs. The Annual Meeting Charter is not a legal document; it relies upon tradition and the COSA purse for final effectiveness.

Our COSA leaders are trusted servants who do not govern the fellowship, but they do need to be empowered to lead, guide, and grow the organization. Concept Seven reminds us to avoid the creation of a single seat of power in our fellowship and our lives, opting instead for balance between different types and sources of power. We are also encouraged to remember the wisdom of trust, respect, and cooperation between groups.

COSA is registered as a nonprofit corporation under the laws of the Commonwealth of Kentucky, USA. Articles of Incorporation were submitted in place of a charter during the incorporation process in 1993; there is no charter on record. The *Bylaws of the International Service Organization of COSA, Inc.* were drafted into existence at the time of COSA's incorporation as a nonprofit organization. They are available on the COSA website for anyone who would like to gain a more thorough understanding of how the business of the fellowship is managed. The bylaws are a physical document which gives the ISO board legal authority over matters related to both the fellowship's business and its service matters.

The annual meeting of the board and delegates, known as the Annual Delegate Meeting, does not have a written charter on record. The delegates are empowered simply by the fact that they are elected by their groups to represent the collective voice of the fellowship and to convey the will of the fellowship to the ISO board at the annual meeting. The traditional representation of the COSA groups by their delegates at the annual meeting effectively grants the delegates sufficient power to balance the legal rights of the ISO board. In representing the many COSA groups, the delegates also represent the financial power of the donations put forth by those groups. In place of a charter, the annual meeting relies on a spirit of cooperation and a quest for unity that are reflected in the collective conscience of our whole fellowship.

Concept Seven helps to ensure that an effective balance of power exists between the board and the delegates. It lays the foundation for the two groups to work together without fear of being overruled or disregarded by the other. The board's legal right to veto or overturn any suggestions or decisions made by the delegates reminds the delegates to make thoughtful, reasonable requests and to act only in the best interests of the groups they serve. The traditional influence of the delegates, along with their power to direct the fellowship's donations toward or away from certain projects, encourages the board to support the delegates whenever they reasonably can. Both the board and the delegates do their best work for the fellowship when they respect each other's power and trust each other to use that power for the benefit of those they serve.

Our personal and professional lives may benefit from our understanding of Concept Seven as well. We all have limitations in our abilities and in our authority in any given situation, and we will likely find ourselves working with other people from time to time. If we approach those situations with respect for our own objectives as well as for the objectives of the other people, we may more easily see how we can help each other. This may lead us to trust others to work on our behalf and encourage us to work on their behalf. Once we have trust and respect, a sense of shared commitment to each other's growth and accomplishment can develop. In such situations, we are aware that both parties have the power to build up or tear down the bonds that join them. Leveraging the balance of power between groups and people almost always results in strong perimeters that surround and unite them instead of walls that divide them.

It is inevitable that we will encounter many sources of power and authority in the world. When we strive to build trust and respect between those sources of power, we cultivate balance as well. The balance exemplified by Concept Seven creates a collaborative environment in which each side can safely exercise its influence without the need to assert its ultimate authority over the other.

Concept Eight

The trustees are the principal planners and administrators of overall policy and finance. They have custodial oversight of the separately incorporated and constantly active services, exercising this through their ability to elect all the directors of these entities.

At the founding of COSA, our Steps, Traditions, and Concepts were adapted from those of AA. Because there are organizational differences between the two fellowships and COSA does not have any separately incorporated services, it is sometimes helpful to draw parallels between the corresponding entities. The *trustees* referred to in Concept Eight are the International Service Organization (ISO) of COSA board members; the *constantly active services* are the board committees like the Convention Committee, Literature Committee, Technology Committee, etc.; the *services rendered* refer to the annual convention, program literature, the COSA website, etc.; and *custodial oversight* refers to a caring, guardian-like stewardship instead of a hierarchical task-based management. The board approves the appointment of each committee chairperson, thus exercising custodial oversight and ensuring appropriate leadership at the committee level.

The ISO board's attention is required for matters relating to the overall direction, policy, and financial health of the fellowship. The board's administration and management of these tasks guide both the fellowship and its service to those who still suffer. So they are not overwhelmed by minutiae or distracted from matters of overall policy, the board members rely on committees to carry out the more active functions such as maintaining the website, providing meeting support, planning the annual convention and delegate meeting, publishing literature, and collecting Seventh Tradition donations. Once the board has approved leadership at the committee level, it humbly steps back and allows the committees the autonomy to manage themselves.

Within each board committee, this same protocol is practiced. Subcommittees may be formed to fulfill the committee's responsibilities and carry out planned service. The committee chairperson provides gentle oversight while encouraging all members to focus on carrying out their own duties, each to the best of their ability. Again, we are reminded that our leaders are but trusted servants; they do not govern.

By distributing power and influence among the members of the fellowship, we keep the foundation strong and stable. This Concept helps to prevent the board from exercising too much direct authority over the service work of the fellowship, which in turn makes the jobs of the board members less demanding. It allows both the board and the board committees freedom to use their unique talents and gifts to do their best service.

In our daily lives we learn to recognize that we are sometimes obliged to focus on overarching topics and delegate more routine tasks to others. If we are involved in a big project at work, we may need to reach out to an associate for assistance in managing our daily responsibilities. We can depend on our families to help with household chores when we are occupied with a job like doing the taxes or focusing on a career path. Discernment around our need to ask for support helps those around us as well. We can be more accountable and dependable when we are not overburdened by the misconception that we can do it all. When we practice the principles of the Twelve Steps, Traditions, and Concepts in all areas of our lives, we have more energy to share with others, and our friends and family members notice our peaceful demeanors.

Our ISO of COSA board members know that they cannot focus on both overall policy and the complexities of providing the myriad of services offered by the fellowship. They give careful consideration to the election of chairpersons who will oversee the board committees and then encourage those chairs to safeguard the work of the committees. This application of Concept Eight helps ensure that the planning and administration of COSA works best for everyone.

Concept Nine

Good service leadership at all levels is indispensable for our future functioning and safety. Primary world service leadership, once exercised by the founders, must necessarily be assumed by the trustees.

Concept Nine tells us it is vital to have sober, sensible, and dedicated leadership at all levels of the COSA fellowship. This is true for the International Service Organization board, board committees, Intergroups, and local meetings alike. This Concept also reminds us that in order to keep the fellowship vibrant, healthy, and safe, we must rotate service leadership. At some point in the early history of COSA, the original founders turned over their responsibility for the board, its committees, and the services they provide, to a new board. It was recognized as part of the natural order of growth and renewal that these new board members would eventually entrust other new board members to carry out the primary world services of COSA, creating sustainable leadership throughout the life of our fellowship.

We can form committees and fill them with volunteers, but without good leadership at all levels, we cannot effectively fulfill our primary purpose. COSA's service structure relies on the many people who manage the myriad of services provided by the fellowship, and like most people, the trusted servants in COSA do their best work when they are guided and encouraged by good leaders. Effective leaders have a thorough understanding of the goal as well as knowledge about the skills and abilities of those with whom they work. They are willing to put principles before personalities. They promote harmony, clarity, and teamwork among group members. They are trustworthy, accountable, and humble.

Special care must be taken to elect service leaders who recognize their primary obligation is to carry out the service plans of the fellowship. Members who accept a service leadership position are accountable to the fellowship, to the ISO board, and to their own Higher Power. A strong leader knows that good ideas can come from anywhere and that sometimes it's best to abandon their own plan in favor of someone else's. A leader's focus must always be on what is best for COSA as a whole. We are all equals in the COSA fellowship and in our service structure. Our leaders do not govern.

Regular communication between leaders and those they serve can help generate new ideas that lead to change and growth. For those who aspire to serve as leaders in the fellowship, regular communication can also create a forum for learning to share their talents. COSA is full of people who are ready and able to provide leadership service. To ensure the smooth rotation of leadership, current leaders reach out to others and invite them to serve, so that the next generation will be ready to assume the role when the time comes.

Over time, it is necessary for even the best and most experienced leaders to step aside and make room for new leaders, thus allowing fresh ideas and perspectives to be brought to the table. Especially when a leader feels unable to continue in their role or to fulfill their duties due to life changes, they can let go of worry and step down before the end of their term, trusting the outcome to their Higher Power. We trust that our Higher Power will ensure the appearance of new leaders when the time is right.

The principles of Concept Nine can also be applied in our workplaces, communities, and families. Healthy leadership supports the stability and growth of the organizations where we work and volunteer, and of the communities in which we live. Great ideas can be talked about and agreed upon, but without leaders who are committed to seeing those visions come to life, such ideas may molder into obscurity. With good leaders at all levels of our organizations, we accomplish more as individuals and as groups.

Concept Nine paves the way for our policy of service rotation, guiding us to avoid seats of perilous power at all levels of the fellowship. Our COSA fellowship will remain strong and sober when we carefully elect good leadership throughout our service structure. Over time, the responsibility for leadership and stewardship must be passed on to others. As we keep our focus on what's best for COSA as a whole, we develop trust, respect, and humility, which serve us well in all areas of our lives.

Concept Ten

Every service responsibility should be matched by an equal service authority, with the scope of such authority well defined.

Concept Ten endows the Twelve Concepts with a crucial principle: accountability through appropriate authority. None of the other Concepts could be honored with much integrity without the sage wisdom of Concept Ten. When a service role is delegated, the tools and permissions required to fulfill that role must also be delegated with clear guidance and boundaries. Accountability can best be expected when authority and responsibility are balanced.

Our COSA fellowship comprises many individuals, and the contributions of every member are important. Concept Ten helps to ensure that each member who accepts a service role is also awarded the authority they need to carry out their task to the best of their abilities. In addition, clear expectations and limits around this authority must be understood by everyone involved. Boundaries other than those established by a job description, the COSA bylaws, or the Twelve Traditions and Concepts may need to be clarified at the outset of a service assignment. At the ISO board and committee level, using the Service

Guide is a helpful tool for consistency within roles. Individual committees have the autonomy to develop their own written guidelines should they choose to do so. This often eases many of the frustrations of micromanagement and frees our trusted servants to use their own unique gifts and talents in service to the fellowship.

For example, when a group treasurer is asked to pay rent due for the meeting space, they need access to the group's funds and permission to deduct the rent from the balance. The treasurer must also understand that only the authorized amount should be withdrawn. Similarly, when a delegate represents their group at the Annual Delegate Meeting, they must understand the group's conscience on the matters being decided and commit to voting accordingly. Some groups entrust their delegate with the right of decision to change their vote should new information become available. Responsibility supported by a well-matched and well-understood authority helps to ensure the best results for our COSA volunteers and the fellowship as a whole.

The principle of delegating appropriate authority to match a responsibility applies equally when the recipient is a board committee, subcommittee, or other group. When the Literature Committee was tasked with writing *COSA Recovery*, they assumed a great deal of authority and autonomy. At the same time, they were given guidelines by the delegates about the content of the book, as well as instructions to focus only on the basic text until it was complete. The application of Concept Ten gave the committee both the creative freedom and the guardrails needed to fulfill this commitment to the fellowship.

When Concept Ten is practiced throughout our service structure, the ISO board and its members can focus on matters of overall policy and international service. They are not distracted by a need to manage every project or committee directly because the people who are managing the day-to-day business of the fellowship are well-equipped to carry out their duties. Delegation of well-defined authority in order to complete a task requires trust between COSA members, between the board and its committees, and between committee chairs and committee members. Our willingness to give and receive this trust is a sign of our growth and recovery. When confusion or misunderstanding occurs, it is an opportunity for us to communicate openly to decide what is best for the fellowship as a whole.

In our daily lives, Concept Ten is important as we strive to achieve accountability in our own actions and as we hope to expect it of others. For instance, when a teenager is hired to mow a yard, they need to have permission to handle the gas can and understand the precautions necessary for doing so safely. An employee who is responsible for the distribution of paychecks is trusted to handle a great deal of confidential data and is expected to closely safeguard each employee's personal information. When people plan an event together and one is tasked with reserving the venue, consensus is more likely if guidelines are agreed upon before the commitment is made. This way, the person in charge of the venue has freedom to make the choice they believe is best with confidence and respect for everyone in the group. We are most able to do our best work when we have authority that is right-sized to our task.

Responsibility without authority can lead to feelings of discouragement and frustration. Authority without clear boundaries can lead to mismanaged resources and chaos. When responsibility and authority are kept in balance, each of our trusted COSA servants is prepared to remain accountable to themselves, to their own Higher Power, and to the COSA fellowship.

Concept Eleven

The trustees should always have the best possible committees, corporate service directors, executives, staffs, and consultants. Composition, qualifications, induction procedures, and rights and duties will always be matters of serious concern.

The overarching spiritual principle of Concept Eleven is *trust*. Without qualified support, the International Service Organization of COSA board cannot execute every task or directive it is given by the delegates and simultaneously carry out the day-to-day business of running the fellowship. Accordingly, this Concept, along with Tradition Eight, reminds us that it is vital to have a trusted support system of committees and individuals, as well as the occasional paid expert, consultant, or special worker. Concept Eleven aims to ensure the board's support system is composed of the best-qualified people and that those people are appropriately introduced to their roles with a clear understanding of their rights and duties.

Sometimes, providing fellowship services requires a talent, specific education, or certification that is not readily available from the current pool of trusted servants. These situations are often temporary or related to a certain project. Examples of people or institutions with special abilities include translators to get COSA literature ready to publish in languages other than English, a certified public accountant to resolve an accounting or tax issue, or legal counsel if needed for any reason. The board demonstrates alignment with the Traditions and Concepts, as well as sobriety in service, when it recognizes a need for specialized support and then seeks a way to get that support.

While the board meets monthly throughout the year, these meetings do not allow adequate time to resolve every issue affecting the fellowship. Committees can continue to carry out the board's work even when the board is not in session. By distributing the work among committees and individuals, more members of the fellowship inherently contribute to decisions and actions taken on behalf of the fellowship; this further ensures adherence to Tradition Two that states, "our leaders are but trusted servants; they do not govern."

It is reasonable to expect the committee members and others working with the board to have the talents and abilities to perform the necessary work successfully. In order to fulfill our primary purpose of carrying the message to those who still suffer, and also because this work contributes to the COSA image presented worldwide, these committee members and workers should be the best-qualified people possible for each job. The importance of their pledge to contribute to the growth and care of the fellowship should be recognized. Their integration into the committee should be handled in such a way that the value and expectations of their work are understood.

Concept Ten reminds us that the scope of the authority associated with each service position must be well-defined. In Concept Eleven, we understand that the rights and duties of each position are also matters of great importance. Volunteers must thoroughly review and respect the job description and sobriety requirements of any service position they apply for. Mentorship of new volunteers by more seasoned committee members helps to ensure a smooth and welcoming transition. Paid contractors and employees must be closely vetted not only for their abilities and talents, but for professionalism and discretion as well. Once workers are carefully selected and approved, equally close attention should be given to integrating them into their roles, ensuring clear expectations, and supporting ongoing communication.

Concept Eleven can be applied in many areas of our lives outside the rooms of COSA. Contemplating the qualifications and duties required by the roles in our lives helps us to honor where we fit best, which helps us avoid situations that may not be healthy for us. Whether we are looking for a job or hiring a new employee, a thorough and respectful interviewing process helps us find the right fit and build strong work teams. Once a decision is made, in-depth onboarding and training will prepare people for professional success. Our homes often run more smoothly when chores are matched to the person who is best suited for the task and responsibilities are clearly outlined. When new jobs are assigned, we teach and guide the learner until they are competent and trustworthy. As we build our network of friends, we find peace and fulfillment with those who appropriately support us and encourage us to be our best selves.

The ISO of COSA board needs the support of committees, individuals, and special workers to ensure the fulfillment of our fellowship's primary purpose. When the members of this support system are carefully selected and equipped for their duties, we all benefit. We trust that the sobriety, growth, and safety of our fellowship are in good hands.

Concept Twelve

The Annual Meeting shall observe the spirit of COSA tradition, taking care that it never becomes the seat of perilous wealth or power; that sufficient operating funds and reserve be its prudent financial principle; that it place none of its members in a position of unqualified authority over others; that it reach all important decisions by discussion, vote, and whenever possible, by substantial unanimity; that its actions never be personally punitive nor an incitement to public controversy; that it never perform acts of government, and that, like the fellowship it serves, it will always remain democratic in thought and action.

Each year, COSA delegates from around the world join the International Service Organization (ISO) of COSA board for the Annual Delegate Meeting. During this event, the board and delegates elect incoming board members and facilitate any other fellowship business that is due for discussion or resolution. With many individuals coming together for a short time during the meeting of the board and delegates, it is vital that those present adhere to the Traditions and Concepts that guide our groups and service work. No principle can be overlooked when COSA unity is at stake.

Generally, the rotation of service positions and the guarantee of traditional rights of decision, participation, and appeal will prohibit unqualified authority from developing. As Tradition Two reminds us, "Our leaders are but trusted servants; they do not govern." Even those individuals who prepare for the Annual Delegate Meeting and facilitate it are not in positions of ultimate authority over anyone in attendance. The meeting is a level playing field where all voices, especially those voices in the minority, are valued.

Conducting the Annual Delegate Meeting requires human, technical, and financial resources. In 2022, the fellowship decided to hold future Annual Delegate Meetings virtually, which will eliminate many of the financial costs. Because the work of the fellowship is ongoing, Seventh Tradition donations collected at the Annual Delegate Meeting that exceed the minimal cost of hosting the meeting can be directed toward fulfilling COSA's primary purpose of sharing the message with those who still suffer.

Concepts One and Two remind us to seek unity and a group conscience whenever possible. In addition, the board has adopted a detailed decision-making process that helps to ensure unanimity and avoid hasty decisions. The traditional rights of decision, participation, and appeal suggested in Concepts Three, Four, and Five also work to keep the balance of power evenly distributed. All delegates and board members who are present for the annual meeting have equal rights in the process of reaching a group conscience on behalf of our fellowship.

As members of the COSA fellowship, we need only the guidance offered in the spiritual principles of the program. There is no need for discipline or judgment during the Annual Delegate Meeting, even when emotions are intense and the discussion is passionate. We each know the value of keeping our own side of the street clean and making amends when we are wrong. We keep the focus of the meeting on COSA and issues affecting the fellowship, while respecting our personal and communal anonymity, so that both personal and public conflict are naturally avoided.

The COSA Traditions remind us that "personal recovery depends upon COSA unity" and "our leaders…do not govern." The inverted triangle that illustrates our service structure emphasizes the democratic, self-governing framework of our fellowship. Whether we are gathered in a local meeting or the Annual Delegate Meeting, we are all equals with no experts present. Regardless if one is a newcomer or an old-timer, the principles of our fellowship apply to all with uniformity. Much of our service work is accomplished via committees or groups that are led by trusted servants who do not dictate or manage the tasks at hand. We focus on our common experience and find hope and healing in COSA, one day at a time.

While it is especially important that the tenets expressed in Concept Twelve be observed at the Annual Delegate Meeting, the real power of this Concept is found when it is honored consistently by the board, our board committees, local groups, and ultimately, by the fellowship as a whole.

INTRODUCTION TO THE TOOLS OF COSA

We enter the rooms of COSA because our lives have been impacted by compulsive sexual behavior. From the start, we hear others in our meetings speak of the tools they use to find peace and healing in their daily lives. The COSA tools often offer our first respite from the upheaval, confusion, and suffering we feel early in recovery.

Our COSA toolbox contains ideas and suggested behavioral adjustments that can immediately help us along our path of recovery. Many of them are unfamiliar to us because we have lived in unhealthy situations for so long. We learn from other COSA members how they use the tools in their lives. Their experiences give us hope by encouraging us to recognize new approaches we can try ourselves.

Some of the tools may immediately make sense to us and help us readily find the willingness to try new behaviors and apply helpful strategies. These may include the tools of journaling about our feelings and experiences or regularly attending meetings, where we are instantly grateful for the COSA tool of confidentiality as we share with others. Other tools, such as setting boundaries with people close to us, can take longer to implement. They may require courage, experimentation, and the support of other COSA members to help us handle the changes that occur in our relationships as a result of our own changed behavior.

Some tools eventually become embedded in our psyche as we work the Twelve Steps of COSA and gain insight around the gifts that these new, healthy behaviors bring to our lives. As we become comfortable using the COSA tools, we develop a new mindset and a new way of responding to life's challenges. We find clarity where before there was mystery or bewilderment regarding the reactions we got from other people and how to best interact with them. Over time, we give back to COSA through the tools of service and sponsorship so that we can carry the message to others. This keeps our own recovery vibrant.

The COSA tools grew out of struggles common to many COSA members, and they were handed down by those who found them helpful in their own recovery. These tools are a gift to all recovering COSAs. The compilation in the following pages is intended to pass along experience, strength, and hope to all COSA members, whether we are trying a tool for the first time, or revisiting one that has long brought us healing on the path of recovery.

Abstinence and Celibacy

We come to COSA because we have been affected by compulsive sexual behavior, and this may impact our sexual intimacy. Those of us living with the effects of compulsive sexual behavior may intuitively reach for the tool of abstinence or even celibacy. It could be equally appropriate any time we feel the need for re-examining our relationship with sex or intimacy.

For some of us, the idea of having sex as we work through the effects of sexual compulsivity on our lives can be frightening and overwhelming. The tool of abstinence and celibacy is used in order to provide space for healing and safety without the pressure, expectation, or fear of sexual relations.

Abstinence refers to the practice of intentionally not doing something that is generally enjoyable or routine in our lives: in this case, engaging in sexual activity. The tool of abstaining may refer to specific sexual behaviors like intercourse, or when used more broadly, may include all forms of sex. The duration of abstinence is left to the individual to decide based on their needs and situation. We can even give ourselves permission to make this decision based on how we feel on a particular day or in a particular moment. Honoring ourselves and how we feel at any particular point can be very healing. Our past experiences can leave us feeling unsafe and confused in many situations, especially those that are sexually intimate. This tool allows us the space to clear our minds, get in touch with our feelings, and continue a life in recovery.

Celibacy is a term that denotes sexual abstinence for a longer period of time; this is often associated with taking a vow. Celibacy may have a religious connotation or significance as well. For some, the vow is until marriage; for others, it is for a lifetime.

Whether abstinence or celibacy is a tool or weapon depends upon how it is used and with what intention. Abstaining from sex in order to punish another person or ourselves will hinder recovery. On the other hand, when used with care, this tool supports our own personal safety and recovery. If we doubt whether we are using this tool in a healthy way, we may rely on prayer, meditation, Step work, or asking our fellow COSAs and sponsors for support and guidance.

For instance, some face concern over personal safety and the possibility of contracting a sexually transmitted infection (STI). By abstaining from sex in such cases, we set boundaries for our physical safety as we determine healthy next steps for ourselves.

Personal safety extends beyond the physical realm to include our emotional, mental, and spiritual safety as well. Abstinence provides a space that we often need in recovery from the effects of compulsive sexual behavior. While abstaining, we use the time to recover, possibly from trauma or emotional wounds. We take time to discover our own self-worth, values, and autonomy. We also seek to clarify and understand healthy sexuality and physical touch in terms of intimacy, consent, and awareness, and to establish new, healthier behaviors around sex.

When needed, abstinence and celibacy can further our recovery by allowing us to take time away from sex to consider and possibly redefine our wants and needs. We learn that our innate humanity is not one-dimensional, solely focused on being sexually appealing or desirable. We also learn that love does not equal sex, and sex does not equal intimacy. Through the careful application of this tool, abstinence and celibacy, we can discover our sense of what is right for us, our intuition, and our voice regarding if and when we have sex. We learn that healthy sex is consensual and considerate. We can develop a deeper personal understanding of both our sexual and emotional intimacy.

Acknowledging Grief

Before we can move forward in our own personal recovery, many of us find we need to acknowledge that we are grieving. Unrecognized grief can be a significant impediment to working the Twelve Steps of COSA. We feel powerless over our grief. Yet it is not healthy to suppress or deny it. Recognizing that we are grieving can often free us from the bondage of being immobilized by unacknowledged, unexpressed grief.

Many of us come to COSA having experienced profound loss. We may have been betrayed. We may be in shock. We are baffled by the depth of pain, sadness, or anger that has entered our minds and hearts. Our lives are in upheaval, and we feel unable to manage them anymore. Our suffering is so paramount that it may be difficult to begin our Step work and to look at ourselves and our personal history in Step One.

Our grief may affect our ability to function in many ways: physically, mentally, and emotionally. Grief can manifest itself in nausea, anxiety, a burning hole in the heart, or a knot in the pit of the gut. Grief often clouds our thinking. Naming what is happening to us and acknowledging that we are grieving brings relief and allows us to move forward in our recovery. Just as we admit in Step One that we are powerless over compulsive sexual behavior, we acknowledge that we are powerless over grief, loss, change, and upheaval in our lives.

When we recognize that we are mired in grief, we can begin to mourn the loss of what we thought we had: the loss of familiarity; the loss of plans for the future; the loss of safety and security; the loss of a relationship as it was, or as we believed it was. The most important foundation of our lives, such as our family unit, may no longer be intact. We may mourn that our children are experiencing upheaval; this is not what we want for them. Even if the relationship with our qualifier continues, we grieve because it will never be the same. We may feel embarrassment and shame. Our self-esteem may suffer.

If we experienced the effects of compulsive sexual behavior as children, we may not have been safe or protected. We grieve that we did not grow up with a sense of security and stability. We grieve our loss of innocence, and we often experience confusion. We may mourn the betrayal of our trust by someone we loved. If it is our child who has engaged in compulsive sexual behavior, we feel devastated for them and for ourselves. If we are affected by compulsive sexual behavior at work or in friendships, we may feel bewildered about how to move forward. We may lose promotions or income in our careers. Our financial well-being or career aspirations may be affected by the decisions we make as a result of another person's sexual behavior.

Many of us experience post-traumatic symptoms. We can't eat, or maybe we overeat. We can't sleep. We lose clarity of thought. We may suffer from depression or feel that we cannot go on. We feel that we will never get over what has happened, that our hearts are permanently broken. Every day feels like a nightmare. We can't believe that this loss has actually occurred. For many of us, the upheaval in our life dominates our thoughts and minds and is the first thing we think about when we open our eyes in the morning after a fitful sleep.

We may hear dismissive comments from others outside of COSA like, "You don't need that relationship anyway. It was not good enough for you." But we know this is not true. Our relationships with our qualifiers may be filled with good times and moments of joy and innocence. Or we might hear, "Everybody does it; just get over it." We may feel misunderstood and judged by others, but we know that there is something else going on. We learn that this person in our lives was overpowered by an addiction. It was the addiction that was running the show and making the choices. We grieve that addiction is controlling the person with whom we believed we were building a relationship of trust and mutual support. We grieve the loss of status quo or the changes in expectations that the discovery of sex addiction brings to our lives. Our life will now follow a new and unfamiliar path, and the challenges feel insurmountable until we discover the gifts of COSA.

The crushing pain of grief can make us feel insane. Many of us struggle with obsessive thought processes. Our lives seem unmanageable. Grief leaves a burning hole in our heart, a void ultimately to be filled by cultivating a spiritual awareness of our Higher Power. Supports like journaling, talking with sponsors, and creating a grief timeline may begin the journey of healing. With the acknowledgment of our grief and the acceptance of our complicated feelings, we can move toward the Steps of recovery in earnest and become ready to heal in COSA.

As we process our grief, the hurtful actions of our qualifiers begin to take up less space in our lives. We realize that our relationships are a part of our lives, but they do not define *all* of our lives. We can view the trauma with an improved perspective, as something that happened to us, something that we experienced, but which is no longer running our lives. We accept that our old relationships have now changed or ended. If we were a participant as a co-addict, our Step work helps us acknowledge our role, and our Higher Power gives us the courage to change. We may find that we must grieve the loss of our old coping mechanisms and character defects. Even our most desperate, wounding losses and discoveries are just a part of our lives. They do not define our lives.

In COSA, we share without judgment. There is no criticism. We feel heard by compassionate witnesses. Recognizing that we are grieving, and sharing it out loud with unconditional acceptance by our sponsors and meeting groups, is a balm for our souls. In COSA, we can acknowledge that we are grieving, find unity in this validation, and move forward together in our recovery.

Anonymity and Confidentiality

Anonymity is a foundational Tradition, principle, and tool in the COSA program. With anonymity, we humbly leave our ego behind and join others on an equal footing in seeking recovery. Being anonymous allows us to be spiritual beings in COSA rather than individuals with a specific worldly identity. Closely associated with anonymity is the act of keeping confidential who we see in our COSA fellowship. We also protect the privacy of every member by keeping confidential the information that is shared with us. Confidentiality means that we do not share what we have heard with anyone, including our partners, friends, or other COSA members.

Anonymity is an essential component of all COSA activities, and its importance is highlighted in our Traditions. In Tradition Twelve, anonymity is deemed "the spiritual foundation of all our Traditions," reminding us to "place principles before personalities." It is imperative that each group and every individual member "guard with special care the anonymity of all Program members," as stated in Tradition Eleven. Feeling assured that our anonymity and personal information are held in confidence, COSA members feel safe sharing in meetings and with a sponsor, which are necessary components of our recovery.

One of the main reasons people are attracted to COSA is the fact that we can participate anonymously. Newcomers take a significant step toward healing and recovery by attending their first meeting. Meeting scripts include a short explanation regarding anonymity, which provides encouragement and comfort. Newcomers are assured that their anonymity is safeguarded, and that maintaining the confidentiality of all information shared with the group is essential to our program. There is unity in our shared anonymity.

We may have difficulty trusting others because of betrayals in our past. However, as we repeatedly observe COSA members' collective respect for anonymity and confidentiality, we come to learn that we can trust the members of the COSA program. We can help newcomers grasp the sanctity of this tool by modeling restraint and redirection in conversations, and by not sharing information about others. This commitment fosters trust and creates a safe place for all of us to share our experience, strength, and hope.

Our program focuses on our inner beings, not our personalities. COSA members come from many walks of life, and are diverse in creeds, colors, nationalities, and backgrounds. We welcome all of these traits into the meeting room because they inform our life experiences, but we also leave at the door any preconceived notions about these parts of ourselves or others. We are here to share, to learn the COSA Steps, Traditions, and Concepts, and ultimately to receive the healing gifts of the Promises. We are reminded at each meeting that we are in a safe space, protected by anonymity, and governed by principles that focus on our spirituality, not our personalities. We recognize that all of us have come to this healing circle because we have been affected by compulsive sexual behavior, regardless of the differences in our outside identities and lives.

We maintain a safe space by using first names only. In COSA we are freed of outside "labels," such as those that relate to our careers, status, and finances. We release our desire to be acknowledged by a particular title or role. We cultivate equality, nurturing patience, compassion, and tolerance for all. We focus on respecting each individual's journey, and we rise above the details. By using the tool of anonymity, we rest assured that our participation will not adversely affect other areas of our lives or those of our partners or families.

Maintaining these boundaries strengthens the group and our response to others. We become less likely to compare, judge, or feel self-righteous, and less likely to feel judged or insecure. We learn to listen to others with love and compassion, without trying to "fix things" or get involved in the details of their personal lives. Being part of a fellowship of equals, we learn that outside labels don't matter because we are all spiritual beings; we all have value; we all come together as equals to share our stories. The power of sharing gives us the reassurance that we are not alone.

Anonymity and confidentiality also extend to other forms of communication and public relations with outside entities. Tradition Eleven is clear that no COSA member may act as a spokesperson on behalf of all of COSA with the press, radio, films, television, and other public media of communication. Because COSA is an anonymous fellowship, no member is authorized to represent the fellowship publicly. COSA as a whole instead puts its collective trust in a Higher Power.

Confidentiality is also crucial between a sponsor and sponsee. There will be times when we need to determine what is private and what is not. Since it can be challenging to navigate anonymity when people are in a web of relationships, sponsors and sponsees communicate about what is appropriate to share when it involves identifying another person. When in doubt, we can decide to keep information to ourselves until a clearer answer emerges. We may eventually come to a solution through studying the Steps, Traditions, or Concepts.

Being accountable for maintaining the anonymity of others strengthens our own personal integrity. We resolutely guard the confidentiality of our COSA fellows. We remain actively aware of the environment surrounding conversations we hold outside of our meeting rooms, our choice of locations for phone calls and video meetings, and how we behave when we happen to come across another COSA member in a public place. We are mindful of the consequences of broken confidentiality and the harm it may cause. We confer with our COSA friends and discuss how best to preserve our mutual anonymity in situations outside of COSA.

While it can be safer to share our stories with people in recovery than with others, we are still human beings who make mistakes or do things without grasping their full impact. We realize that there is no such thing as perfect safety when depending on the behavior of others. If someone inadvertently violates the confidentiality that we expect, we know that safety also comes from our reliance on a Higher Power and our faith that we will be okay no matter what. Bringing such issues to a group conscience at meetings can remind us all of the guiding principle of anonymity and the underlying necessity of confidentiality.

As we strengthen our practice of anonymity in COSA, we may begin to see that we have violated the confidentiality of others in our outside personal or business relationships. Perhaps we have gossiped or shared others' private information, harming both their and our own reputations through these actions. We may be able to make amends, repair our integrity, and earn trust back from those with whom we have broken it.

We also seek guidance from our Higher Power about how best to respect another person's feelings, and how to avoid causing additional harm if we approach them about our transgression. It builds character when we practice the principle of anonymity in all areas of our lives. As we do this, our relationships become more trustworthy and intimate.

In COSA, we cultivate a deep understanding of anonymity and confidentiality, and we cherish these values. Practicing anonymity and confidentiality strengthens our recovery, bringing authenticity and integrity to our relationships with others, both in COSA and in the rest of our lives. We are humbled and our appreciation for humanity broadens when we recognize that we are truly all equals. This is made more evident to us as we use the COSA tool of anonymity.

Attending COSA Meetings

Attending a COSA meeting is usually our first introduction to the COSA program. We may arrive at the meeting with preconceived ideas, fears, hopes, and confusion. Yet, as we look to expand our recovery, COSA meetings become a vital lifeline for our healing.

Tradition Three describes what it means to be a member of COSA: "The only requirement for COSA membership is that our lives have been affected by compulsive sexual behavior. The members may call themselves a COSA group, provided that, as a group, they have no other affiliation." Meetings are a safe place to share how our lives have been affected by compulsive sexual behavior. Many of us experience tremendous relief and comfort in meetings as we find true support and understanding, without judgment or unsolicited advice, from others who have been there.

COSA meetings provide opportunities to practice and deepen our personal recovery. Other COSA members share their experience and model strength and hope. This helps us to learn self-care and healthy relationship behaviors, so that we have alternatives to the unhealthy or dysfunctional behaviors that may be more familiar to us. In meetings, we can hear our fellow COSAs share their experience, strength, and hope around program fundamentals such as the Steps, Traditions, Concepts, and other tools. We learn to listen for similarities rather than differences, and to tune in to others rather than becoming hung up on specific situations. We learn to take away what helps us, and without judgment, leave the rest. By reaching out and offering support to newcomers, we continue to strengthen our own recovery through the Step Twelve practice of service.

In the early stages of recovery, many of us follow the practice of attending 90 meetings in 90 days or variations thereof, such as 60 in 60 or 30 in 30, to help us find our way through especially challenging times. The COSA website offers a rich resource to help members find meetings of all types: face-to-face (if available in our area), phone, videoconference, or online. Many COSAs work a strong program solely through attendance at phone or online meetings, especially when face-to-face meetings are not yet available in their area. Attending meetings at least once each week, or more often if possible, helps us let go of denial, learn from our fellow COSAs, gain support, and become open to receiving the gifts of the program.

In strong and sober meetings, members are working the Steps, sponsoring, being sponsored or cosponsored, using COSA literature during the meeting, actively serving, and holding regular business meetings. Members strive to apply the spiritual guidance of the Traditions in all of the different types of meetings. Within these group meetings, service positions are filled and rotated regularly between members. Members share their progress with Step work and their use of COSA tools during meetings. Additionally, the application of the Traditions, Concepts, and other tools to one's personal life is often a focus of discussion. A key component in conducting sober meetings is that all newcomers are warmly welcomed.

We can also find healthy guidelines for meetings on the COSA website. These resources give detailed guidance on conducting a variety of meetings. One type is the business meeting. Regularly scheduled business meetings with a clear focus and agenda are an important part of maintaining a healthy, sober meeting. At these meetings, everyone has a chance to give input on specific topics, issues, or action items. In this way, all members contribute to healthy group decisions and outcomes. Additionally, we gain experience in conducting ourselves with emotional sobriety, which can then be applied in our personal lives.

Regular attendance at COSA meetings is truly a foundational tool for COSA recovery and sobriety. Using the tool of consistent meeting attendance, we can find the support we need to successfully pursue our COSA recovery. Many of us choose a home meeting that especially resonates with us. We often gain confidence through sharing, listening, and taking on specific service roles such as meeting secretary, treasurer, or literature person. Meetings give us the opportunity to forge healthy, loving relationships with our fellow COSAs. With regular meeting attendance, we come to feel a true sense of belonging—often in a way we have never felt before. Meetings can be a refuge from the outside world where we may often feel misunderstood or unsafe; instead, meetings offer a place where we can show up and truly feel at home being who we are. Through regular meeting attendance, we can deepen our understanding and practice of the spiritual recovery principles of the COSA program.

Boundaries

Understanding and applying boundaries is an important part of our recovery. Boundaries are the foundation of self-care, sobriety, and serenity. Healthy boundaries are an extension of our personal values and support our recovery intentions. They create the environment we need in order to be effective and to feel safe physically, emotionally, sexually, mentally, and spiritually.

What exactly are these foundational elements of our recovery? Boundaries are the safe parameters or limits that we establish to help take care of ourselves in our personal life and in our relationships with others.

Establishing boundaries can be compared to "drawing a line in the sand" between what's healthy and nurturing for us and what does not serve us well. Standing firmly on the side of what's right for us helps maintain balance and sobriety in all our relationships. We can set boundaries with other people, and we can also set boundaries for ourselves in our own behavior. Boundaries keep us focused on our self-care and recovery, not the behavior of others.

It may seem paradoxical, but boundaries actually foster greater intimacy. Consider our Tradition of anonymity. When we enter a COSA meeting or have a recovery conversation with another COSA member, we make an implicit promise to hold everything said in confidence, thereby protecting one another's anonymity. That powerful boundary—of not repeating anything outside of the meeting—creates a trust-filled space where we may safely and vulnerably share without fear.

This same principle also benefits us in our personal relationships. When there are clear boundaries within a relationship, it fosters healthy energy and communication. For example, we become resentful when we give of ourselves against our wishes in order to please another. A healthy boundary is honoring what is right and true for us.

In addition to creating a safe environment where we can navigate our world, the process of setting boundaries helps us find our truth and our voice. This awakens our personal power. Setting and maintaining boundaries helps us gain greater self-esteem by honoring and meeting our own needs. For example, to nurture our self-care we may set time for ourselves to exercise or to use our creativity instead of taking on additional responsibilities.

Despite all the benefits that boundaries provide, we may have been hesitant about setting them. We may have been exposed to systems where having boundaries was viewed as selfish or egotistical. We may have been subjected to inappropriate boundaries set by others. We may have been confused about the difference between control and self-care. Saying a simple "no" or standing up for ourselves was considered impolite or even disrespectful. Such an atmosphere led to confusion and powerlessness. Fear of rejection, abandonment, or other perceived losses may have held us back as well.

In recovery we learn that we have the right to say "no" to things that are not right for us. We have a responsibility to ourselves regarding the conduct of our lives. We decide how to allocate our time, money, talents, and even our emotions.

Setting boundaries does not make us selfish or rude; it makes us responsible for ourselves, our actions, and our personal choices.

Our boundaries often impact others in our lives, and relationships may change as a result. We are mindful that healthy boundaries do not punish or control another's behavior. Many of us have experienced betrayals, which can make setting boundaries confusing, create fear of abandonment, and present us with many questions. How do we know if we are setting a healthy boundary or trying to control? We can begin by examining our motives. Does the boundary align with our personal values and our recovery intentions? Or, is it an attempt to control an outcome or to change someone else's behavior? Are we seeking to simply avoid facing another person or situation? Self-reflection, meditation, and prayer can help us gain clarity. Our sponsors or other trusted COSA friends who practice healthy boundaries may also provide valuable insight.

Expressing our needs and boundaries may cause some people in our lives to chafe at or resist our request for what we need. We can share with them how the boundary is important to our values and well-being. Many will respect our boundaries and support us. Some may need time to adjust to this new way of interacting. Others may choose to no longer be in our lives once we begin setting boundaries with them. This can be especially difficult when it's someone we love and want to keep in our lives, such as adult children. We hope that by modeling healthy behaviors it will bring them back to us. We remind ourselves that the best thing we can do for others is to be our healthiest selves.

When establishing healthy boundaries, we may find it helpful to take some quiet, meditative time and check in with ourselves mentally, emotionally, physically, and spiritually. We take into consideration what we need to help us feel grounded and safe. When considering these needs, we listen to our inner voice, instincts, and even how our bodies react when we explore particular situations. We begin to get clarity on what boundaries are right for us. Clarity is especially important when we need to ask someone else to have a role in supporting our boundaries. Just as our concept of a Higher Power may evolve and change over time so too our boundaries may evolve and change over time with the help of our sponsors, fellow COSAs, Step work, and COSA literature.

Sometimes a healthy boundary is as simple as speaking a truthful "no" to a triggering question or request. Other times we may need to decline certain invitations or situations that feel triggering or emotionally loaded. Perhaps there's a work-related or family event that could be troublesome for us. We can set a time limit or other conditions in advance to create a safe exit strategy. For example, if someone exhibits unwanted flirtatious or sexual overtures not in line with our recovery, we will have already decided in advance how to take care of ourselves. Then it is simpler and easier for us to honor our pre-set boundary.

We may need specific boundaries regarding sexual behaviors. We can set a boundary with a sexual partner not to touch us while we are sleeping. We may need a period of sexual abstinence with a partner while we rebuild trust. We may wish to set boundaries for ourselves that give us time to develop a relationship before becoming sexual with a new partner.

What can we do when someone crosses one of our boundaries? We can communicate our needs to them and ask them for their support going forward. We can seek the experience, strength, and hope from a meeting, phone calls with our sponsor, or other trusted COSA members who model healthy recovery and boundaries. We can ask our Higher Power for guidance and comfort. We can remind ourselves that it is appropriate to take care of ourselves.

We compare boundaries to a "line in the sand." Unlike something set in stone, boundaries can change as we grow in recovery. Situations and relationships may have changed, too, allowing us to reexamine our needs and draw a new line to suit the changes. We have the right and responsibility to take care of ourselves and make choices that support our serenity and sobriety. Healthy boundaries are at the heart of honoring what is right for us.

Defining and Maintaining Sobriety

In our attempts to cope with the havoc compulsive sexual behavior brings to our lives, many of us engage in unhealthy or codependent behaviors. Some of us become obsessed with stopping someone else from sexually acting out. We may find ourselves compulsively snooping, checking on the addict's whereabouts, or attempting to manage their recovery. Others turn to drugs or alcohol to numb the pain. We may overeat, isolate, or commit acts of self-harm. We may rage, become destructive, or withdraw completely from our loved ones. When we act in these ways, we may feel out of control or not in our right minds.

Even behaviors that do not seem to be addictive can be destructive to us and those around us. Some of these are behaviors that we employ to deal with the pain and trauma brought into our lives by sex addiction; others are coping mechanisms we developed at other points in our lives. Whatever the cause, with the help of the Twelve Steps, our Higher Power, and the COSA fellowship, we come to see that these behaviors affect our lives negatively, and we find the desire to change. As we work our Steps, we learn to focus on the one person whose behavior we *can* change—ourselves—and let others be responsible for their own recovery. We begin to relinquish our damaging and controlling behaviors and let go of outcomes, trusting our Higher Power to guide us on our journey.

Sobriety in COSA is deeply personal; we do not have a single definition that fits everyone because our experiences have affected us in different ways. So, with the help of a sponsor or another COSA, we identify our unhealthy behavior patterns and define what our emotional sobriety will look like. We may document our discoveries by writing a list, creating a chart or spreadsheet, or drawing a diagram.

Many of us find using sobriety circles helpful in defining and maintaining our sobriety. We begin by drawing a diagram of three concentric circles. In the innermost circle, we write those problematic actions that we do not wish to engage in anymore. We are sober when we abstain from these behaviors. Rather than creating an exhaustive list of our shortcomings, we focus on those actions that are causing the most harm in our lives right now. A short and specific sobriety list is easier to remember and accomplish.

In the middle circle, we list those behaviors, thoughts, situations, and emotions that tend to lead to the inner circle behaviors. For each inner circle behavior, we ask ourselves: "What situations trigger me to respond that way? What emotions do I notice just before engaging in that behavior? What action usually precedes it?" We put those things in our middle circle, where they serve as a warning that we are in dangerous territory. Something as simple as skipping lunch could be a middle circle behavior if we recognize that allowing ourselves to get overly hungry leads to poor behavior later in the day.

We may be tempted to include unpleasant emotions in our inner circle, but we are reminded that only actions belong there. Instead, it's the middle circle where we can list emotions that tend to lead us to unhealthy choices. For example, we may feel angry and respond by breaking things in our home. Feeling anger is not a loss of sobriety but can be a middle circle emotional trigger—responding by damaging things is the inner circle action.

The outer circle helps us cope with our middle circle triggers in healthy ways that lead to serenity. Here we list those healthy actions that bring us joy and draw us away from our inner circle behaviors. We write down as many things as possible in the outer circle. We want to have a long list of activities that soothe us in the moment as well as those that reinforce our long-term sobriety. We include our favorite physical activities like exercise, sports, or playing with our pets. We list poems or affirmations we find comforting. Attending meetings and connecting with other COSAs are important components of our outer circle, as are journaling, prayer, meditation, and other COSA tools. Our outer circle might be rounded out with activities that engage our five senses, such as listening to music, smelling freshly cut grass, running our hands over a soft blanket, drinking a cup of our favorite tea, or looking at a special piece of art.

If we can't decide in which circle a given behavior belongs, becoming more specific often helps. For example, sex can be a confusing topic for some COSAs—perhaps it is healthy in some situations but not others. By being more specific, we might realize that having sex when feeling pressured or in an attempt to keep an addict from acting out is an inner circle behavior, but having sex when feeling connection with an emotionally available partner is in our outer circle.

Once defined, we put our sobriety plan into action and seek our Higher Power's help to discontinue our inner circle behaviors. We keep the list of outer circle activities close at hand, perhaps in our phone or wallet, so that when we find ourselves in our middle circle, we can take action to move toward the outer circle and our sober behaviors. We may say a prayer, call our sponsor or a COSA friend, or engage in other outer circle activities.

As our recovery deepens, we learn to identify our patterns more quickly. Where we once may have caught ourselves just as we were beginning to engage in self-destructive behavior, eventually we recognize those physical or emotional symptoms in our middle circle that warn us before the behavior begins, and we redirect ourselves into thoughts and activities that are healthy and healing.

In our COSA sobriety, we learn to keep the focus on ourselves instead of obsessing over or controlling sex addiction. We come to a better understanding of the motives that drive our own behaviors and develop the ability to see alternatives in our responses to the world. We learn to affirm our feelings and act from a new position of self-awareness.

With the help of our sponsors, we find it useful to occasionally revisit and update our sobriety circles. Behaviors that were difficult to avoid early in our recovery may subside and perhaps no longer need our attention. With the growth and healing recovery brings us, we gain the strength and wisdom to address additional concerns, and we may add new things to our inner circle. Along the way, we discover many new outer circle activities that help guide us toward serenity and peace.

Detachment

Before we came to COSA, many of us thought that being in a relationship with anyone—friends, parents, children, spouses, and especially the addicts in our lives—meant taking on their problems, their emotions, and their opinions of us. Whether we took on these things out of love, a sense of duty, or long habit, it leads to negative consequences: loss of sanity, futile attempts to control, and a loss of our own sense of self and worth.

Many of us struggle with maintaining healthy boundaries. We may become enmeshed with, or have an unhealthy relationship with, an addict. We may devote significant energy to managing the addictive dynamic in our lives and can suffer emotionally and spiritually. In COSA, we learn to redirect our emotional energy toward our own spiritual growth, which requires knowing how and when to detach.

When those around us experience difficulties or blame us for their discomfort, we struggle to leave responsibility for their situation with them. Many of us have not learned to disengage from hurtful patterns or to ask for what we want because we fear a negative response. We frequently neglect our own needs and emotions when we attempt to manage things or control outcomes for others.

If someone comes to us for comfort and we instead offer unsolicited advice, try to manage their emotions, or attempt to take on the problem, we create more difficulty for ourselves and for those we are attempting to help. If we forget that the solution will emerge through the other person's recovery and their relationship with a Power greater than themselves, we expend unnecessary energy trying to work out a solution to something we cannot fully understand. If we step in to manage a situation that isn't ours, and when we haven't been asked, we end up disrespecting the other person's abilities, dignity, and right to be responsible for their own choices and feelings.

While detachment is a helpful tool, many of us have experienced particular difficulty in detaching from the sex addicts in our lives. We may have taken on feelings of shame that were not ours to carry. We may have avoided setting a boundary or expressing a need out of fear of upsetting them or facing possible rejection. We may have thought that we could fix them through our own efforts. But the addicts' recovery is not our job. In our attempts to manage them, we fail to treat them as independent adults; we rob them of the opportunity to learn from the consequences of their own actions and deny them the growth that facing their own struggle offers them. In our desperate efforts, we can lose track of ourselves and our own sanity. When we notice this happening, we know it is time to detach and focus on our *own* recovery.

In COSA we discover that detachment is the key to removing ourselves from over-involvement and over-responsibility. We learn to step back and allow emotional space between ourselves and those around us—a space that gives us room to feel our own feelings and experience our own lives. As a result, we gain perspective. We begin to remove ourselves from those places we don't belong. We learn to listen without offering to help. We practice *caring* without *caretaking*. We stop doing for others what they are capable of doing for themselves. We let go of the urge to manage others, manipulate their responses, or protect them from the consequences of their own actions. Instead, we turn people and situations over to a Higher Power.

COSA offers us many safe opportunities to practice the skill of loving detachment. We can practice this tool in our meetings, in conversation with our recovery friends, and with sponsees. We learn to resist the urge to overwhelm the newcomer with advice, tell another COSA how to feel, or attempt to fix a sponsee's situation for them. We do our best to listen with empathy; offer our experience, strength, and hope; and then compassionately detach and allow others to find their own path to hope and healing.

In all aspects of our lives, detachment helps us recognize when we are called to take action and when we can step away. We learn to let go of attachment to a desired result and instead entrust outcomes to our Higher Power.

We practice detaching from escalating patterns of conflict in which we habitually used to become involved. When we recognize these cycles beginning, we step back—kindly, lovingly, but firmly. We no longer need to defend ourselves or justify our feelings and actions. Instead, we can say, "this conversation (or situation) is becoming unhealthy for me. I'm going to take a break." We give ourselves and our loved ones the gift of time and space; we re-enter the discussion when we are calm and centered.

Detaching can also protect us from the false and injurious words or actions of unhealthy people. Some of us have been subjected to verbal, emotional, or physical abuse. Detaching from these messages spiritually and emotionally—and when necessary, removing ourselves entirely from unsafe relationships—can be necessary to establish safety, restore clearer thinking, and allow us to move forward in our recovery.

As we learn to step back from trying to rescue or control our loved ones, the chaos around us decreases. Things fall into place without our involvement. Our relationships become healthier as we respond to others in appropriate ways and allow them the opportunity to take responsibility for themselves. And as we turn our attention away from where it doesn't belong, we find the freedom to focus on our own emotional and spiritual well-being. Our minds calm, our capacity for joy returns, and we welcome peace into our lives.

Honesty

Honesty is vital for meaningful recovery. The more deeply we can practice honesty, the further we can take our recovery. For real change and growth to occur, we must be willing to open our eyes and hearts to the whole truth about how we feel, who we are, and how we have behaved.

While honesty helps us to more genuinely work the Steps, practicing the Steps gives us ongoing opportunities to work on honesty. In Step One, we become truthful with ourselves about our powerlessness and the unmanageability of our lives. Steps Four through Ten require us to be honest with both ourselves and others, especially when we make amends. Steps Two, Three, and Eleven emphasize honesty with a Higher Power. The Steps challenge us to engage in keen and balanced self-reflection, to acknowledge how our behaviors have affected us and others, and to be accountable.

Most of us came into COSA with broken trust and a distorted sense of truth. We had been lied to repeatedly, which made it difficult to know the truth and to trust our own sense of reality. Some of us had been lied to by parents or the people to whom we looked for our care when we were young. To feel safe and accepted, we learned to ignore our gut feelings, often trading our truth for someone else's.

When we discovered that the addicts in our lives had deceived us with a web of lies, we felt shocked, deeply wounded, furious, betrayed, disrespected, or even abused. Perhaps we tried to shield ourselves from our pain, shame, and grief by holding tightly to illusions of well-being, thus failing to acknowledge how compulsive sexual behavior had affected our lives. To stay in the (false) comfort of denial, we shut ourselves off from reality. This may have felt safe in the moment, as it served to protect us temporarily from experiencing devastating hurt and sadness. Yet that sense of safety was deceptive, because denial limits our ability to experience the intimate emotional and spiritual connection that comes with vulnerability. Ultimately, denial leaves us feeling empty, lonely, and lifeless.

Without honesty, our feelings and experiences are shallow, and we miss out on the richness of true joy and happiness. When we face reality, we open ourselves to fully experience life.

In COSA, instead of focusing on the sex addict's behaviors, we pay attention to our self-care and trust that our Higher Power will let us know what we need to know when we need to know it. We can listen to and trust our Higher Power's guidance. We can discuss concerns with our sponsors and other COSA members. As we begin to recognize that some people may not currently have the ability to be honest, we can accept our powerlessness over them. We learn to stop obsessing over the actions of others. Instead, we concentrate on working the Twelve Steps ourselves.

As we recover in COSA, we learn that we do not have to forfeit our own truth and power when what we are being told doesn't feel right. We practice trusting our intuition. We can refuse to buy stories that seem to us to be spun from deception and manipulation.

Our sponsors and other COSA members model honesty for us by speaking their truth and setting boundaries, even when it's difficult. We hear and see how they trust their inner wisdom and Higher Power, and we feel hopeful and motivated to do the same. We discover healthier ways to deal with situations in which we feel unsafe or sense that others are not being honest with us.

Some of us are able to be truly honest for the first time in COSA. Our program's Traditions and guidelines help to ensure that meetings are safe places where members can freely share from the heart. COSA's emphasis on anonymity and a judgment-free zone, where "crosstalk" or advice-giving are discouraged, allows many to feel secure enough to be profoundly vulnerable.

On the other hand, we may struggle with knowing just how much of ourselves to share. We may have overshared in the past, especially when we needed relief from our emotional burdens. It is true that once we tell a secret, it can never be untold. We may ask for support and guidance from our Higher Power, sponsors, and fellow COSA members while we learn how to assess the safety of situations, identify our boundaries, regain our sense of authenticity, and recover the ability to trust. We can be gentle with ourselves and listen to our inner voice.

Many of us struggle with whether to share the truth about the effects of sex addiction with family members, friends, or others outside of COSA. We practice patience as we listen to the experience, strength, and hope offered by others, and we work to determine what is best for our situation. Being authentic does not mean we must reveal all the details of our lives to everyone, even if we are pointedly asked. We take care of ourselves by learning to listen to our inner truth and to discern when and where we feel safe. Sometimes the most honest approach is to state that we do not feel comfortable sharing about it.

Recovery requires rigorous honesty. In order to heal, we must become honest with ourselves about both our current situation and our past. When it comes time to make amends, our authentic acceptance of who we are and what we have done allows us to feel true remorse and empathy. This might require us to acknowledge things that we would rather forget. Until we can recognize and accept all aspects of ourselves and our lives, our shame will hold us back. Secrets feed shame and shame thrives in the darkness. Honesty is the pathway into the light.

Spiritual connection and honesty are intricately entwined. We can have a clear and genuine connection with our Higher Power only when we are completely honest about who we are. The more honest we can be, the more connected we are to our Higher Power. And conversely, the more we connect with our Higher Power, the closer we get to accessing our own truth and inner knowing.

Often honesty requires courage and discernment. Sometimes we may not recognize that we are being dishonest, or we may not know how to be honest. We need to be patient with ourselves. Honesty is an unfolding process. As we grow in our recovery, our understanding of honesty grows. When we are unsure of our own truth, we can pause and seek an intuitive connection with our Higher Power. Honesty removes distortions and frees us to regain a connection to our true thoughts and feelings. Gradually, we learn to trust in ourselves.

Some of us spent a lot of time and energy trying to build a false or inaccurate persona. We feared that if others saw the "real" us, we would be rejected or excluded. Some of us masked our denial of reality by calling it optimism. We put on a happy smile and told others that we were OK and that all was well, when really, it was not. Deep down, we were betraying our true feelings.

When we deceive ourselves by denying our truth and ignoring our feelings, we bury our authenticity. This deep denial of self tends to result in reactions such as anger, rage, stress, resentment, depression, and grief. Swallowing our truth can suffocate the essence of who we are. We cannot celebrate and love ourselves when we are locked in the shadow of deception, afraid to acknowledge our very being.

In contrast, we honor ourselves when we embrace our truth. When we get in touch with our feelings, thoughts, and fears, the very core of who we are is set free.

Honesty is necessary for authentic relationships. We cannot experience full acceptance from others when we hide away our true selves. Only when we are honest with ourselves can we allow other people to know, accept, and love us for who we really are. When we are honest and open, we lower our barriers and allow ourselves to connect completely with another's heart. The person we are on the inside is aligned with the person we present to the outside world.

When we do not want to face difficult or uncomfortable feelings, it might seem easier to fabricate a story than to admit the truth. But in the long run, lies and fabrications harm us. Even if we aren't telling an outright lie, we lack honesty when we are not direct and forthright or when we withhold important, relevant information. We are dishonest when we tell white lies, maybe in the guise of protecting another's feelings. We may wish to head off a potential conflict or try to protect someone from disappointment. While we might mean well, when we play with the facts instead of being direct, we disrespect the other person and ourselves. When we withhold significant information, we sabotage intimate and authentic relationships.

Instead of trying to change reality, to present a different version of it, or to insincerely please someone, we validate ourselves by speaking the truth.

With authenticity and true intimacy as our goal, we are careful to be honest with ourselves about our motives in communicating. Honesty is not a license to self-righteously judge, criticize, or punish others. Honesty is not an excuse for passing our anxiety and anger onto others instead of practicing emotional self-regulation. If something bothers us and we are not sure how to handle it, we may take some time to pause and reflect on our options and reasoning before taking action. We may call our sponsor or another COSA member to consider our perceptions and motivations and to practice expressing ourselves as we learn new behaviors. We may ask our Higher Power for guidance.

As we learn to be honest in our recovery, we can shed all pretenses of who we want to be and embrace who we truly are. We move toward a life of self-acceptance, honor, and dignity. Our self-esteem, self-confidence, and self-love grow. We need honesty for self-care and to set healthy boundaries.

Honesty is not just telling the truth; it's living the truth. It's seeing the situation for what it is, not for what we want it to be. Recovery is not about getting what we want. It is about moving forward and finding joy no matter what our reality is. As we step out from hiding behind a cloak of mistruths, honesty helps us move into the ease of sincerity and authenticity. Trust in ourselves returns only when we are honest. We feel whole and can make choices from a place deeply centered in knowledge of self and our Higher Power's guidance. Recovery helps us live life on life's terms. Honesty opens the door to a greater sense of true peace and joy.

Outreach Calls

Before recovery, isolation was a common experience for many of us suffering from the effects of compulsive sexual behavior. As our secrets deepened, we may have retreated into silence, since exposure could mean ruined reputations, jobs at risk, severed family ties, or a feeling of shame we could not bear. We may have tried sharing our experiences with others, only to find that some people were unsafe, judged us, gave unhelpful advice, or did not understand what we were going through.

In COSA, we find a welcome reprieve. We discover it is safe to share with others who have similar experiences and seem to understand just what we are feeling and going through. We feel the relief of not being alone.

One powerful tool we learn to use is making outreach calls to other COSA members. Group members encourage us to "reach out" and call them during times of distress or confusion, or simply to make a positive connection. Many groups keep current phone lists with members' contact information. We can expand our pool of safe, healthy people beyond our local meeting when we attend COSA phone meetings, videoconference meetings, regional retreats, and conventions (all of which may have contact lists). We begin using our contact list to call between meetings or we save members' phone numbers to access easily, especially in times of crisis or stress.

We know all too well that these experiences can crop up at any time. It could be an unexpected disclosure from our addicted partner, our addicted child calling us "out of the blue," or a personal bout of overwhelming grief, despair, crippling fear, or red-hot rage. These occurrences and feelings can threaten our serenity and propel us into our own destructive and debilitating behaviors. It can help us to hear how others have handled similar experiences, or perhaps we just need some support in the form of validation and affirmation. We learn that reaching out and calling others in such times helps us ground ourselves in reality, reconnect with our recovery, and re-center ourselves spiritually.

Initially, we may hesitate to reach out to others for a variety of reasons. Growing up, many of us had little support, and we learned to be self-reliant or show a façade of perfectionism to hide family secrets and shame. Breaking our isolation and reaching out for support may be very difficult, especially in early recovery. We may fear being judged, misunderstood, or shamed, as these *were* our experiences prior to recovery. Or, we may worry about being a burden to fellow COSAs and hesitate to reach out in times of crisis, in the middle of a hectic workweek, or when we are hurting and feeling alone.

However, phone calls offer us an opportunity to strengthen our recovery. Some members may use the traditional "90 in 90 tool" (90 meetings in 90 days), adjusting it to 90 phone calls in 90 days. Creating a new habit of reaching out for help begins to break old, destructive habits of isolation, obsession, and fear. Rather than engaging in an old behavior, such as snooping on the addict, spending an afternoon ruminating on a recent (or past) betrayal, shaming our partners, or arguing with the addict, we pick up our phone and call a COSA friend. We begin sharing our pain and refocusing on *what we can change*.

There are times when a phone call is not possible. Fortunately, our modern world and its technology offer us many ways to reach out to other COSA members. COSAs who live in different countries can connect using international calling options such as videoconferencing. Wherever we live, there are times when difficult experiences arise in the middle of a busy day or when we are in a public place, unable to make a private phone call. At these times, some of us find it helpful to email or text our sponsors or other program friends, thus ensuring we receive support when we need it most. While digital media can be uniquely helpful at these times, we work to be honest with ourselves and not avoid a longer phone call when that is needed.

Whatever our challenges, our group members and recovery friends continue to encourage us to reach out. In time, we learn that support is vital to the recovery process. Not one of us recovers alone; rather, we recover together in a shared fellowship with members we come to love and trust. We begin to feel safe enough to reach out and ask for help. We are reassured when those members tell us they, too, receive a gift when we call. They are able to share their own experience, strength, and hope, thereby enhancing their own recovery. We learn that we are not a burden but a loved and loving human being with a special connection to ourselves, our Higher Power, and others in recovery.

When we first come to COSA, outreach calls offer us relief from our immediate difficulties, and we feel heard and validated. But over time, another transformation occurs. As COSA members lovingly witness our process, we come to hear *our own stories* with more understanding and compassion. We clarify our wants and needs, and we grow in acceptance of ourselves and others. We see our Higher Power working in miraculous ways, and we discover what it truly means to live and to love our own lives.

Practicing Gratitude

Gratitude was probably the last thing on our minds when we first entered the COSA rooms. Many of us were experiencing more pain, anger, and devastation than we thought it possible to endure. But as we progressed in our recovery and listened to the experience, strength, and hope of other COSA members, we came to understand how practicing gratitude could be a valuable tool in our recovery.

Practicing gratitude is about shifting our perspective, finding moments of joy, and then savoring them. By practicing gratitude, we have the ability to turn our day around. We move our attention away from everything that is wrong in our lives so that we can better appreciate the beauty and abundance of the day. We might experience a complete shift in our energy as we focus on our strengths and the blessings in our lives and begin to recognize peace and abundance.

We might have to start small with our gratitude practice. Prior to recovery, many of us found ourselves feeling hopeless and defeated. Recognizing just one blessing, such as a bird singing outside our window or the sun shining on a wildflower, opens our hearts to a new appreciation of other gifts. Gratitude might serve to lift us from the lowest depths. With practice, living in gratitude becomes a way of life for many of us.

We can develop our gratitude practice by paying attention to the present moment and to our current environment. Pausing to take stock of things that bring us joy might help us feel relaxed and calm. Some of us write in a daily gratitude journal, jot things for which we are grateful down on pieces of paper to put in a gratitude box, or record them using an app. During difficult times, we may refer to our gratitude lists to help us cope. Some of us have established a daily practice of emailing our sponsors about things for which we are particularly grateful. Or we may simply thank our Higher Power each morning for the day in front of us.

Practicing gratitude helps us remember that we do in fact have choices. We don't have to play the victim or wallow in self-pity. We can fixate on our problems, or we can choose to cultivate an "attitude of gratitude." Since there is no such thing as a "perfect" life, imperfections are always there for us to find. We can so easily focus on what's going wrong in our lives when we complain or fall into negative self-talk. It is when we accept imperfections as a part of life, and instead choose to turn our focus to the things that bring us joy, that our gratitude practice steers us away from negative emotions such as dissatisfaction, envy, fear, and regret, and toward happiness, joy, beauty, and freedom.

Some of us might have a tendency to try to warp our lives into a fairytale in an attempt to avoid painful feelings. Practicing gratitude doesn't mean that we are living in denial and ignoring our problems or our feelings of anger, sadness, or pain. But we don't have to stay in a place of misery either. We might even find ourselves being grateful for our various life challenges, recognizing that they present us with opportunities to grow.

When practicing gratitude, many of us experience a profound appreciation for our COSA program. When newcomers hear other COSA members talk about gratitude for the program, they might experience shock, disbelief, or maybe even anger. But if not for the effects of compulsive sexual behavior in our lives, we would not have found COSA. And if not for COSA, we would not have received the priceless gifts of experience, strength, and hope from our sponsors and other COSA members, renewed our connection with our Higher Power, or undergone a spiritual awakening.

Our gratitude practice deepens and intensifies the gifts we receive when we work the Twelve Steps of COSA. This tool can help us begin to let go of negative thoughts and feelings so that we can courageously move forward in our Step work. We may find that a dose of gratitude allows us to dig a little deeper and work a little harder.

When we do service in our program or help others, we might experience a sense of gratitude for who we are and what we can contribute. By pausing to appreciate the opportunity to help others, we recognize a sense of purpose and find deeper fulfillment in our lives.

We may practice gratitude by articulating our thanks to other program members or to our families and friends. When we stop to tell another, "Thank you," "I appreciate it," or even "I appreciate you," we may become more aware of the love we have for others and of the care we might be receiving from them. And who knows? Our gratitude might be contagious!

Over time, we might develop gratitude toward those for whom we hold strong resentments, such as the sex addict in our lives. Finding gratitude when we're feeling resentful may take patience and grace. Our sponsors might remind us that we can be grateful for someone and at the same time feel frustrated with them. The slogan, "It's hard to be hateful when I am grateful," can hold a lot of wisdom for us when we're being dragged down by our anger and resentment.

Our gratitude practice doesn't have to include big important events or monumental moments, and often it doesn't. If we wait for those big gifts to materialize, we may very well be missing out on all of the small things that pass our way moment by moment. Practicing gratitude is often helpful to those of us who tend to worry about what's to come or who ruminate on regrets from the past. It can also be a powerful tool when we're feeling irritated, sad, or disconnected. When we are able to focus on our minute-by-minute blessings, we are better able to appreciate and enjoy what's directly in front of us. We remember that it's the myriad of little moments that actually make up our lives.

As human beings walking the earth, we are, no doubt, receiving our Higher Power's gifts every day. Even on our most difficult days, the gifts are abundant. Sometimes we miss opportunities to be mindful of our gifts. But with the tool of gratitude practice, our recovery, our days, and even our moments are endowed with the precious gift of appreciation. This cultivates our awareness of the beauty and joy that surround us.

Prayer and Meditation

Prayer and meditation are at the heart of the Twelve Steps and play an important role in our COSA recovery. We come to COSA with backgrounds and experiences unique to each of us. Some of us are familiar with prayer and meditation from our religious or spiritual upbringings, and we may comfortably continue or even expand these practices. Those of us who have not had previous experience with prayer or meditation may feel uneasy or doubtful. Still others may have had negative experiences that turned us away from these practices. Or we may not practice meditation and prayer, simply for philosophical or other reasons.

Whatever our backgrounds, COSA offers us a place to safely explore our spirituality. In Steps Two and Three, we come to believe and build trust in a Power greater than ourselves. Because COSA is a program for our spiritual development and not a religious program, we are free to discover a Higher Power of our own understanding. We may call this power God, Higher Power, the Universe, the Source, Spirit, or by another name that we acknowledge as divinity. We may start by simply recognizing the grace of "good orderly direction" (G.O.D.). As we navigate this spiritual journey, we may seek support and guidance from our sponsors and other COSA members. COSA meetings are a safe haven where we may discuss our experiences with prayer, meditation, and our Higher Power without judgment.

We use prayer and meditation to seek our Higher Power's guidance and loving care as we work the Steps. We begin to surrender our will and our lives. Prayer and meditation help us experience loving compassion for ourselves as we review our histories and face our pain and defects of character. Even when tasked with making amends to those we've harmed, prayer and meditation help us gain clarity and cultivate willingness and courage. Step Ten teaches us how to seek our Higher Power's guidance on a daily basis. Step Eleven invites us to deepen our personal relationship with our Higher Power. Prayer and meditation are the tools we use to improve our conscious contact with the God of our understanding.

Prayer is a way for us to communicate with our Higher Power. We can safely express who we are, how we feel, and what and whom we love. We can say what we are grateful for and what we would like to receive, including God's guidance. Our approach might build upon our previous experiences, such as invoking traditional prayers or revisiting religious teachings with a new perspective. Or we may redefine old concepts, or even start from scratch, integrating new prayer and meditation practices into our developing spirituality.

Prayer may be considered a kind of deep connection—to ourselves, to our Higher Power, and to others. Meetings typically start and end with the Serenity Prayer or other prayers. Many of us find that when we pray together, we feel more open or experience a sense of belonging. Holding hands with other COSA members as we pray together can soften our hearts and gently remind us that we are not alone on our recovery journey.

We may also use prayer to center ourselves spiritually and experience our Higher Power's presence. In times of sadness, distress, or despair, we can find solace in our decision to turn our lives over to God's care. We turn to our Higher Power with our pain, fear, and needs and express ourselves honestly through prayer. We surrender outcomes to our Higher Power's loving care. As we work the Steps, our prayers become less motivated by our desires and more aligned with the knowledge of God's will for us and the power to carry that out.

Some people pray in quiet invocation, with heads bowed. Others recite or sing prayers or chants aloud, together. As we develop our personal relationship with God in COSA, all of us can open ourselves to new possibilities, allowing prayer to take many forms. We can light a candle and reflect on our wishes for ourselves and our loved ones. We may experience spiritual moments while listening to music or walking in nature. Writing in a gratitude journal, playing an instrument or singing, painting and creating—all of these may feel like prayerful expressions of our inner being. Even during everyday moments like laughing with our children, doing the dishes, or taking a break outside during the workday, we can feel spiritually connected.

If prayer is expressing ourselves to our Higher Power, meditation can be thought of as listening to our Higher Power. When we quiet ourselves and listen within our bodies, minds, and hearts, we open ourselves to receive insight and spiritual nurturing. Some of us experience our Higher Power's presence by taking a moment alone to become still, bringing our awareness fully to the present moment. In this way, we quiet our minds, focusing on our breath and sensory experience. Alternatively, we can try forms of moving meditation, such as walking a labyrinth or walking in nature, noticing and silently appreciating the details around us.

It may be helpful to meditate with others, in a recovery setting or other group, where we feel less alone and can more easily settle into ourselves. Some meetings incorporate group meditation time. Recovery conventions and retreats often provide a meditation room. In moments of group meditation, we may find a greater sense of connection to others and our Higher Power.

Alternately, we may focus internally by slowing our minds and becoming aware of how we feel, physically and emotionally. This may happen during a peaceful flow in yoga, while playing our favorite sport, or in a dance or exercise class. In these moments, we experience the spiritual bliss of letting go of fear and being one with body, mind, and spirit.

We may also experience our Higher Power's expressions to us through other means. Perhaps we feel moved by a heartfelt share in a meeting or enjoy connecting with a friend. The kindness of a stranger, a happy coincidence, or a peaceful moment with a family member can remind us we are not alone on our journeys.

In meditation, we learn to truly listen to ourselves: our hearts, our instincts and intuition, and even what our bodies are trying to tell us. We may have spent years ignoring and neglecting ourselves, shutting down our feelings and intuition, and seeking our truths from other people rather than connecting to our own inner truths. Through prayer and meditation practices, we learn to reconnect to parts of ourselves that may have felt lost. We come home to ourselves.

Spiritual practices are not always easy and at times may be unsettling. Sitting quietly with ourselves and our Higher Power may take considerable effort and may feel counterintuitive when we lead such busy and demanding lives. When we quiet our minds and hearts, we may discover difficult feelings or wrestle with accepting our Higher Power's loving care and guidance for us. As with any spiritual endeavor, the more we practice prayer and meditation, the more easily we can relax into peace and serenity. From this place, we can reach a state of being in which we are open to our Higher Power's will for us. We remember that in COSA we are never alone, and that at any time in our spiritual journey, we can reach out to fellow COSA members to hear their experience, strength, and hope.

At first occasionally, and then more frequently, we notice gifts and miracles beginning to appear in our lives. We start to feel more grounded and centered. We notice a sense of stability and peace growing within us. Especially when we are struggling, our spiritual practices offer us a safe place to share our hearts and receive help, love, and guidance from our Higher Power. Whether in times of distress or joy or in our day-to-day routine, prayer and meditation help us experience moments of inspiration and hope. Through these practices, we come to feel a deep sense of love and connectedness with ourselves, others, and our Higher Power.

Service

Service is a powerful recovery tool. As an integral part of our recovery work, it is woven into our Steps and Traditions. (Step Twelve: *"Having had a spiritual awakening as the result of these steps, we tried to carry this message to others, and to practice these principles in all areas of our lives."* Tradition Five: *"Each group has but one primary purpose—to carry its message to those who still suffer. We do this by practicing the Twelve Steps ourselves."*)

COSA could not function, nor could we attract and help newcomers, if not for our members generously giving their time and energy. This recovery path is created for us and by us, working with a Higher Power, to offer recovery and spiritual awakening to all whose lives have been affected by compulsive sexual behavior. The fact that the COSA fellowship is available to us is a direct result of the service of those who have come before us.

There are innumerable ways to be of service, including but not limited to attending and sharing at meetings, greeting a newcomer, helping to set up or stack chairs after a meeting, or supporting our fellow COSAs by listening attentively. We can take on an "official" service role at our home meetings such as serving as secretary, treasurer, literature person, intergroup representative, or delegate. We can sponsor and encourage our sponsees to be of service. We can take on an intergroup service role such as chair or treasurer. We can serve on an International Service Organization (ISO) committee such as the Literature, Outreach, Finance, or Technology Committee. We may desire to serve on the ISO Board or participate on the COSA convention committee. Some serve through written contributions to the COSA *Balance* newsletter or on the Literature in Development Committee. There are many possibilities!

Being of service sets our course on a journey of self-discovery that supports our continued growth no matter how long we've been in recovery. Service adds a richness to our COSA experience. It provides a sense of belonging, meaning, and purpose—a sense that we are contributing to something greater than ourselves. Many of us find that service in COSA is a safe and sober way to learn how to best balance our individual needs with the needs of the group. Service is a chance to learn how to establish healthy boundaries with saying "yes" to what our Higher Power wants for us, instead of automatically defaulting to our previous habit of saying "yes" to anything and anyone who asks something of us. With the help of our sponsor, and the COSA community, we learn to respect each individual's decisions about service and make no judgments about their choices. It is up to each of us to decide how to negotiate our path and balance our needs with the needs of the fellowship. Many of us find that when we first start to be of service, our old unhealthy patterns kick in. We overdo it and assume more than our share of responsibility. Over time, through our sponsors' guidance and working the Steps, service offers us the chance to learn healthier, more balanced options. We celebrate when we find we can apply that learning to other areas of our lives.

Utilizing service as a tool can provide an opportunity to build confidence, responsibility, and commitment toward recovery. We often have the opportunity to find and develop our strengths, learn about our weaknesses, and see or hear examples of how to deal with situations differently. Service gives us the chance to learn about ourselves in a safe setting; our COSA community practices mutual support and acceptance rather than perfection. We are given an amazing opportunity to learn new skills, create friendships, and become closer to our fellow COSAs. We develop self-confidence that carries over to all areas of our lives. For many of us, taking service roles at our meetings gives us the extra commitment we need to make sure we attend meetings regularly. When we serve at the intergroup or ISO level, we enhance our recovery experience by learning so much more about COSA at the regional, national, and international level; we see how we as a fellowship are "carrying the message." This, in turn, helps us to enrich our local and home group meetings. Performing service brings numerous recovery gifts, all of which combine to strengthen our recovery. The learning, connection, and growth that we gain from service combine to strengthen our recovery and infuse our lives with newfound joy and confidence.

Slogans and Wise Sayings

Slogans are wisdom conveyed in shorthand—a few simple words cleverly strung together. The messages they carry can be so wise and powerful, while their wit and simplicity make them easy to remember.

A slogan often sticks in our minds, making it easier for us to call on its wisdom when it is helpful to us. The subtle analogy found in some slogans can carry a message straight to our hearts. When we easily remember and recite a slogan, we can readily share it with other COSA members, offering hope and inspiration to anyone who needs encouragement.

Some slogans shine brightly for us. Others we might pick up and put back down, acknowledging their value for some COSA members, but not for us—at least not right now. We **"take what we need and leave the rest."** Slogans leave room for our individual interpretations. We can find our own meaning in a slogan, or we may have a shared understanding with others. If one slogan doesn't fit for us, there's a good chance that another one will.

We learn about slogans from a variety of sources. We may encounter them in COSA readings or hear them in meeting shares. We sometimes inherit bits of wisdom from our sponsors and can pass them along to our sponsees.

Many of us have found creative ways not only to embrace slogans in our hearts, but also to incorporate them into our day-to-day environments. We may place them on our mirrors or computer screens as reminders, or blend our favorites into artwork that we hang on our walls. Some of us have slogans stamped onto jewelry to wear as a constant reminder or even tattooed onto a wrist. We might make bookmarks with the phrases we find the most helpful. Some of us have a slogan box from which we can pull a printed slogan to read every morning and focus on throughout our day.

Slogans keep us moving forward in times of despair. Their gentle nudges can give us the courage and hope we need when we are feeling triggered, emotionally reactive, or out of control. They can help redirect our thinking during times of conflict, indecision, or trauma. Slogans often bring us back to what is really important to us—our relationship with our Higher Power and our spiritual centeredness—reminding us that we are not alone.

Equipped with the slogans in our COSA toolbox, we can pick and choose which words of wisdom work for us at various times in our recovery. As the miracles of the program emerge in us, we can pass these precious, powerful words on to others. **"We have to give it away to keep it."**

Slogans and Wise Sayings with Explanatory Text

The slogans and sayings compiled in this chapter do not represent a complete list of all COSA slogans. Some may be quotes adapted from popular culture that have become helpful program slogans for some of our fellowship, and some might not be considered slogans by all COSA members. The determination is up to the individual. In seeking to be as inclusive as possible, we hope that all COSA members can find phrases that give guidance in many recovery and life situations and challenges.

. . .

"HALT—Hungry, Angry, Lonely, Tired" reminds us to take care of ourselves. Sometimes we are so triggered, upset, or busy that we forget about our own needs. We may be distracted and so focused on others that we neglect ourselves. Some of us are still learning how to identify what we need or even recognize that we have needs. *"HALT"* helps us on our self-care journey by reminding us to take care of our most basic requirements. We can ask ourselves, "Am I hungry, angry, lonely, or tired?" If the answer is yes, we can then embrace the reminder and figure out what to do next for our self-care.

. . .

"Just do the next right thing." "First things first." When things feel uncertain and overwhelming, we can use these reminders to put one foot in front of the other. When we get too far ahead of ourselves, we can feel paralyzed by fear or doubt. These slogans remind us to face our lives in small increments and to be mindful of what is presently in front of us. ***"Keep it simple"*** is another slogan that reminds us not to overthink a situation.

. . .

"One day at a time." The wisdom of this slogan helps many of us through times when pain and sadness engulf us, and we don't know how we can go on. When one day at a time is too much to consider, we focus on one minute, or even one breath, at a time—identifying only where we are today and putting aside our concerns about the future. We can also use this slogan to remind us to stay present in joyful times, and to live mindfully with gratitude each day. Taking life in small bites can help us better savor the delicate flavors of each moment.

. . .

"This too shall pass." The wisdom in these simple words offers us hope. As COSA members in recovery, we may have experienced intense emotional pain and even trauma. This slogan reminds us that everything is temporary, including feelings; that we will get through our challenges; and that we can look toward better tomorrows.

. . .

"Feelings are not facts." This slogan reminds us that our emotional responses may not be based on reality. If we start to immerse ourselves in crazy making "what if" and "if only" thought processes, this reminder can help pull us out. We can learn to sit with our feelings and notice the sensations in our physical body. We can pray and meditate, asking our Higher Power to help us see what is truly real. Recognizing that our brains can hijack us while trying to protect us helps us learn to allow our feelings to flow through us and dissipate.

Some acronyms allow us the creativity to choose for ourselves the words that resonate deep within our beings. One acronym with multiple meanings is "*FEAR*":

"*FEAR is—False Evidence Appearing Real.*"
"*FEAR—Face Everything And Recover.*"
"*FEAR—Fantasy Encourages Abandonment of Reality.*"
"*FEAR is—Forgetting Everything is All Right.*"

Sometimes when we are afraid, we can forget that our Higher Power is always by our side. These phrases can help us turn worry or dread into productive thought processes, ground us in reality, and may help us act instead of feeling immobilized.

• • •

"**Serenity is not peace after the storm but peace amid the storm.**" Recovery is the boat that holds us as we weather the storm. We are learning that we cannot control those around us; people will do what they are going to do. When our own stormy feelings threaten our serenity, we can use our COSA tools and the Serenity Prayer to maintain a sense of peace and perspective even during times of anger and sadness. With help from our Higher Power and our COSA recovery, we are developing the courage and strength to face our challenges. We do not have to postpone joy as we work through our problems.

• • •

"Let go and let God." The message of the Serenity Prayer, as well as much of our Step work, is succinctly captured in these five words. This reminds us to align our own will with our Higher Power's will for us. Prior to recovery, we may have tried to fix every problem we came across. The lesson we learn in recovery, simply put in this slogan, is that when we develop the faith to turn our will and our lives over to our Higher Power, we find serenity and peace. Another variation on this saying is ***"I can't, God can, so I'll let God"***; this reminds us of the first three Steps.

...

"Take the actions; let go of the results." Sometimes we have trouble moving forward when we think ahead and try to second-guess how another person might respond or whether an outcome will be to our liking. We can't control others and their reactions to us. Nor can we control how situations will play out for us as a result of our own decisions. This slogan guides us to do our own work and to let our Higher Power take it from there. Otherwise, worry and indecision can stop us in our tracks. When we remember we're not all-powerful and that there are many things we can't control, it can be much easier to let go of outcomes and take action. This slogan reminds us to use our recovery tools, detach, set boundaries, and take care of ourselves. The people in our lives will react based on their own experiences and perceptions, and this is not our responsibility. We learn in COSA to step back and observe the results and accept "what is."

...

"Live and let live." This slogan advises us to focus on our own conduct, recovery, and lives. When we stop judging and criticizing others and instead practice tolerance, we become free to attend to our own needs and desires.

· · ·

"An expectation is a premeditated resentment," "Expectations are resentments waiting to happen." We have no right to impose our expectations on another person. When we set goals for others, we are opening ourselves up to disappointment and even despair. These slogans also offer a healthy reminder to set aside the expectations we might have for another person's recovery work. We are reminded not to expect something from someone who does not have it to give. We learn in COSA to pray for the clarity and strength to follow our Higher Power's will, rather than praying for our own specific desires and expectations.

· · ·

"Resentment is like drinking poison and expecting someone else to die." This saying reminds us that holding onto resentment harms *us* rather than the person or situation we resent. Refusing to forgive and remaining stuck in anger and blaming hinders our own recovery. This can be useful to remember, especially as we work Steps Four and Eight. We must take ownership of our own actions before we can fully heal and find peace in our lives.

· · ·

"Ego is not my Amigo," "EGO—Edging God Out." These slogans offer us the powerful reminder to set our self-will and ego aside so that we may know our Higher Power's will for us.

· · ·

"Humility is not thinking less of yourself but thinking of yourself less."
"A little humble pie will never give you indigestion."
"Higher Power is my source."

The humility we develop in COSA helps us remember that our recovery is spiritual. We learn to humbly ask that our Higher Power's will be done.

. . .

"GOD—Good Orderly Direction."
"GOD—Grace Over Drama."
"GOD—Grace Over Darkness."

We can define this acronym in any way that spiritually suits us, just as we make our own decisions about the terminology we choose to describe our understanding of our Higher Power.

. . .

"Is it odd, or is it God?" As we learn to have faith in our Higher Power, we might come to believe that coincidences, or unusual or unexpected events, are spiritual reminders that our Higher Power is always with us. **"Rejection is God's protection"** also helps us remember that when things do not go our way, our Higher Power may be guiding us toward something better.

When we make a request to our Higher Power, we can expect one of these three replies: *"1. Yes. 2. Yes, but not right now. 3. No, because I have a better plan for you,"* or **"Yes; No; Wait."** These valuable slogans help us remember to let go and trust that Higher Power is by our side, and that things will work out as they are supposed to.

. . .

"Progress not perfection." Many of us spent our pre-recovery days striving to be perfect. After all, if we were perfect, we would have the perfect love, family, and work situation; and life for us would be perfect. We are learning in recovery that there is no such thing as perfection. When we expect ourselves to accomplish something perfectly, our unreasonable expectations might stop us from taking any action at all. When we fall short of our goal, which of course we will if our goal is perfection, we might be hard on ourselves and give up. By instead focusing on our progress, our goals become attainable, and we can celebrate our successes and feel motivated to keep going. We may use our mistakes and challenges as opportunities for growth, thus cutting the word "failure" out of our vocabulary. We can then joyfully anticipate what our Higher Power has in store for us. Other slogans with similar messages include:

"Perfection, procrastination, paralysis."
"I have enough. I do enough. I am enough."
"We are human beings, not human doings."
"I am perfectly imperfect."

. . .

"Stay on my side of the street." In other words, mind our own business! Many of us have been avid caretakers for other people's problems. This slogan can serve as our reminder to set boundaries and emotionally detach from others' chaos. We can let them find their own guidance from their Higher Power. By focusing on ourselves, we are empowered to practice self-care, live our own lives, and contribute to our own well-being. We can do the most good on our own side of the street, the side on which our Higher Power resides. ***"Stay in my own Hula-Hoop"*** provides additional imagery that helps us recognize our own boundaries.

. . .

"Not my circus, not my monkeys." Some slogans bring a smile to our face as they carry an invaluable message. The striking image of circus monkeys can bring to mind a lot of shenanigans and nonsense. We can embrace the lesson that we no longer have to be caught up in chaotic situations that steal our serenity.

* * *

"The Three Cs: I didn't Cause it, can't Control it, can't Cure it." Many of us are learning in recovery that someone else's addiction and acting out behaviors are not ours, and we are powerless to change them, as hard as we might try. We don't have to carry the weight of the world around on our shoulders. We are only responsible for ourselves. Some of us contemplate a **Fourth C, "I can Contribute to it,"** reminding us that our own unhealthy behaviors can enable an addictive dynamic to continue. When we try to control another's behavior by pushing or shaming them, we do ourselves and them a disservice. Each individual is responsible for working their own program. *"There's no reason to change if there's no reason to change"* reminds us that unless we move out of the way and cease our caretaking of others, we will impede the natural incentive for others to seek improvements in their lives. Similarly, we cannot expect others to rescue us from our own pain and addictive behavior. *"Bless them; change me"* opens our hearts to appreciating others as they are. For some of us, the **Fourth C** is *"I can Cope with it!"*

* * *

"If I am not the problem, I have no solutions." "I can only fix problems that are my own." In other words, we can stop trying to fix things for other people. We only have control over ourselves and our own problems. Sometimes we struggle to figure out which problems are ours, or when our involvement might

actually be meddling. With the help of our Higher Power, we develop the *"wisdom to know the difference."* If we stop trying to fix or control others, we can let go, relax, and spend our precious moments taking care of ourselves.

• • •

"Detachment not amputation." Many of us are learning in recovery to stop caretaking and fixing. But when we detach, some of us go too far. In our attempts to cease interfering in another person's recovery or life experiences, we might refrain from any interaction or discussion at all, when offering our feedback or support might actually be helpful. Detachment is not abandonment, but this distinction can be difficult to gauge. In COSA, we learn to ask if feedback is desired, and we learn to accept a refusal, without judgment or facial grimaces. We can have respectful conversations with our loved ones, letting them know we care but that we are not invested in a particular outcome. We remember to **"Detach with love."** We can care enough about another person to allow them to learn from their mistakes while still accepting them, loving them, and wishing the best for them.

• • •

Some have found it helpful to use the phrase **"Do no harm"** as a reminder that our recovery work should not injure ourselves or others. Taking our Fourth Step inventory is not about beating ourselves up. And our Ninth Step amends are intended to free us from the bonds of past transgressions or flawed behaviors, but without causing collateral damage. We are also reminded that each Step of our recovery work occurs when we are ready and that our pace is gentle, not punishing or harmful to ourselves.

• • •

"'No' is a complete sentence." Those of us who are people-pleasers have a hard time saying no. We don't want to let other people down. We're afraid they'll think poorly of us or even abandon us. This slogan can motivate us to set, enforce, and maintain healthy boundaries. It is not always necessary to provide an explanation when we want to respond with "No" to a request, even when we find ourselves fearful about how the other person will react. We know what is right for us, and that is enough. When we stop assuming responsibility for others' feelings, we can respond with thoughtful choices rather than reacting from a place of fear and trying to please others.

. . .

"Your worth doesn't depend on another's opinion."
"Others' opinions about me are none of my business."
"Don't let someone else determine your value."
"Keep the focus on myself."

We can waste so much time and energy trying to please others, to the point where we ignore ourselves. These slogans are mighty reminders to shift the focus onto ourselves. We are precious human beings. We do not have to do or be anything to be worthy of love.

. . .

"Look back but don't stare."
"It's OK to visit the past, just don't set up your tent."
"Give up the need for a better past."

Some slogans encourage us to use our prior mistakes as opportunities and lessons. When we "*Accept the things we cannot change,*" we are better able to let them go and move on. Many slogans provide a succinct and wise message to come to terms with our past and maybe even find gratitude for where we've been and where we are now.

· · ·

"Worry doesn't prevent tomorrow's tragedies. It only steals today's joys." When worry overwhelms us, this slogan can remind us to let it go so that we can joyfully embrace this one day. Other sayings that keep us focused on our life today include:

"Today is my day."
"Keep your head where your feet are."
"The joy is in the journey."

· · ·

"Say what you mean; mean what you say; don't say it mean."
"THINK—Is it Thoughtful? Helpful? Inspiring/Informative/Insightful? Necessary? Kind?"
"How important is it?"
"Would I rather be right or happy?"
"Would I rather be right or relational?"

Some slogans offer messages to help us keep things in perspective as we interact with others. They can help us with our communication and point us toward a more spiritual life. If we have a tendency to react impulsively when we are feeling angry or afraid, these slogans can remind us to pause, to consider how powerful our words can be, and to respond gently and intentionally.

· · ·

"Cultivate an attitude of gratitude."
"It's hard to be hateful and grateful."

The importance of gratitude and having appreciation for even the smallest gifts in our lives helps us reframe our point of view. Gratitude can keep us going in dark times and allow us to see a light glimmering at the end of the tunnel. It can help us stay in the present moment, even if things are very difficult or challenging. When we're reminded of our blessings, we can adjust our attitude and shift our focus.

...

"Patience takes patience."
"Don't just do something; sit there!"

Many of us are sometimes quick to want to jump into action. Out of desperation resulting from past traumas, we may want to fix a situation before we take the time to problem-solve or develop a full awareness of it. We learn in recovery that if we move too quickly or try to force a solution, we may be pushing our own will and missing out on our Higher Power's will for us. But if we are patient and give ourselves the time and space to become aware, we will be better able to take action that is relevant, thoughtful, intelligent, and aligned with God's will for us. Our Higher Power may even resolve situations for us without any action on our part. Other slogans that encourage patience and pensiveness include:

"Time takes time."
"Change is a process, not an event."
"God is in the pause."

...

"The Three A's: Awareness, Acceptance, Action." This slogan can offer invaluable guidance when we are facing a challenge or anticipating a change. It helps us remember to open our eyes and be patiently still, knowing that change is a process. We observe and become more aware, remembering not to judge ourselves or others. The Three A's teach us to consider the entire situation and to connect with our Higher Power before we take action.

...

"Keep an open mind" and ***"Denial is not a river in Egypt"*** can help us when we find uncomfortable truths in our awareness. As we allow light to shine into the darkness of confusion and discomfort, we can acknowledge our situation and work toward acceptance.

Acceptance can be challenging for us, and we are asked to admit our powerlessness as early as Step One in our recovery work. In time we become willing to embrace what is, even if we don't like it. This can require emotionally charged work and is an important part of the grieving process. ***"Feel your feelings"*** reminds us that we are allowed to acknowledge our feelings and our grief as we walk the path of recovery. Numbing ourselves suppresses our feelings and directs us away from the work that needs to be done.

...

"HOW—Honest, Open, Willing." When we are honest, we can be grounded in reality rather than immersed in denial. When we are open-minded we can more easily hear and accept our Higher Power's will for us. When we are willing, we can find the courage to take the Steps necessary to our recovery. ***"Willingness is the key"*** and is essential for us to make progress in our recovery work, show up at meetings, and follow our sponsors' suggestions.

...

"You're only as sick as your secrets." This slogan reminds us about the importance of honesty. When we bring our secrets out of the darkness and into the light, they lose their power. We can begin this process by being honest with ourselves, and we continue to heal as we eventually share our Fifth Step with our Higher Power and our sponsor. While we guard the confidentiality of others, the anonymity we experience in COSA gives us the safety to share with honesty. We feel our shame diminish. COSA welcomes us into the sunlight!

• • •

"Insanity is doing the same thing over and over again and expecting different results."
"Don't go to the hardware store to buy bread."
"Nothing changes if nothing changes."
"Fake it 'til you make it."
"Act as if."

These slogans help us remember that in order to effect change, we must start somewhere. We will not experience lasting improvements in our lives if we do not take any action. If we continue with our same old approaches, or go to the same people who cannot fulfill our relationship needs, we will arrive at the same outcomes. These phrases can be particularly helpful to us in Step Six, when we experiment with new behaviors or thought processes so that we can become entirely ready to ask our Higher Power to guide us toward a life with healthier behaviors. *"You can't think your way into a new way of behaving; you have to behave your way into a new way of thinking."*

• • •

"I don't want you to save me; I want you to stand by my side." Many slogans give us clarity as we attend meetings, develop recovery relationships, and work the Steps with our sponsors or our Step groups. They often remind us why we entered recovery and that we are not alone. Other helpful sayings about staying the course in COSA unity include:

"If I quit, I will be right back where I started, and when I started, I was desperately wishing I was where I am now."
"Don't quit before the miracle happens."
"I am sick and tired of being sick and tired."
"I entered the rooms for someone else, and I stayed for myself."
"We all come in on different ships, but we're all in the same boat."
"CPR—Call, Pray, Read."
"It's a 'we' not a 'me' program."

. . .

Some slogans give us courage and determination to keep working our COSA program. *"Recovery is a journey, not a destination."*

"You don't have to understand the Steps to work them; you have to work them to understand them."
"The only wrong way to work the Steps is not to work them."
"Keep coming back! It works if you work it, so work it — you're worth it!"

These powerful words bring many COSA meetings to a close. Recovery takes hard work and our dedication to the task can falter if the rewards are not evident. There's not an instant cure for us, but when we see light in others' recovery, we feel inspired to follow their example. And we learn to value ourselves. We are worth it!

Slogans and Wise Sayings Categorical Index

Anxiety
"Feelings are not facts."
"Serenity is not peace after the storm but peace amid the storm."

Being Gentle with Ourselves
"Progress not perfection."
"I have enough. I do enough. I am enough."
"We are human beings, not human doings."
"I am perfectly imperfect."

Boundaries and Detachment
"Live and let live."
"An expectation is a premeditated resentment."
"Expectations are resentments waiting to happen."
"Stay on my side of the street."
"Not my circus, not my monkeys."
"The Three Cs: I didn't Cause it, can't Control it, can't Cure it."
"Bless them; change me."
"If I am not the problem, I have no solutions."
"I can only fix problems that are my own."
"Wisdom to know the difference."
"'No' is a complete sentence."

"*I don't want you to save me; I want you to stand by my side.*"
"*I entered the rooms for someone else, and I stayed for myself.*"
"*Detachment not amputation.*"
"*Take the actions; let go of the results.*"
"*Stay in my own Hula-Hoop.*"

Caretaking vs Caring
"*Live and let live.*"
"*Stay on my side of the street.*"
"*The Three Cs: I didn't Cause it, can't Control it, can't Cure it.*"
"*Bless them; change me.*"
"*I don't want you to save me; I want you to stand by my side.*"
"*Stay in my own Hula-Hoop.*"

Dealing with Chaos and Challenges
"*First things first.*"
"*Just do the next right thing.*"
"*Keep it simple.*"
"*One day at a time.*"
"*This too shall pass.*"
"*Serenity is not peace after the storm but peace amid the storm.*"
"*Let go and let God.*"
"*Progress not Perfection.*"
"*Stay on my side of the street.*"
"*Not my circus, not my monkeys.*"
"*Rejection is God's protection.*"
"*'No' is a complete sentence.*"
"*The Three A's: Awareness, Acceptance, Action.*"
"*Keep an open mind.*"
"*Change is a process, not an event.*"
"*Insanity is doing the same thing over and over again and expecting different results.*"
"*Don't go to the hardware store to buy bread.*"

Denial

"Keep an open mind."
"Denial is not a river in Egypt."
"HOW—Honest, Open, Willing."
"Rejection is God's protection."
"There's no reason to change if there's no reason to change."
"The only wrong way to work the Steps is not to work them."
"We will not regret the past nor wish to shut the door on it."

Ego

"Ego is not my Amigo."
"EGO—Edging God Out."
"A little humble pie will never give you indigestion."
"Humility is not thinking less of yourself but thinking of yourself less."
"Your worth doesn't depend on another's opinion."
"Others' opinions about me are none of my business."
"Don't let someone else determine your value."
"I have enough. I do enough. I am enough."

Fear

"FEAR is False Evidence Appearing Real."
"FEAR—Face Everything And Recover."
"FEAR—Fantasy Encourages Abandonment of Reality."
"FEAR is Forgetting Everything is All Right."
"Feelings are not facts."
"Just do the next right thing."
"I have enough. I do enough. I am enough."
"Higher Power is my source."

Feelings
"Feel your feelings."
"Feelings are not facts."

Focusing on Ourselves
"Live and let live."
"Your worth doesn't depend on another's opinion."
"Others' opinions about me are none of my business."
"Don't let someone else determine your value."
"HALT—Hungry, Angry, Lonely, Tired."
"Stay on my side of the street."
"I don't want you to save me; I want you to stand by my side."
"Stay in my own Hula-Hoop."
"Keep the focus on myself."

Gratitude
"Cultivate an attitude of gratitude."
"We will not regret the past nor wish to shut the door on it."
"Rejection is God's protection."
"It's hard to be hateful and grateful."
"One day at a time."
"The joy is in the journey."

Healthy Communication
"Do no harm."
"'No' is a complete sentence."
"Say what you mean; mean what you say; don't say it mean."
"THINK—Is it Thoughtful? Helpful? Inspiring/Informative/Insightful? Necessary? Kind?"
"How important is it?"
"Would I rather be right or happy?"
"Would I rather be right or relational?"

"Stay on my side of the street."
"Keep an open mind."

Higher Power's Presence
"Is it odd, or is it God?"
"GOD—Good Orderly Direction."
"GOD—Grace Over Drama."
"GOD—Grace Over Darkness."
"God is in the pause."
"Higher Power is my source."

Higher Power's Will for Us
"Let go and let God."
"1. Yes. 2. Yes, but not right now. 3. No, because I have a better plan for you."
"Yes; No; Wait."
"I can't, God can, so I'll let God." or "I can't, God can, so I'll let Him (Her) (Them)."
"Rejection is God's protection."
"EGO—Edging God Out."

Honesty
"HOW—Honest, Open, Willing."
"You're only as sick as your secrets."
"Say what you mean; mean what you say; don't say it mean."

Humility
"Ego is not my Amigo."
"EGO—Edging God Out."
"A little humble pie will never give you indigestion."
"Humility is not thinking less of yourself but thinking of yourself less."
"Rejection is God's protection."
"Higher Power is my source."

Impulsivity
"Say what you mean; mean what you say; don't say it mean."
"THINK—Is it Thoughtful? Helpful? Inspiring/Informative/Insightful? Necessary? Kind?"
"How important is it?"
"Would I rather be right or happy?"
"Would I rather be right or relational?"

Letting Go of Outcomes
"Let go and let God."
"Take the actions, let go of the results."
"Live and let live."
"An expectation is a premeditated resentment."
"Expectations are resentments waiting to happen."
"Resentment is like drinking poison and expecting someone else to die."
"Stay on my side of the street."
"Not my circus, not my monkeys."
"The Three Cs: I didn't Cause it, can't Control it, can't Cure it."
"If I am not the problem, I have no solutions."
"I can only fix problems that are my own."
"Accept the things we cannot change."
"Look back but don't stare."
"It's OK to visit the past, just don't set up your tent."
"Give up the need for a better past."
"Rejection is God's protection."
"1. Yes. 2. Yes, but not right now. 3. No, because I have a better plan for you."
"Yes; No; Wait."
"I can't, God can, so I'll let God." or *"I can't, God can, so I'll let Him (Her) (Them)."*

Not Trying to Save or Fix Others
"Live and let live."
"An expectation is a premeditated resentment."
"Expectations are resentments waiting to happen."
"Stay on my side of the street."
"The Three Cs: I didn't Cause it, can't Control it, can't Cure it."
"Bless them; change me."
"I don't want you to save me; I want you to stand by my side."
"Stay in my own Hula-Hoop."
"A Fourth C: I can Contribute to it."
"There's no reason to change if there's no reason to change."
    "A Fourth C: I can Cope with it."
"Keep the focus on myself."

Pain and Sadness
"One day at a time."
"This too shall pass."
"Feel your feelings."

Patience
"Patience takes patience."
"Don't just do something; sit there!"
"Time takes time."
"Change is a process, not an event."
"God is in the pause."
"Rejection is God's protection."

Perfection
"Progress not perfection."
"Perfection, procrastination, paralysis."
"I have enough. I do enough. I am enough."
"We are human beings, not human doings."

"I am perfectly imperfect."
"Recovery is a journey, not a destination."
"Take the actions; let go of the results."

Resentments
"An expectation is a premeditated resentment."
"Expectations are resentments waiting to happen."
"Resentment is like drinking poison and expecting someone else to die."
"Rejection is God's protection."
"Live and let live."
"Look back but don't stare."
"Give up the need for a better past."
"Keep the focus on myself."

Self-care
"HALT—Hungry, Angry, Lonely, Tired."
"Take the actions, let go of the results."
"Keep the focus on myself."

Self-love
"Your worth doesn't depend on another's opinion."
"Others' opinions about me are none of my business."
"Don't let someone else determine your value."

Service
"We have to give it away to keep it."

Staying in the Present Moment
"First things first."
"Just do the next right thing."
"Keep it simple."

"One day at a time."
"Worry doesn't prevent tomorrow's tragedies. It only steals today's joys."
"Today is my day."
"Keep your head where your feet are."
"The joy is in the journey."
"It's OK to visit the past, just don't set up your tent."
"Give up the need for a better past."
"1. Yes. 2. Yes, but not right now. 3. No, because I have a better plan for you."
"Yes; No; Wait."
"The Three A's: Awareness, Acceptance, Action."
"Feel your feelings."
"HOW—Honest, Open, Willing."

Step One

"The Three A's: Awareness, Acceptance, Action."
"Keep an open mind."
"Denial is not a river in Egypt."
"HOW—Honest, Open, Willing."
"The only wrong way to work the Steps is not to work them."

Step Two

"GOD—Grace Over Drama."
"GOD—Grace Over Darkness."
"Is it odd, or is it God?"
"Insanity is doing the same thing over and over again and expecting different results."
"Higher Power is my source."

Step Three
"Let go and let God."
"I can't, God can, so I'll let God." or *"I can't, God can, so I'll let Him (Her) (Them)."*

Step Four
"Resentment is like drinking poison and expecting someone else to die."
"Do no harm."
"HOW—Honest, Open, Willing."
"Progress not perfection."

Step Five
"You're only as sick as your secrets."

Step Six
"Willingness is the key."
"HOW—Honest, Open, Willing."
"Insanity is doing the same thing over and over again and expecting different results."
"Don't go to the hardware store to buy bread."
"Nothing changes if nothing changes."
"Act as if" or *"Fake it till you make it."*
"You can't think your way into a new way of behaving; you have to behave your way into a new way of thinking."

Step Seven
"EGO—Edging God Out."
"A little humble pie will never give you indigestion."
"Humility is not thinking less of yourself but thinking of yourself less."

Step Eight

"Resentment is like drinking poison and expecting someone else to die."
"HOW—Honest, Open, Willing."
"It's hard to be hateful and grateful."
"Willingness is the key."

Step Nine

"Do no harm."

Step Ten

"One day at a time."
"The Three A's: Awareness, Acceptance, Action."

Step Eleven

"1. Yes. 2. Yes, but not right now. 3. No, because I have a better plan for you."
"Yes; No; Wait."
"GOD—Good Orderly Direction."
"Higher Power is my source."
"I can't, God can, so I'll let God." or "I can't, God can, so I'll let Him (Her) (Them)."

Step Twelve

"We have to give it away to keep it."

Taking Action

"The Three A's: Awareness, Acceptance, Action."
"Insanity is doing the same thing over and over again and expecting different results."
"Don't go to the hardware store to buy bread."
"Nothing changes if nothing changes."

"Act as if" or "Fake it till you make it."
"Willingness is the key."
"You can't think your way into a new way of behaving; you have to behave your way into a new way of thinking."
"There's no reason to change if there's no reason to change."
"Keep coming back! It works if you work it, so work it—you're worth it!"
"Recovery is a journey, not a destination."
"You don't have to understand the Steps to work them; you have to work them to understand them."
"The only wrong way to work the Steps is not to work them."
"Take the actions, let go of the results."
"Progress not perfection."
"Perfection, procrastination, paralysis."
"Don't quit before the miracle happens."

Unity vs. Being Alone

"I don't want you to save me; I want you to stand by my side."
"If I quit, I will be right back where I started, and when I started, I was desperately wishing I was where I am now."
"I am sick and tired of being sick and tired."
"I entered the rooms for someone else, and I stayed for myself."
"We all come in on different ships, but we're all in the same boat."
"It's a 'we' not a 'me' program."
"Principles before personalities."
"CPR—Call, Pray, Read."

Worry

"Worry doesn't prevent tomorrow's tragedies. It only steals today's joys."
"Serenity is not peace after the storm but peace amid the storm."

Sponsorship

When we come to our first COSA meetings, most of us find a reprieve from our pain, loneliness, and trauma—a place where we are finally understood and supported. In the loving company of our fellow COSAs, we can finally breathe again, discovering to our great relief that we are not alone.

As time passes, we notice that many of our fellow COSAs with the greatest peace and healing have done more than just attend meetings; they work the Steps. Seeing these results, we long to move toward our own peace and healing by working the Steps ourselves. We do not do this alone; in COSA we seek the guidance of a sponsor.

A sponsor is a person in the program who serves as our guide as we work the Twelve Steps of COSA. This is someone with whom we can share our story more fully, and who shares their own experience, strength, and hope with us.

It can be daunting to ask another COSA member to be our sponsor. We may be unused to asking for things for ourselves or worried about imposing upon another person's time. However, asking someone to sponsor us is an important growth opportunity for us, in which we learn to advocate for ourselves and trust that anyone we ask to be our sponsor will demonstrate their own healthy boundaries. Because of the close nature of the relationship, we avoid asking those with whom the potential for romantic or other inappropriate interest may exist.

Some of us are drawn to the recovery of a person in our regular meetings and know immediately that we want to ask them to be our sponsor. Others take more time to find someone whose outlook on recovery inspires us. We may need to ask multiple people before we find someone who is available to be our sponsor. Those who do not find available sponsors in local meetings may find someone through phone or Zoom meetings, retreats, or COSA's annual convention. When sponsors are not available, we may enter into co-sponsorship with another COSA with whom we can work the Steps in tandem, or we may form a Step Group of several COSAs working the Steps together.

Some of us begin with a temporary sponsor. Others find that the roles of our sponsor relationships change at various points in our recovery. If we ever need to change or end a sponsor/sponsee relationship, we do our best to do so lovingly, forthrightly, and with the guidance of our Higher Power.

No matter what path leads to finding our sponsor, we find the benefits of this close relationship to be a great help in working the Steps. Our sponsors guide us in our Step work, sharing the resources and practices they found most helpful on their journeys. They are often the first people we turn to when recovery becomes difficult or our path unclear. Our sponsors listen with loving acceptance to our personal narratives and our Fifth Steps; they help us identify our unmanageable behaviors and character defects. They are the ones with whom we carefully plan our Ninth Step amends. They are accountability partners for our emotional sobriety and a source of safe and loving support as we navigate our recovery. Our sponsors should not become our Higher Power; rather, they guide us toward the loving care of our true Higher Power.

Eventually, our sponsors encourage us to pass on the gift of recovery by becoming sponsors ourselves. Some of us may hesitate to take on what seems like a great responsibility, but we realize that the best way to show our gratitude for the loving gift of our sponsor's time and guidance is to pay it forward to someone else.

We are reassured that all we have to do is follow the example our own sponsors set for us: to listen with love and acceptance, to offer guidance when needed, and to share our own experience, strength, and hope in working the Steps. We are careful to guide our sponsees without giving directives or unsolicited advice, since it is not our responsibility, and we do not have the expertise or the right to make decisions for our sponsees. Instead, we remind them to always seek the guidance of their Higher Power.

We tell our sponsees that we are one source of support for them but not their sole support. It is to our benefit to "spread a wide net"—to have a whole network of COSAs we can contact for emotional and recovery support. Our meeting phone lists are a good source of contact information for COSAs that can be part of our support network.

As we pick up the mantle of sponsorship, the gifts of the program multiply, and our own recovery deepens. Guiding our sponsees through the Steps provides us greater insight into our own Step work. We may even hear ourselves saying to a sponsee the exact thing we ourselves need to hear at that moment.

Sponsorship challenges us to continue to grow: in assisting someone else to see themselves more clearly, we learn to look at ourselves in greater depth. As we support our sponsees in identifying their shortcomings, we can be brought face-to-face with our own most persistent defects of character. In encouraging our sponsees to turn their lives and their wills over to the care of their Higher Power, we may find we are more easily able to let go of our own troubles. There are also times when our sponsees share with us insights and lessons that are new to us.

We discover that we can be of the most benefit to our sponsees when we don't just tell them about the tools of recovery, but demonstrate through our own actions how to live them. In being of service this way, we strengthen our own recovery.

When we feel unsure of what to do or question whether we are up to the task, our own sponsors continue to give us guidance. We are reminded that the journeys of our sponsees are their own to walk—we can show the way but not walk it for them. Their achievements and their disappointments are their own—their challenges are not ours to fix, nor their growth ours to claim. We are afforded many opportunities to practice turning our sponsees over to the care of their Higher Power. Just as our sponsors did with us, we practice loving detachment that gives our sponsees room to learn and grow on their own. We celebrate their successes with them and comfort them when they cry over their losses. And when the time comes, we teach them how they, too, can best keep what they have been given by giving it away.

The Serenity Prayer

God, grant me the serenity
to accept the things I cannot change,
courage to change the things I can,
and wisdom to know the difference.

This simple but profoundly powerful prayer has become a trusted tool for COSA as well as for fellowships of recovering people all over the world. It's no wonder, because the few short words of the prayer engage a wealth of recovery principles that can be applied to any situation.

The Serenity Prayer offers us a moment in which to pause, become emotionally centered, spiritually grounded, and connected to our Higher Power. The prayer guides us through a problem or situation using a recovery-based process. Many recovering COSA members use this universal prayer to start or end the day. We can turn to it whenever we need clarity, peace, and the reminder that we are neither alone nor helpless.

We can look at each part of the Serenity Prayer separately to gain insight into how this tool helps us in tough situations and in our daily life.

GOD, GRANT ME THE SERENITY TO ACCEPT THE THINGS I CANNOT CHANGE,

Early in our recovery we may have found it hard to grasp that we could have serenity in the midst of situations we were powerless to control or change. We may have spent a great deal of our lives fighting against the swift currents of circumstances we did not like, including the behaviors of others. With the Serenity Prayer as a guide, we can examine whether or not we can change situations that challenge us.

We learn in recovery that we cannot change another person, regardless of our efforts, desires, or good intentions. No matter how often we ask, how hard we try, or how desperate we are, there are many things we cannot change.

We can use the Serenity Prayer in the most challenging of situations, such as discovering compulsive sexual behavior that affects our lives. We may feel anguished upon realizing that all our efforts to "help" have failed. Recovery and healing will come to others only when they are ready and want it for themselves. With this awareness, it becomes clear that we are not responsible for charting another person's path, for sparing them from the consequences of their actions, or for cleaning up the aftermath of their behaviors. While we may feel fear and discomfort at first, we detach from the false sense of responsibility and illusion of control. We ask for the serenity to *accept* what we cannot change. The Serenity Prayer might help us arrive more calmly at acceptance. We let go and trust our Higher Power to work it out for the greatest good. Along with this acceptance, we receive the gift of a peaceful, inner calm that we know as serenity.

COURAGE TO CHANGE THE THINGS I CAN,

In recovery we come to understand that what we *can* change is ourselves. The second part of the Serenity Prayer shifts the focus to examine what we can change, thus illuminating a pathway toward action.

Because change can be unsettling and difficult, we ask our Higher Power for courage as we endeavor to break out of our comfortable but self-defeating behaviors. We need courage to move from inertia into action.

Having accepted that we cannot change someone else does not mean there is nothing we can do. We can take action and make powerful changes that improve our lives, regardless of the circumstances of compulsive sexual behavior that are around us. In the Serenity Prayer, we ask our Higher Power to grant us courage to make changes such as prioritizing ourselves and our recovery, finding our voice, speaking our truth, standing up for ourselves, setting healthy boundaries, and asking for what we need.

AND WISDOM TO KNOW THE DIFFERENCE.

In the midst of difficult, confusing, or emotionally charged situations we may not be able to see options and solutions clearly. In the last portion of the prayer, we ask our Higher Power for clarity to discern between what we can change and cannot change. Seeking wisdom from a Higher Power means we are not relying merely on ourselves. We may find wisdom through prayer and meditation or from the experiences of others.

The wisdom we receive helps us to understand what we can and cannot change and provides direction for our next steps: either acceptance and letting go, or change and growth. The beauty of the Serenity Prayer as a recovery tool is that either course of action can bring us lasting serenity.

Using the Twelve Steps to Work Through a Specific Situation

INTRODUCTION

As we learn to apply the Twelve Steps of COSA in all areas of our lives, we are able to approach challenges differently than we did in the past. With the Twelve Steps as our guide, we can resolve difficulties in our daily lives and avoid the traps of our old way of thinking. When we feel paralyzed, overwhelmed, reactive, or triggered, we can work the Steps with a focus on the particular situation affecting us. Using the Steps this way is a tool that can bring us clarity, comfort, direction, and relief.

This tool is not intended to replace our comprehensive Step work, in which we examine our life as a whole. The Twelve Steps section of this book provides detailed information about each Step and may be a helpful resource for putting this chapter into action, especially if we experience difficulty applying a particular Step to a situation.

This chapter offers questions to consider when working each Step around a specific circumstance. How we utilize the suggested questions is a personal choice. We may work with a sponsor or COSA friend who can provide guidance and support as we untangle complicated situations. Our sponsor or friend might also help us recognize and take responsibility for any part we may have played. We may come up with additional questions and considerations to help us apply the Twelve Steps to address the situation.

Before we begin, many of us find it helpful to say the Serenity Prayer and ask our Higher Power for guidance. We then write a concise description of the situation with which we are struggling. We focus on our role in the situation rather than on the behaviors of others, and we refrain from assigning blame to others. Answering the questions in this chapter may help us gain a better perspective about the issue at hand and develop deeper insights that can support our recovery.

THE TWELVE STEPS

1. Step One: "We admitted we were powerless over compulsive sexual behavior, that our lives had become unmanageable."

    Related Questions:
    a. What people, places, and things am I powerless over in this circumstance?
    Identifying relevant sources of frustration may provide insight when answering this question.
    b. What, in particular, am I powerless to change or control in this situation?
    c. How is this situation making my life unmanageable?
    d. How might my reaction to this situation create unmanageability in my life?
    e. How has this unmanageability affected my serenity?

2. Step Two: "Came to believe that a Power greater than ourselves could restore us to sanity."

   Related Questions:
   a. Am I doing anything self-defeating, unhealthy, or potentially fueling the problem in this situation? If so, what?
   b. How can I invite my Higher Power into this situation?
   c. Do I believe my Higher Power can restore my sanity in this situation? If so, how might that look and feel?

3. Step Three: "Made a decision to turn our will and our lives over to the care of God as we understood God."

   Related Questions:
   a. What is my will in this situation?
   b. Am I willing and ready to turn my will about this situation and its outcome over to the care of my Higher Power?
   c. What does "the care of God" mean in this situation?
   d. Am I willing and ready to accept my Higher Power's will for me? If not, what do I need to become willing and ready? Am I willing to be willing?
   The following prayer may be helpful: "Higher Power, help me surrender my will in this situation." Writing an affirmation may also be helpful; for example, "I now turn my fear and anxiety over to my Higher Power."
   e. How will I know my Higher Power's will for me in this situation?

4. Step Four: "Made a searching and fearless moral inventory of ourselves."

   Related Questions:
   a. Am I behaving as I have in the past and expecting different results?
   b. What am I doing that might be preventing me from experiencing sanity?
   c. What resentments, hurts, or fears do I have about this issue?
   d. To whom and what do I feel resentment?
   e. Am I in denial or being dishonest with myself or others?
   f. What part, if any, have I contributed to this situation?
   g. Which of my character defects or unhealthy coping mechanisms may be in play in this situation?
   h. Which of my assets can I recognize or use in this particular situation?

5. Step Five: "Admitted to God, to ourselves, and to another human being the exact nature of our wrongs."

   Related Questions:
   a. Do I have fears about admitting my part in this situation to myself? If yes, what are they?
   b. What is the exact nature of my wrongs?
   c. What harmful core beliefs about myself are coming up in this situation? (for example, "I am bad," "I am not enough," "I am unlovable, unwanted, unsafe," etc.)
   It may be helpful to share the responses with a sponsor or trusted COSA friend. Starting with a prayer invites Higher Power into the discussion and provides a reminder that this is a spiritual practice.

6. Step Six: "Were entirely ready to have God remove all these defects of character."

    Related Questions:
    a. What are the negative consequences of my character defects, learned behaviors, or unhealthy coping mechanisms? How are they hurting me and others in this situation?
    b. What benefit am I receiving from continuing to practice the defects?
    c. What are the potential positive consequences of surrendering these defects?
    d. Do I feel entirely ready to turn these defects over to my Higher Power? If not, what is preventing me from moving forward? Am I willing to be willing?
    e. Can I imagine how I might think, feel, and behave if my shortcomings were removed or lifted? *It may be helpful to consider the slogan "Act as if."*

7. Step Seven: "Humbly asked God to remove our shortcomings."

    Related Questions:
    a. How might I humbly ask God to remove my shortcomings in this situation?
    It may be helpful to write a brief letter or speak this request aloud to emphasize a willingness to have the shortcoming(s) removed. Also, it may be beneficial to share the letter or request with a sponsor or COSA friend.

8. Step Eight: "Made a list of all persons we had harmed, and became willing to make amends to them all."

   Related Questions:
   a. Have I harmed myself or anyone else in this situation?
   b. How have I caused harm?
   c. Am I willing to make amends to each person, including myself?
   d. Do I need to forgive myself or anyone else before I feel willing?
   e. What else can I do to become ready to make amends?
   It *may be useful to employ tools such as journaling, meditation, and prayer. Praying for the other person and the willingness to make amends may be especially helpful. The prayer or blessing could be as simple as "God bless _____ (someone on my resentment list) and heal me." Some COSA members write a "venting letter" to be destroyed rather than sent.*

9. Step Nine: "Made direct amends to such people wherever possible, except when to do so would injure them or others."

   Related Questions:
   a. How can I make amends for the harm I have caused in this situation?
   b. Do I need help becoming ready to make amends?
   c. If I don't feel ready, whom will I consult for guidance?
   d. Might living or symbolic amends be appropriate in this situation?
   e. Can I commit to making these amends?
   f. What will I do and when?
   g. Can I ask my sponsor or another COSA member to act as an accountability partner or someone with whom I can check in before and after I make my amends?

10. Step Ten: "Continued to take personal inventory and when we were wrong promptly admitted it."

    Related Questions:
    a. Is anything related to this situation left unfinished? If so, what?
    b. What changes might I make to help me avoid or address similar situations in the future?
    c. How can I use my daily inventory to continue to understand and learn from the situation and others similar to it?
    d. When taking personal inventory, am I focused on only my part and my spiritual progress—recognizing that I cannot change others' behaviors, their roles, or how the situation affects them? *Checking in with a sponsor often helps us stay on track toward finding serenity.*
    e. What am I doing well?
    f. What can I improve?

11. Step Eleven: "Sought through prayer and meditation to improve our conscious contact with God as we understood God, praying only for knowledge of God's will for us and the power to carry that out."

    Related Questions:
    a. What is my Higher Power's will for me in this particular situation?
    b. Am I willing to continue to ask for guidance and strength from my Higher Power about this over the next few days or weeks?
    In addition to prayers for knowledge of God's will and the power to carry it out, prayers may include reflecting on and expressing gratitude for Higher Power, the fellowship, the program, a sponsor, and this tool.

12. Step Twelve: "Having had a spiritual awakening as the result of these Steps, we tried to carry this message to others and to practice these principles in all areas of our lives."

    Related Questions:
    a. How do I feel about the situation now that I have used the Twelve Steps to work through it?
    b. What lessons have I learned?
    c. Have I experienced a spiritual awakening or gained spiritual insight as a result of using this tool?
    d. How can I use my acquired insight to serve others?
    e. What message can I carry, and how might I do that?
    It may be beneficial to write a brief affirmation that encapsulates the lessons learned by using this tool and to review it as needed.

Writing and Journaling

We come to COSA having been affected by compulsive sexual behavior. Our experiences of living with addiction are fraught with confusion and pain. Especially when we first come to COSA, we may feel emotionally and physically drained. Many of us have experienced trauma, and starting our recovery work can seem overwhelming.

Writing or recording our experiences helps us make sense of our lives and find clarity. We may use writing in many different ways in our journey of healing and recovery. We do not have to consider ourselves a writer to benefit from using this tool to record our thoughts and experiences, nor do we need to compare our writing to what we think a good writer would produce. If we are not initially comfortable with writing, we start where we can with the help of our Higher Power, our sponsors, and our COSA community.

We remember to begin by taking things one day at a time. Writing out lists helps us clarify what we have control over and what we do not. For example, to manage our day-to-day responsibilities, we can use lists of what we want to accomplish for the day. When we think through changes in our lives, lists of pros and cons help us sort through situations. We discover that making lists also helps us focus directly on what's in front of us. It helps us to process what is going on and reassures us that our experiences are real and valid, especially for those of us who have been manipulated by others.

In early recovery, our thoughts may be scattered. We've got so much on our mind. Being new to the program, we may worry so much about "doing it right" that we end up saying and doing things that feel inauthentic or that are not right for us. Writing is one way of working through the confusion. We connect and get to know the truth about who we are, rather than who we think we have to be or how we want people to perceive us. Healing begins when we can show up authentically. So we must take the time to get to know ourselves well. The more we get to know ourselves through writing, the more clarity we gain.

As we work through our Steps, we see how much our recovery benefits from writing. In Step One, some members write at length, perhaps creating a personal narrative of their COSA story; others may compile lists of what they are powerless over and how their life has become unmanageable. Step Four asks us to create a moral inventory of ourselves. Step Eight suggests we write a list of all persons we have harmed. We look deep within ourselves, become aware of our patterns, and thus are better prepared for amends work in Step Nine. In Step Ten, many use written lists as a way to take daily personal inventories. Writing regularly is a practical way of putting our Step work into action. It helps us work toward clarity around what has happened, how we feel about it, and what our part has been in any given situation. Our writing may even gently point us toward additional recovery work we have yet to do.

As we grow in self-awareness on our recovery journeys, there may still be times when we aren't sure what we need or how we feel. All we know is that something is bothering us and we need an outlet. If it concerns another person, writing is a way to express ourselves without directly confronting them when we aren't ready or if that is not the right move. Expressive writing such as poems, stories, or stream-of-consciousness writing can help us when we are confused. Our writing doesn't need to have an end goal. We can use it to air out our grievances or cleanse the built-up hurt and resentment we feel. Expressive writing isn't limited to negative feelings but may include joyful expression as well. With expressive writing, we find our authentic voice as we process our thoughts and feelings in a safe space. Ultimately, this can help us remove blocks to our healing process.

Sometimes life can feel overwhelming, and we may find ourselves occasionally slipping into a victim mentality by blaming our challenges on the actions of others. This can blind us from acknowledging our true power over our situation and seeing the good things in our lives. We may end up in a downward spiral that can harm our mental and physical health, as well as our relationships with others. In these situations, gratitude writing—recording things for which we are grateful—can energize us and transform our thinking. This can be as simple as a list we carry in our pocket to pull out when we need a positive reminder of all the great things going on. It can also be a daily practice of journaling or meditating on what we appreciate in our lives. We may even choose to share our gratitude with our fellow COSA members and bring a hopeful message to our meetings.

Some of us write letters to others, with no intention of sending them, as a way of working through our feelings and confusion. We may even write letters to our future or past selves, acting as a loving best friend. Thinking of the encouragement and comfort we extend to our friends, we are reminded to extend that same level of kindness to ourselves as well. By acting as our own best friend, we can get in touch with parts of ourselves that need healing the most. We are more able to make sense of past traumas, develop self-compassion, and gain clarity.

In Step work, letter writing helps us address situations where we cannot directly make amends, such as when a person has died or when direct amends would be unsafe or otherwise inappropriate. Our intention is to write a letter from a genuine and authentic place, even though we cannot send it to them. This provides a form of cleansing as well. Some read the letter at the gravesite or create a healing ritual at home, such as lighting a candle and reading the letter as a prayer.

Reflective writing, such as journaling, gives us the opportunity to write out our thoughts and feelings, also allowing us to examine our experiences with more depth and inquiry. These discoveries about ourselves are keys to opening new doors in our recovery. For example, once we know where we are struggling (whether that be with fear of abandonment, anger or bitterness, self-will, or maybe even denial and dishonesty), writing helps us gain the clarity we need to move forward. We can overcome denial and face difficult truths in our lives or relationships that we didn't wish to see before or were not able to see. Many of us find that a daily journal entry is a beneficial start or end to our day or a great way to take our Step Ten inventory. We find the most healing and empowerment when we keep our writing focused on our sobriety and sanity and when we abstain from obsessing over what others are doing.

Sometimes we run into challenges with writing about our experiences, especially if our boundaries have been violated in the past. We may fear having our writing seen or feel shame about what we've been through. If we have been betrayed in the past, or our privacy and confidentiality have been breached, we may fear writing down our thoughts. One way to overcome this is to find a place or writing technique that makes us feel comfortable and safe, such as writing on a protected electronic device. Or we may find a private, safe space to keep paper journals. We can ask fellow members how they choose to protect their writing. Sometimes writing with the intention of destroying the document later can symbolize surrender and promote healing.

We are careful that we don't use our writing in a way that could be harmful to our recovery or the addicts around us. While we want to see others around us doing well in their lives and making healthy choices, if we use our writing to focus on another person's behaviors or their own program work, this may be a form of control. Writing in this way can take us further away from our own sobriety and sanity. However, when we keep the focus on ourselves, we are free to write about our feelings, thoughts, and reactions to others' behaviors as we further explore our own recovery process.

There may be times when we aren't inspired to write or feel we have nothing to write about. The focus of our writing depends on what we want to accomplish at that moment. We may seek inspiration and guidance from our sponsors or other COSA members, from reciting the Serenity Prayer, or from reading recovery literature that invites us to reflect on specific topics.

Because patterns may emerge over time, writing serves as a way of tracking our progress. We no longer need to rely on our old, broken coping skills. We can look back at how we approached conflicts or challenges in the past and observe how far we've come. We can address our defects and have gratitude for our assets.

Our lives transform as writing enables us not only to express what's going on inside ourselves but also to communicate with others and connect with them authentically, as well. Our courage increases as writing takes us on an enlightening and rewarding journey inside our hearts and minds and out into the world.

APPENDIX

The Twelve Steps of COSA

1. We admitted we were powerless over compulsive sexual behavior—that our lives had become unmanageable.
2. Came to believe that a Power greater than ourselves could restore us to sanity.
3. Made a decision to turn our will and our lives over to the care of God as we understood God.
4. Made a searching and fearless moral inventory of ourselves.
5. Admitted to God, to ourselves, and to another human being the exact nature of our wrongs.
6. Were entirely ready to have God remove all these defects of character.
7. Humbly asked God to remove our shortcomings.
8. Made a list of all persons we had harmed, and became willing to make amends to them all.
9. Made direct amends to such people wherever possible, except when to do so would injure them or others.
10. Continued to take personal inventory and when we were wrong promptly admitted it.

11. Sought through prayer and meditation to improve our conscious contact with God as we understood God, praying only for knowledge of God's will for us and the power to carry that out.

12. Having had a spiritual awakening as the result of these steps, we tried to carry this message to others, and to practice these principles in all areas of our lives.

. . .

The Twelve Steps of Alcoholics Anonymous have been reprinted and adapted with the permission of Alcoholics Anonymous World Services, Inc. ("AAWS"). Permission to reprint and adapt the Twelve Traditions does not mean that Alcoholics Anonymous is affiliated with this program. A.A. is a program of recovery from alcoholism only—use of A.A.'s Traditions or an adapted version in connection with programs and activities which are patterned after A.A., but which address other problems, or use in any other non-A.A. context, does not imply otherwise.

THE TWELVE STEPS OF ALCOHOLICS ANONYMOUS

1. We admitted we were powerless over alcohol—that our lives had become unmanageable.
2. Came to believe that a Power greater than ourselves could restore us to sanity.
3. Made a decision to turn our will and our lives over to the care of God as we understood Him.
4. Made a searching and fearless moral inventory of ourselves.
5. Admitted to God, to ourselves, and to another human being the exact nature of our wrongs.
6. Were entirely ready to have God remove all these defects of character.
7. Humbly asked Him to remove our shortcomings.
8. Made a list of all persons we had harmed, and became willing to make amends to them all.
9. Made direct amends to such people wherever possible, except when to do so would injure them or others.

10. Continued to take personal inventory and when we were wrong promptly admitted it.
11. Sought through prayer and meditation to improve our conscious contact with God as we understood Him, praying only for knowledge of His will for us and the power to carry that out.
12. Having had a spiritual awakening as the result of these steps, we tried to carry this message to alcoholics, and to practice these principles in all our affairs.

The Twelve Traditions of COSA

1. Our common welfare should come first; personal recovery depends upon COSA unity.

2. For our group purpose there is but one ultimate authority—a loving God as expressed in our group conscience. Our leaders are but trusted servants; they do not govern.

3. The only requirement for COSA membership is that our lives have been affected by compulsive sexual behavior. The members may call themselves a COSA group, provided that, as a group, they have no other affiliation.

4. Each group should be autonomous except in matters affecting other groups or COSA as a whole.

5. Each group has but one primary purpose—to carry its message to those who still suffer. We do this by practicing the Twelve Steps ourselves.

6. A COSA group ought never endorse, finance, or lend the COSA name to any related facility or outside enterprise, lest problems of money, property and prestige divert us from our primary purpose.

7. Every COSA group ought to be fully self-supporting, declining outside contributions.

8. COSA should remain forever non-professional, but our service centers may employ special workers.

9. COSA, as such, ought never be organized; but we may create service boards or committees directly responsible to those they serve.

10. COSA has no opinion on outside issues; hence the COSA name ought never be drawn into public controversy.

11. Our public relations policy is based on attraction rather than promotion; we need always maintain personal anonymity at the level of press, radio, films, television, and other public media of communication. We need guard with special care the anonymity of all Program members.

12. Anonymity is the spiritual foundation of all our traditions, ever reminding us to place principles before personalities.

・・・

The Twelve Traditions of Alcoholics Anonymous have been reprinted and adapted with the permission of Alcoholics Anonymous World Services, Inc. ("AAWS"). Permission to reprint and adapt the Twelve Traditions does not mean that Alcoholics Anonymous is affiliated with this program. A.A. is a program of recovery from alcoholism only—use of A.A.'s Traditions or an adapted version in connection with programs and activities which are patterned after A.A., but which address other problems, or use in any other non-A.A. context, does not imply otherwise.

THE TWELVE TRADITIONS OF ALCOHOLICS ANONYMOUS

1. Our common welfare should come first; personal recovery depends upon A.A. unity.
2. For our group purpose there is but one ultimate authority—a loving God as He may express Himself in our group conscience. Our leaders are but trusted servants; they do not govern.

3. The only requirement for A.A. membership is a desire to stop drinking.
4. Each group should be autonomous except in matters affecting other groups or A.A. as a whole.
5. Each group has but one primary purpose—to carry its message to the alcoholic who still suffers.
6. An A.A. group ought never endorse, finance, or lend the A.A. name to any related facility or outside enterprise, lest problems of money, property, and prestige divert us from our primary purpose.
7. Every A.A. group ought to be fully self-supporting, declining outside contributions.
8. Alcoholics Anonymous should remain forever nonprofessional, but our service centers may employ special workers.
9. A.A., as such, ought never be organized; but we may create service boards or committees directly responsible to those they serve.
10. Alcoholics Anonymous has no opinion on outside issues; hence the A.A. name ought never be drawn into public controversy.
11. Our public relations policy is based on attraction rather than promotion; we need always maintain personal anonymity at the level of press, radio, and films.
12. Anonymity is the spiritual foundation of all our traditions, ever reminding us to place principles before personalities.

The Twelve Concepts of COSA

1. Final responsibility and ultimate authority for COSA world services should always reside in the collective conscience of our whole Fellowship.

2. The Annual Meeting of Delegates and the ISO Board of COSA has become, for nearly every practical purpose, the active voice and the effective conscience of our whole Society in its world affairs.

3. To insure effective leadership, we should endow each element of COSA, "the Annual Meeting", the International Service Organization of COSA and its service committees, contracted worker, and executives with a traditional "Right of Decision".

4. At all responsible levels, we ought to maintain a traditional "Right of Participation" allowing a voting representation in reasonable proportion to the responsibility that each must discharge.

5. Throughout our structure, a traditional "Right of Appeal" ought to prevail, so that minority opinion will be heard and personal grievances receive careful consideration.

6. The Annual Meeting of the board and delegates recognizes that the chief initiative and active responsibility in most International service matters should be exercised by the trustee members of the Annual Meeting, acting as the International Service Organization.

7. The Charter and Bylaws of the International Service Board are legal instruments, empowering the trustees to manage and conduct international service affairs. The Annual Meeting Charter is not a legal document; it relies upon tradition and the COSA purse for final effectiveness.

8. The trustees are the principal planners and administrators of overall policy and finance. They have custodial oversight of the separately incorporated and constantly active services, exercising this through their ability to elect all the directors of these entities.

9. Good service leadership at all levels is indispensable for our future functioning and safety. Primary world service leadership, once exercised by the founders, must necessarily be assumed by the trustees.

10. Every service responsibility should be matched by an equal service authority, with the scope of such authority well defined.

11. The trustees should always have the best possible committees, corporate service directors, executives, staffs, and consultants. Composition, qualifications, induction procedures, and rights and duties will always be matters of serious concern.

12. The Annual Meeting shall observe the spirit of COSA tradition, taking care that it never becomes the seat of perilous wealth or power; that sufficient operating funds and reserve be its prudent financial principle; that it place none of its members in a position of unqualified authority over others; that it reach all important decisions by discussion, vote, and, whenever possible, by substantial unanimity; that its actions never be personally punitive nor an incitement to public controversy; that it never perform acts of government, and that, like the fellowship it serves, it will always remain democratic in thought and action.

. . .

The Twelve Concepts of Alcoholics Anonymous have been reprinted and adapted with the permission of Alcoholics Anonymous World Services, Inc. ("AAWS"). Permission to reprint and adapt the Twelve Traditions does not mean that Alcoholics Anonymous is affiliated with this program. A.A. is a program of recovery from alcoholism only—use of A.A.'s Traditions or an adapted version in connection with programs and activities which are patterned after A.A., but which address other problems, or use in any other non-A.A. context, does not imply otherwise.

THE TWELVE CONCEPTS OF ALCOHOLICS ANONYMOUS

1. Final responsibility and ultimate authority for A.A. world services should always reside in the collective conscience of our whole Fellowship.
2. The General Service Conference of A.A. has become, for nearly every practical purpose, the active voice and the effective conscience of our whole society in its world affairs.
3. To insure effective leadership, we should endow each element of A.A.—the Conference, the General Service Board and its service corporations, staffs, committees, and executives—with a traditional "Right of Decision."
4. At all responsible levels, we ought to maintain a traditional "Right of Participation," allowing a voting representation in reasonable proportion to the responsibility that each must discharge.

5. Throughout our structure, a traditional "Right of Appeal" ought to prevail, so that minority opinion will be heard and personal grievances receive careful consideration.
6. The Conference recognizes that the chief initiative and active responsibility in most world service matters should be exercised by the trustee members of the Conference acting as the General Service Board.
7. The Charter and Bylaws of the General Service Board are legal instruments, empowering the trustees to manage and conduct world service affairs. The Conference Charter is not a legal document; it relies upon tradition and the A.A. purse for final effectiveness.
8. The trustees are the principal planners and administrators of over-all policy and finance. They have custodial oversight of the separately incorporated and constantly active services, exercising this through their ability to elect all the directors of these entities.
9. Good service leadership at all levels is indispensable for our future functioning and safety. Primary world service leadership, once exercised by the founders, must necessarily be assumed by the trustees.
10. Every service responsibility should be matched by an equal service authority, with the scope of such authority well defined.
11. The trustees should always have the best possible committees, corporate service directors, executives, staffs, and consultants. Composition, qualifications, induction procedures, and rights and duties will always be matters of serious concern.
12. The Conference shall observe the spirit of A.A. tradition, taking care that it never becomes the seat of perilous wealth or power; that sufficient operating funds and reserve be its prudent financial principle; that it place none of its members in a position of unqualified authority over others; that it reach all important decisions by discussion, vote, and whenever possible, substantial unanimity; that its actions never be personally punitive nor an incitement to public controversy; that it never perform acts of government; that, like the Society it serves, it will always remain democratic in thought and action.

The Three Circles

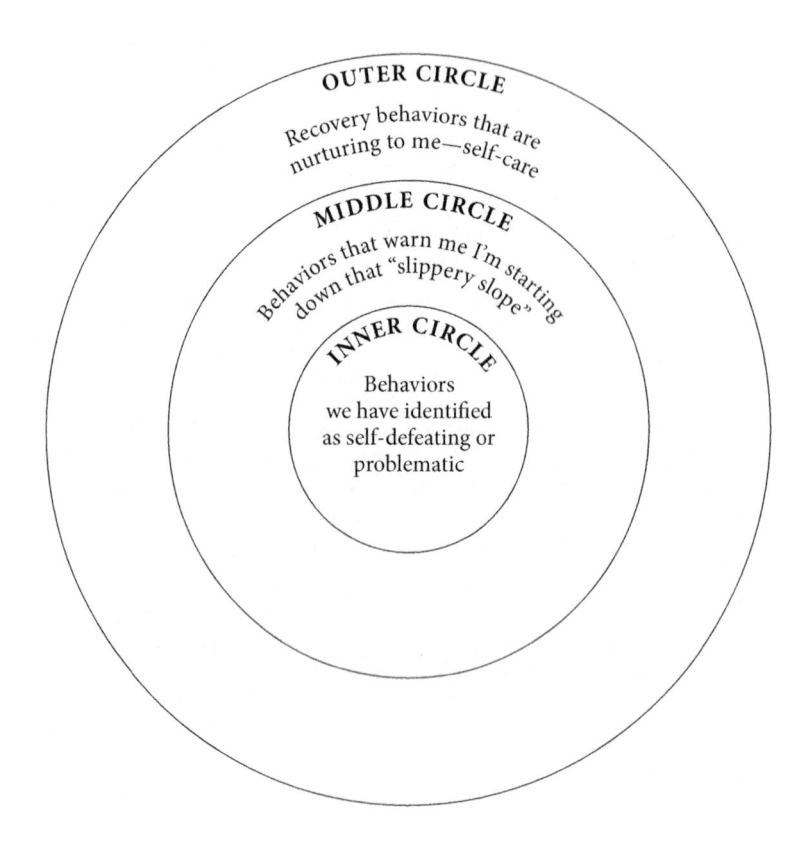

OUTER CIRCLE
Recovery behaviors that are nurturing to me—self-care

MIDDLE CIRCLE
Behaviors that warn me I'm starting down that "slippery slope"

INNER CIRCLE
Behaviors we have identified as self-defeating or problematic

The Three Circles concept is © copyright 1991 Sex Addicts Anonymous. All rights Reserved

Confidentiality Statement

The anonymity and confidentiality of COSA meetings offer a sense of security rarely found in other environments. Many COSA members discover that COSA meetings are the first place they have ever felt safe to tell their stories. Anonymity is a "spiritual foundation" of COSA, established by our Traditions, and should be respected to the greatest extent possible, however, COSA membership does not guarantee immunity from any laws or legal jurisdictions.

Since membership in COSA does not bestow special legal rights or protections, we remind you that you are the steward of your own confidentiality and anonymity in COSA where local regulations are concerned. You may want to consider this when sharing specific details in meetings or with other members.

We remind you that our Traditions also state that COSA is "forever non-professional." As such, COSA members enter meetings solely as a person in recovery. Matters of legality are beyond the scope of COSA and so the ISO of COSA does not offer legal guidance. Please contact a professional if you have legal concerns regarding confidentiality.

The Inverted Triangle Structure of COSA

The Second Tradition reminds us that "Our leaders are but trusted servants; they do not govern." The organizational structure of the ISO of COSA reflects that. The informed Group Conscience is communicated to the trusted servants, and decisions are made which reflect that Group Conscience. See the Inverted Triangle in the graphic below:

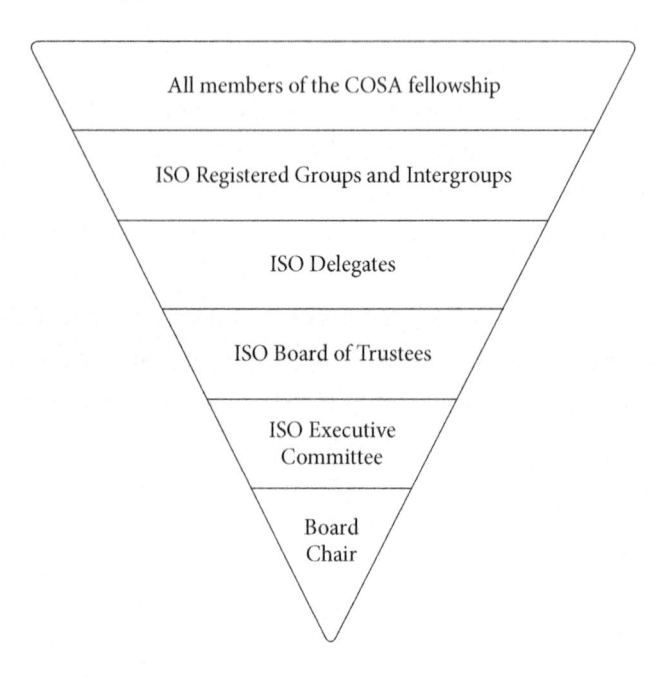

All members of the COSA fellowship

ISO Registered Groups and Intergroups

ISO Delegates

ISO Board of Trustees

ISO Executive Committee

Board Chair

Printed in Great Britain
by Amazon